Checkerboards and Shatterbelts

Checkerboards & Shatterbelts

The Geopolitics of South America

Philip Kelly

 University of Texas Press   Austin

Requests for permission to reproduce material
from this work should be sent to Permissions,
University of Texas Press, Box 7819,
Austin, TX 78713-7819.

∞ The paper used in this publication meets the
minimum requirements of American National
Standard for Information Sciences—Permanence
of Paper for Printed Library Materials,
ANSI Z39.48-1984.

Library of Congress Cataloging-in-Publication Data

Kelly, Philip, 1941–
    Checkerboards and shatterbelts : the geopolitics
of South America / Philip Kelly. — 1st University of
Texas Press ed.
        p.   cm.
    Includes bibliographical references and index.
    ISBN 0-292-74327-0 (cloth : alk. paper). —
    ISBN 0-292-74328-9 (paper : alk. paper)
    1. Geopolitics—South America.   2. South
America—Foreign relations.   I. Title.

F2231.K45   1997
327.1´098—dc20   96-41600

Contents

Preface

Two motivations prompted me to write this book. Following publication of the volume I coedited with Jack Child, *Geopolitics of the Southern Cone and Antarctica* (1988), I wanted to create another version of South American geopolitics, one that extended beyond the Southern Cone to cover the entire continent and the strategic relationships that swirl within the Western Hemisphere. I also wanted to describe certain contemporary transitions in diplomacy as well as the traditional geopolitical concepts and theories more systematically than had been possible in the earlier book.

For the most part, South America lacks a continentwide geopolitics. Rather, one normally sees geopolitics in national and subregional settings. My title, *Checkerboards and Shatterbelts*, helps explain this fragmented application of the term by pointing to two important geopolitical concepts, the first regional in scope, the second both regional and strategic, each having an effect on the environment in which South American diplomacy must work. *Checkerboards* appear as multipolar balance-of-power structures that reveal a fragmentation relative to the dictum, "My neighbor is my enemy, but my neighbor's neighbor is my friend." These phenomena have appeared throughout the foreign affairs of republican South America as, at times, Brazil, Chile, and Colombia have aligned against their immediate neighbors, Argentina, Peru, and Venezuela. Such structures have prevented continental unity like that in the United States of North America.

Shatterbelts are regions where military rivalries between outside great powers tie into local contentions and bring the possibility of conflict escalation.[1] The Soviet alliance with Cuba that challenged the United States and its Caribbean and Central American allies, for example, caused a shatterbelt to form in Middle America from approximately 1960 until the late 1980s. Frequently, checkerboards create the political divisions among nations that make shatterbelts possible.

Although shatterbelts at present do not operate within South America, they continue to affect South American geopolitics in several ways. For example, shatterbelts of the Amazon and La Plata estuaries during colonial and postindependence times helped prevent Brazil and Argentina from spreading their territories to the Pacific; instead, they caused the persistent checkerboard design that checkmated the expansion of both powers. Likewise, Caribbean shatterbelts have restricted contact between the northern and southern continents, and the Yankee fear of shatterbelts in Latin America led to the Monroe Doctrine, a policy bent on keeping America free of European alignment. Nonetheless, Norberto Ceresole (1988) observed a cold war shatterbelt in the South Atlantic that violated the United States' desire for Southern Cone support against the Soviet bloc. In all instances, shatterbelts have stalemated a unified South American geopolitics and have prevented a strategic projection of power beyond the continent.

South America's world location is peripheral, distant from the power centers and resources of temperate Eurasia and North America. The continent's wealth, industry, and technology are quite meager in comparison. Instead, frontier disputes, checkerboards, and shatterbelts have characterized the continent's geopolitical perspective, although at present a gradual integration of common economic policies among the Southern Cone republics seems to be replacing the traditional multipolar diplomatic structure. Notwithstanding occasional wars and frontier tensions, the continent normally lives at peace, a benefit created in part by its isolation and the difficult terrain between nations, the cost of warfare in an area of restricted domestic resources, the cushioning function of several buffer states bordering the larger powers, the fear of U.S. intervention to prevent the creation of a Latin American shatterbelt, the existence of the checkerboard pattern that threatens to escalate conflict, and the possibility of two-front warfare. In all of these cases, geopolitics offers an insightful tool for studying the continent's foreign affairs.

Chapter 1 begins with definitions, characteristics, and theories appropriate to the discussion of South American geopolitics. Here, I tie relevant concepts and hypotheses to specific examples of the continent's foreign affairs. In chapter 2, I offer largely my own ideas on individual countries' geopolitics. Chapter 3 inventories the viewpoints of leading South American geopolitical writers. In chapters 4 and 5, I investigate regional geopolitical views, for instance, frontier conflict and war, economic cooperation, comparisons of industrial development, and the territorial expansion of Brazil. United States – South American relations compose chapter 6, followed by a summary and geopolitical projections in the final chapter.

This book is dedicated to two of my geopolitical mentors, Col. Howard Pittman of the U.S. Marine Corps, and Gen. Carlos de Meira Mattos of the Brazilian army. "Howey," who died in the fall of 1993, made initial contacts between North and South American geopolitical scholars and assembled a mass of data and sources in his monumental dissertation, "Geopolitics in the ABC Countries: A Comparison" (1981a). I could not have authored the present account without Howard. General Meira Mattos spawned my initial interest in Brazilian geopolitics and served as a funnel to other South American writers and sources. I have learned more about geopolitics from him than from any other single source.

I thank Dr. Barbara Shortridge and Tobi Steinberg of the University of Kansas Cartographic Service for developing the geopolitical maps and the Research and Creativity Committee at Emporia State University for its funding of my cartographic needs. My appreciation also goes to Shannon Davies and others on the staff of the University of Texas Press.

Note

1. Shatterbelts are defined in several ways. In "Geopolitics in the New World Era," Saul B. Cohen (1994: 32) seems to subscribe generally to my description (Kelly 1986a), although elsewhere he appears at greater variance (1973). Paul Hensel and Paul Diehl (1994) offer a good review of the term also.

Checkerboards and Shatterbelts

▪▪▪▪ Geopolitical Definitions,
ONE
▪▪▪▪ Characteristics, and Theories

I n this chapter, two introductory topics will be examined: geopolitical definitions and characteristics that are pertinent to the South American environment; and major concepts and theories that will assist the reader in understanding the geopolitical descriptions in subsequent chapters.

Defining Geopolitics

Geopolitics signifies the impact of certain geographic factors on a country's foreign policy. In this book we will concentrate on the position and location of the South American states; their access to resource wealth; and a country's space, size, terrain, climate, and demography as these influence national diplomacy and the continent's international affairs.

For visualizing this mix of geography and foreign affairs, the following offer good examples of recent South American geopolitics.

Checkerboards and the 1982 Malvinas/Falklands War

After the Argentine occupation of the British-held Malvinas/Falkland Islands, a diplomatic checkerboard pattern once again emerged in leapfrog fashion in South America as neighboring states became opponents, and neighbors of neighbors became confederates. Peru and Venezuela gave Argentina diplomatic support, Brazil equivocated, while Chile offered the English its communications facilities to use against the Argentines. Based on national position and international conflict, a checkerboard of allies and opponents was revealed once more in the continent's fragmented foreign relations.

Shatterbelts and the End of the Cold War

The collapse of the Soviet empire ended the Caribbean shatterbelt—that intermingling of rivalry between Russia and the United States and struggle among the Middle Americans—reduced the United States' strategic vulnerability in Latin America, and weakened South America's bargaining position with the Yankees in security and economic matters. Will this change in world politics hinder Latin America's quest for better access to the North American Free Trade area, or might a multipolar globe strengthen the southerners' hand?

Threat at Itaipú

The giant binational hydroelectric power complex at Itaipú on the frontier Paraná River is shared by Brazil and Paraguay and provides vital energy to industrial southern Brazil. Antonio Pecci (1990) alleges that Brazil would invade an unstable or rebellious Paraguay if electricity flow were disrupted. Recent history lends credence to this assertion, for Brazilian forces occupied a disputed area north of Itaipú in 1965 when the Paraguayans resisted their neighbor's demands for a greater share of this vital resource (Da Rosa 1983: 82). For some, Itaipú represents the strategic core of South America.

From Manifest Destiny to Rapprochement: Brazilian-Argentine Relations

Brazil's alleged desire to extend its boundaries to the Pacific coast has kept South American foreign relations stirred up since colonial times. For a variety of reasons, among these the opposition of Argentina, Brazil's quest has failed. The Brazilian-Argentine rivalry for regional leadership has solidified the continental checkerboard, made shatterbelts more likely, kept frontier tensions high, and prevented regional integration. Yet, of late, because of the potential for profit through South American economic integration and a diplomatic cooling between Brazil and the United States, conflict has changed to cooperation between the two states. This represents a monumental reversal of traditional geopolitics, and the two countries' foreign policies and resources now seem to be melding into an integrative structure of regional peace.

Narcotics Wars and Cooperation between Two South American Enemies

At the isolated "triple point" area at Güepi, where Peru, Ecuador, and Colombia touch, a Peruvian army patrol in 1993 suffered casualties after being ambushed by an armed force of cocaine producers. The Ecuadoran army provided medical assistance to the Peruvian wounded. This friendly gesture contrasted with the ongoing and long-running frontier conflict between the two nations for resources and access to the Amazon River.

Territorial Disputes throughout South America

From Caribbean islands to the Antarctic, from coastal fringes to the interior, most international conflict in South America has originated over disputed territory. Poorly drawn colonial boundaries, disputed lands taken as prizes of war, access to newly discovered natural wealth in border zones, and recent immigration to formerly vacant areas are the causes. Such geopolitical discord extends over maritime areas as well. Peace now seems in place throughout the continent.

Interior Transport Systems

Most South Americans live near ocean coasts. Interior road and canal facilities have begun to penetrate the almost empty hinterland. The recently completed Hidrovía river barge system now links "Mediterranean," or landlocked, Bolivia and Paraguay to the South Atlantic to a network via canals and the Paraguay, Paraná, and Plata Rivers. A series of trans-Amazon highways, including the controversial "export corridors" from southern Brazil to Bolivia and Paraguay, link coastal Brazil to most of its Spanish neighbors. Such transport access may heighten tensions over resources, enliven checkerboard rivalries, increase trade and industrial development, and contribute to both continental conflict and cooperation.

Brazil's World Status and the Plata Basin Common Market

Worldwide, Brazil ranks fifth in size, seventh in population, eighth in national power, and ninth in gross national product (Kurian 1990), despite the "lost decade" of the 1980s. The nation's geopolitical writers boast of world prominence. Ironically, Brazil's rise in status has prompted Southern Cone free-market cooperation with Argentina, and momentum toward joint development and trade expansion in the Mercado Común del Sur (MERCOSUR, South American Common Market) integration plan seems quite promising.

The 1993 Massacre of Venezuelan Indians by Gold Miners

In 1993 gold prospectors seeking new claims decimated Yamomani villages on the southeastern Venezuelan frontier. The vast, vacant space, the resources and new highways, plus an already tense international frontier between Venezuela and Guyana make this an incident of geopolitical significance.

"Applied" Geopolitics in South American Foreign Policy

Often, leading South American geopolitical writers hold major governmental offices; hence, they appear positioned to influence developmental and foreign policy. For instance, Gen. Augusto Pinochet of Chile served his country as president, Gen. Edgardo Mercado Jarrín of Peru governed as prime minister and foreign minister, Gen. Golbery do Couto e Silva of Brazil functioned as chief advisor to three presidents, and Gen. Juan Enrique Guglialmelli of Argentina headed the National Development Agency.

Two Additional Definitions of Geopolitics

Definitions of geopolitics abound (see Atencio 1986; Guglialmelli 1986; and Briano 1977). But two examples beyond the one I have given might provide further background for examining the term and its application.

Jack Child and I originated this description of the concept (1988: 2–3):

> Geopolitics is the impact on foreign security policies of certain
> geographic features, the more important being locations among
> countries, distances between areas, and terrain, climate, and
> resources within states. Geopolitics might also be described
> as the relationship between power politics and geography.
> The usefulness of geopolitical analysis derives in part from
> the formulation of broad linkages or theories among these

geographic features and policies, linkages that bring insights to international relationships. Geopolitics, we believe, represents one method for studying foreign and strategic affairs, and it relates as much to planning for peace as it does to military involvement.

The foreign and security policy aspect, the geographic traits that influence policy (position, location, distance, terrain, climate, and resources), the connections between theory and policy, and the emphasis on peace and conflict all appear important to this portrait.

Jorge Atencio of Argentina, in his influential book *¿Qué es la geopolítica?*, contributes this definition of geopolitics (1986: 41; all translations are mine unless otherwise noted):

> Geopolitics is the science that studies the influence of geographic factors in the life and evolution of states, with an objective of extracting conclusions of a political character . . . [Geopolitics] guides statesmen in the conduct of the state's domestic and foreign policy, and it orients the armed forces to prepare for national defense and in the conduct of strategy; it facilitates planning for future contingencies based on consideration of relatively permanent geographic features that permit calculations to be made between such physical realities and certain proposed national objectives, and consequently, the means for conducting suitable political or strategic responses.

Atencio's South American version contrasts in several areas with the Kelly-Child definition. In common with other South American renderings, but one that stimulates controversy in the United States because of its determinist implication, he depicts geopolitics as a "science." His reference to "the life and evolution of states" offers geopolitics an organic format in which states take on a human or living characteristic, a trait again not found in U.S. writings but inherent in South American descriptions. Finally, Atencio dynamically links both international and domestic policy considerations to geopolitics as a means of measuring and balancing national resources against foreign-policy objectives.

The German impact on South American geopolitics gives one explanation for variations between the two definitions. For example, the 1938 German text *Einfuhrung in die Geopolitik*, by Richard Hennig and Leo Körholz, later issued in Spanish as *Introducción a la geopolítica* (1977), closely reflects the work of Atencio and other

South American geopolitical writers. It contains many references to geopolitics as, for example, "scientific," "organic," and "space conscious." The German text is widely approved in geopolitical circles throughout the Southern Hemisphere, and many military schools require it. Other reasons for the contrasting descriptions of geopolitics are discussed later in this chapter.

All three definitions contained in these introductory pages have merit.

Characteristics of South American Geopolitics

I shall broaden the geopolitical perspective by outlining certain characteristics of the term I have found to be inherent to South America.

The Uniqueness of South American Geopolitics

South American geopolitics seems particularly conditioned by disputed frontiers, checkerboards, shatterbelts, and regional cooperation. Boundary protection and expansion, a preoccupation of geopolitical writers, appear throughout the history of republican America; they are the heritage of erratic border demarcations, distant and isolated frontiers, and small coastal, concentrated population clusters that resisted the settlement of the hinterland. Countries fought major wars to annex or protect exposed and valuable territories.

Checkerboards have performed as the dominant balance-of-power structure among the leading countries of South America for the past two hundred years. Shatterbelts, as noted in the Preface, have helped block continental expansion, caused Yankee intrusions, isolated North and South America from each other, and prevented a unified South American voice in global diplomacy. Regional integration, only now emerging although a traditional goal, features lowered trade barriers and free-market cooperation, as well as multinational collaboration in resolving regional problems and encouraging wider development. These four factors—frontiers, checkerboards, shatterbelts, and regional cooperation—represent keys to interpreting the geopolitics of South America.

South America is more isolated from the major events of the northern hemispheres than are the states of the Caribbean and Central America. Not currently part of a sphere of influence or shatter-belt, South America exists largely beyond the command of the great European powers and the United States. Such autonomy has not always been the case. Spain and Portugal for centuries controlled the continent and created shatterbelt rivalries there, as did, later, Great Britain and the United States. But the present isolation enhances the unfolding of a distinctive genre of geopolitics, a traditional and in-digenous, even classical, structure of buffer states, heartlands, and checkerboards, of frontier tensions, choke points, and illegal immi-gration, of competition and cooperation for access to resources, trade, and development.

Rugged terrain, harsh climates, and extensive unoccupied spaces, all geopolitical factors, likewise have affected South American events (map 1). For example, most major river systems penetrate areas without substantial potential for settlement, and rivers are ill-placed for linking South America's subregions, as happens in North Amer-ica. The Andes restrict transcontinental communication; jungles and deserts impede transportation as well. Accordingly, the Por-tuguese and, later, the Brazilians never succeeded in extending their territories to the Pacific or the Caribbean. Nor did Chile or Argen-tina become bicoastal. Imagine the difference today in hemispheric diplomacy had a South American colony or republic been able to grow to continental proportions.

Hence, a continent of twelve sovereign nations has resulted, and no single country or area dominates the region's politics and eco-nomics, although Brazil clearly has emerged as the leader. South America has diverse geopolitical sections, each drawn differently ac-cording to the reporter's perspective. For example, Gen. Julio Lon-doño of Colombia saw four "confederations" and a Plata basin as distinct parts of South America (map 2). Brazilian general Golbery do Couto e Silva partitioned the continent differently, with larger Amazonian and Plata areas in addition to two Brazilian sectors and a "continental welding zone" (map 3). Spanish diplomat Carlos Badía Malagrida envisioned four distinct "countries" (map 4), and Ber-nardo Quagliotti de Bellis of Uruguay also found four parts (map 5). One visualizes sections as all having a dominant river or sea, a po-litical and economic culture, and a historical heritage. Balances of power, distance, terrain, and a growing sense of nationhood have kept the four primary buffer states (Ecuador, Bolivia, Uruguay, and Paraguay) independent, and these have added balance and perhaps

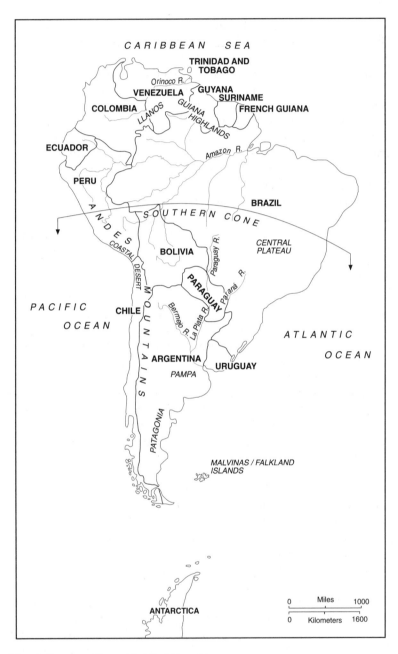

Map 1. Topographic and Political Place Names

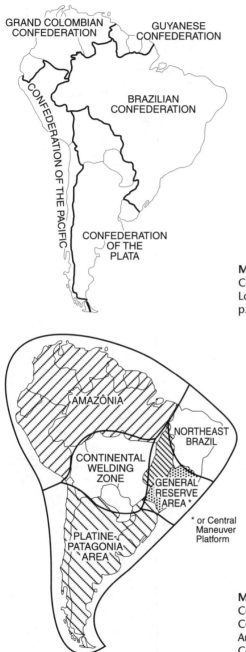

GRAND COLOMBIAN
CONFEDERATION

GUYANESE
CONFEDERATION

BRAZILIAN
CONFEDERATION

CONFEDERATION OF THE PACIFIC

CONFEDERATION
OF THE
PLATA

Map 2. The South American Confederations of Gen. Julio Londoño (after Londoño 1977, p. 34)

AMAZÔNIA

NORTHEAST
BRAZIL

CONTINENTAL
WELDING
ZONE

GENERAL
RESERVE
AREA *

PLATINE-
PATAGONIA
AREA

* or Central
Maneuver
Platform

Map 3. General Golbery do Couto e Silva's Geopolitical Compartmentalization of South America (after Golbery do Couto e Silva 1981, p. 88)

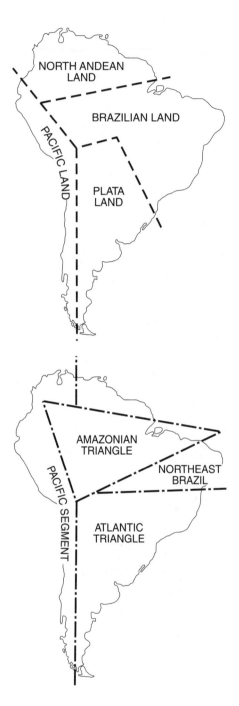

Map 4. The Geographical Factor in South America (after Carlos Badía Malagrida 1919 in Quagliotti de Bellis 1976d, p. 29)

NORTH ANDEAN LAND

BRAZILIAN LAND

PACIFIC LAND

PLATA LAND

AMAZONIAN TRIANGLE

NORTHEAST BRAZIL

PACIFIC SEGMENT

ATLANTIC TRIANGLE

Map 5. The Geopolitical Factor in South America (after Bernardo Quagliotti de Bellis 1975, p. 15)

stability to the traditional checkerboard structure that has inspired much of the continent's strife and diplomacy.

South America has less natural wealth than other continents, for instance, Australia, southern Africa, North America, and Eurasia. Resources are scattered throughout the region: oil in the northern Andes; iron in the Amazon, Orinoco, and Plata basins; tin and copper in Peru, Chile, and Bolivia. Fertile farmlands occur in the Southern Cone and in isolated valleys elsewhere. Yet, with the limited exception of the South Atlantic coast, the resources mix necessary for globally significant industry is not present in South America.

Most population since colonial times has clustered along ocean coasts; and the continental center is still sparsely inhabited. Difficult physical access and the lack of economic incentives hinder interior colonization and development. The vacant hinterland, nevertheless, is steadily disappearing, particularly of late, because of road and canal systems that penetrate previously impassable topography and in many cases damage the virgin landscape. Examples of this epic transformation of the interior abound: the Hidrovía system connecting the Paraná and Paraguay Rivers to Bolivia; the planned Bermejo barge canals of northern Argentina; the overland "corridor" highways linking coastal southern Brazil to Bolivia and Paraguay; the not-yet-completed "El Marginal" road through the jungle from Venezuela to Bolivia; the Brazilian superhighway network; even the outrageous "Amazon lake" proposal of the Hudson Institute, which would flood the continent's core and allegedly connect by lake transport the South American subregions.

These and other geographic features, when they affect foreign policy, describe the contribution of South American geopolitics. Several other geopolitical features, these dealing more with theory and application of the term, also need mention.

Development of the Study of South American Geopolitics

South American geopolitical scholars cover indigenous as well as international themes: the imperial nature of the Inca and Arucanian peoples; Columbus' discoveries and the early explorers, *conquistadores*, and slave masters (*bandeirantes* in Brazil); the struggle for independence and Simón Bolívar's dream of a united continent; wars, border conflicts, territorial cessions, and checkerboard patterns; Brazil's expansionism and the Bismarckian manipulations of the Baron Rio Branco; the potential for U.S. interference; and the recent issues of integration, development, smuggling, rebellion, immigration, and democracy.

Many South American writers have cited leading western philosophers—Aristotle, Bodin, Montesquieu, and Machiavelli, for instance—whose accounts contain occasional references to geopolitics. But South American geopolitics received its greatest theoretical inspiration from turn-of-the-century scholarship on European and U.S. political geography, where modern geopolitics first originated. Two principal ideas prevailed (Parker 1985: 10): that major political upheavals and transformations would occur during the twentieth century, and that "scientific" and "organic" theories would help explain such disorder and prescribe solutions. Inspired by Friedrich Ratzel and other mostly German writers, evolutionist writers took hold in South America and placed citizens, the state, and other pertinent features of the political landscape within a biologically conceived corporate structure of survival and determinism. In the international realm, the larger states, if they resembled healthy, dynamic organisms, would expand economically and territorially to absorb weaker, unprotected neighbors.

These ideas of *lebensraum*, or the natural urge and right of states for territorial growth, were broadened by U.S. geostrategist Adm. Alfred Thayer Mahan, who argued in 1897 that world empire depended on sea power as a mechanism for spatial expansion. The French school of Vidal de la Blache, less expansionist and strategic in nature but as motivated as the Germans to locate organic laws that governed societies, also would influence South American geopolitics.

Of considerable influence on South American geopolitics as well was Halford Mackinder, an Englishman who originated the first worldwide geopolitical theory. He saw recurring competition for world domination between land powers and sea powers (1904; 1919). The "heartland," or center of the "world island," that great expanse of land and resources in Central Asia, invulnerable to sea attack and able to capitalize on internal unity and maneuverability, posed the key to global empire. Mackinder warned western leaders that the world's power equilibrium had shifted from the maritime democracies to the continental autocracies, primarily because new land transportation and communications technologies gave strategic advantage to the centrally located land powers. Once these possessors of the heartland, most likely Germany or Russia, could successfully develop the greater Eurasian land mass, annex the "inner crescents" of China, India, the Middle East, and western Europe, and achieve a sea power capacity to enhance their continental strength, "the empire of the world would be in sight" within the aegis of the continental bloc of states.

The Karl Haushofer–Munich group of theorists rose during the interwar period and combined Ratzel's expansionism ideas and the organic theses of the state with Mahan's and Mackinder's grand visions of world power emanating from land power and maritime power. This school advocated the correctness of "youthful" nations bent on *lebensraum* expanding into less-populated spaces and absorbing the territory of weaker countries. Haushofer and his colleagues strongly favored German alignment with Russia and Japan, and they were among the first to note the importance of the Pacific basin in world affairs (Ael 1988).

These general sources of geopolitics, particularly the German, came to South America during the early decades of the twentieth century in military missions sent to South America or as South American officers received military schooling in Europe and the United States. Officer intellectuals in the advanced military schools and civilian instructors associated with such academies introduced geopolitical concepts into local doctrines (Guglialmelli 1986; also Nunn 1992). Because of the military impact on most governments, these geopolitical doctrines readily contributed to state policy, and thus found a positive and legitimate reception.

Two disclaimers require comment. First, I do not claim that geopolitics figures as the best or sole describer of international relationships. Rather, the theory is just one among a variety that may assist in describing, explaining, and predicting foreign affairs. Geopolitics might be useful, for instance, in showing the effects of geographic position on states' international behavior, whereas the approach may not be at all appropriate in modeling patterns of decision making or trade regimes.

Second, a direct cause-and-effect relationship between the impact of geopolitics and actual day-to-day decision making cannot be precisely gauged; hence, no concrete proof of this relationship appears in this text. I contend, nonetheless, that such a connection indeed does exist. One could partly substantiate geopolitics' contribution to policy by noting these examples: (1) the general reputation of geopolitics in South America is quite positive; (2) geopolitics is taught in many public and private schools and in most South American military academies; (3) many of the outstanding South American geopolitical writers were or are influential in government; and (4) many facets of South American foreign policy, for example, checkerboard structure, boundary conflict, and access to natural resources, appear to correspond to the geopolitical format.

Variations between South American and U.S. Geopolitics

The geopolitics of North and South America differ widely in terms of respectability and content. In South America, the term finds a friendly reception among most policy groups, wherein influential elites explore pertinent geopolitical ideas and theories from a wide spectrum of viewpoints and international origins. Active geopolitical associations appear in most of the countries, and these sponsor research centers and publications that apply and advance the concept. For example, in 1986 and again in 1989–1990, I participated in the meetings and research projects of the Instituto Paraguayo de Estudios Geopolíticos e Internacionales (Paraguayan Institute of International Geopolitical Studies). This group of academic and government intellectuals, in part financially supported by German and U.S. sources, holds seminars on diplomacy and integration, publishes monographs on geopolitics and democratic elections, and administers a resource and research center in downtown Asunción.

Such acceptance of geopolitics simply is not encountered in the United States. In fact, geopolitics attracts steadfast opponents who attribute to it a Nazi taint and allege a Machiavellian realpolitik of greed, corruption, and power not suited to democratic values. One rarely hears geopolitics discussed in a positive sense in the North, even though geopolitics seems to underlie the prime strategic dimensions of U.S. foreign and security policy. When geopolitics appears free of pejorative bias, it normally receives a "great-power politics" label, which likewise distorts the more appropriate definitions. North American geopolitical journals do not exist, although articles and books with a geopolitical designation in the title or as a subject now appear in greater numbers and enjoy a more positive reputation (Hepple 1986).

The two continents' geopolitics contrast in content as well. South America's geopolitics shows primarily a regional and subregional emphasis—on frontier pressures, national development and access to resources, territorial expansion, and regional conflict and cooperation. In contrast, the U.S. vision continues to be strategic or intercontinental and maritime, focused on maintaining an equilibrium of power in Eurasia and on isolating Latin America from involvement in Asian and European alliances.

Several explanations may account for these differences in geopolitical evolution. Certainly, the English colonial heritage of North America instilled a world vision on later U.S. policymakers that focused on sea power and strategic balances in Europe. The Spanish and Portuguese international scripts likewise came originally wrapped in strategic and maritime themes. However, the European intellectual traditions of South Americans, and the prominence of German, French, and Italian military missions, lent a strong continental thrust to southern geopolitical viewpoints, which one can easily observe in the literature. This continental impact, having reached receptive South Americans, represents a major point of departure between the two American interpretations of geopolitics.

Probably of greater significance, however, is the perspective of position and location. The United States directly confronts an encircling Eurasia from the European, polar, and Asian directions. Consequently, its location necessitates a strategic focus that considers the effects of a Eurasian balance or favorable imbalance on American security. Likewise, greater U.S. resources and a more unifying North American topography enable a strategic preoccupation with rimland Eurasia.

In contrast, the South Americans dwell in a more peripheral isolation. Their extracontinental ties focus more on Africa and North America, the former nonthreatening or of little global importance, the latter interventionist but distracted in East-West pursuits. Eurasia, the dominant world continent in traditional geopolitical terms, remains distant, buffered by the United States, and does not pose a security concern. Even if directly threatened by outsiders, the divided and, in most cases, militarily weak republics possess little power to exert a significant impact on northern affairs. In sum, positional and resources aspects contribute also to the different geopolitical directions of the two continents.

Location and Position As Vital to Geopolitics in South America

Location signifies place occupied: South America is located in the southern hemisphere of America. *Position* denotes relative placement or arrangement among an assortment of states: Latin America occupies the southern frontier of the United States. These two geopolitical attributes appear frequently in the literature, and they are vital to the understanding and use of the term.

The location of countries reflects the influence of environment on policy. For instance, based on traditional geopolitical hypotheses, states located on seacoasts or along large rivers may exert more of an impact on regional and world trade than do states located in the interior. Further, they tend to be less isolated from current technologies and cultures than countries located in the interior might be. South America's location, in the global sense, seems peripheral to Northern Hemisphere currents; as a result, its geopolitics focuses more on national and subregional events.

Position is utilized to appraise leverage or pivotal impact in international relationships. Certain countries are found in central or middle positions and, thus, may enjoy certain advantages in trade, resources access, and leadership. They may, in turn, suffer the disadvantages of possible border insecurity, foreign invasion, and dismemberment.

Location and position clearly have an impact on each other. Brazil's location in the center of South America motivates a tendency in foreign policy for balancing one neighbor against another. In contrast, Venezuela's peripheral location has insulated the republic from warfare with regional neighbors. In position, the centrally located buffer countries—Ecuador, Bolivia, Uruguay, and Paraguay— have suffered intrusions and dismemberment from more powerful neighbors; unfortunately for them, their isolated placements have not kept them free of damaging regional involvement.

The Importance of Maps to the
Study of South American Geopolitics

Maps show location and position, access to natural resources, areas of strategic importance, obstacles to and facilities for communication, and sources of conflict and cooperation. In the great majority of cases, the cartographic descriptions of South American writers validly render the continent's geography and geopolitics, and they assist interpretation of relationships between geographic factors and foreign policy.

Such depictions, however, may exhibit biases that expand an author's viewpoint, sometimes to the point of distortion. For instance, on map 6, Gen. Julio Londoño of Colombia sees the "Communist ideas" of the Southern Cone countries moving toward the "democ-

racies" of the northern-tier states. Likewise, Brazilian Golbery do
Couto e Silva alleges on map 7 a global antagonism between Communist forces (of course, in black) and the western nations. In similar terms, Gen. Edgardo Mercado Jarrín of Peru warns against Brazilian imperialism, as portrayed on map 8. His mapmaking depicts
an evil and threatening Brazil (note his configuration of arrows).
Finally, Venezuelan theorist Rubén Carpio Castillo accuses North
America of plotting the formation of a buffer state between its
southern frontier and revolution-prone central Mexico (map 9).

Three other examples of slanted cartography seem pertinent to
this discussion. Ricardo Riesco of Chile demonstrates in map 10
what seem to be racist overtones in his presentation of a possible
Asian "invasion" of South America, and he drafts a clear distinction between "dark-tropical" and "white-temperate" South America.
Chilean writers use the "Arc of the Southern Antilles" (map 11) to
draw on a series of Antarctic islands and flows of ocean current to
help justify Chile's claim against Argentina to maritime territory in
the South Atlantic, although, of course, this interpretation is not
sanctioned by the Argentines. Rubén de Hoyos contributes a final
example in map 12, a design meant to reveal NATO's alleged coveting of the Malvinas/Falkland Islands.

The Military Contribution to Geopolitics

Many South American geopolitical writers and practitioners come
from the armed forces, and most relevant topics revolve around defense matters. Geopolitics receives much attention in schools of professional military training, and active and retired officers as well as
civilians tied to the defense establishment sponsor geopolitical seminars, edit journals, head research clearinghouses, and publish books
and monographs. With the arrival of democracy to South America
and the new emphasis on development through regional integration, the military impact has become less visible within contemporary geopolitics than previously.

The "National Security State" doctrine merits our attention here
because it examines an important feature of military geopolitical
thinking. As stated by Jack Child (1988a: 42–43): "There appears to
be a close link between the organic theory of the state [the state as
a living entity], the National Security Doctrine, and geopolitical
thinking in the Southern Cone . . . As perceived by many South
American military professionals, the basic purpose of the state is to

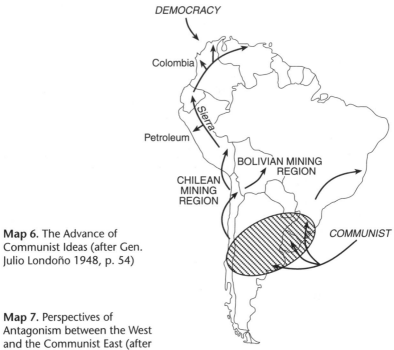

DEMOCRACY

Colombia

Sierra

Petroleum

BOLIVIAN MINING
REGION

CHILEAN
MINING
REGION

COMMUNIST

Map 6. The Advance of
Communist Ideas (after Gen.
Julio Londoño 1948, p. 54)

Map 7. Perspectives of
Antagonism between the West
and the Communist East (after
Golbery do Couto e Silva 1981,
p. 188)

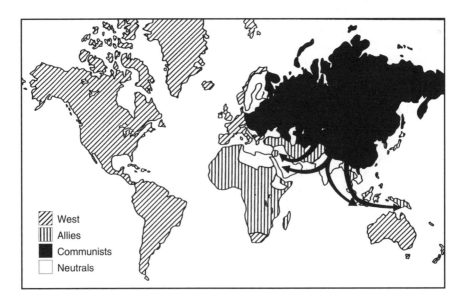

West

Allies

Communists

Neutrals

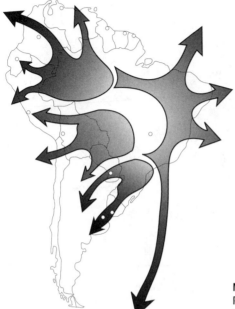

Map 8. Brazil's Geopolitical Projections (after Gen. Edgardo Mercado Jarrín 1979, p. 7)

Map 9. Buffer State Proposed by the U.S. Ambassador (after Rubén Carpio Castillo 1961, p. 60)

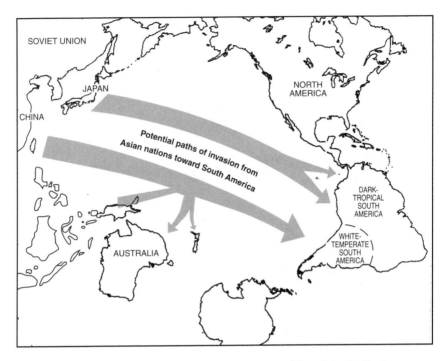

Map 10. Chile's Role in the Newly Developing Geopolitics of the Pacific Ocean, after Ricardo Riesco as adapted by César Caviedes in Kelly and Child 1988, p. 21.

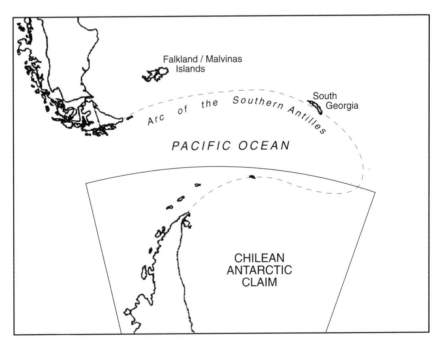

Map 11. The Arc of the Southern Antilles (after Child 1988b, p. 188)

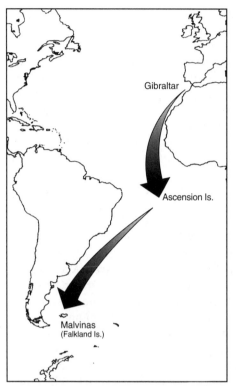

Map 12. Malvinas/Falklands: An Overflow of NATO? (after Rubén de Hoyos 1988, p. 238)

increase its power in order to provide for its security, and geopolitical thinking provides a pseudoscientific basis for it to do so." In the Darwinian and cruel world in which the organic states struggle to survive, neighbors are seen as potential adversaries, and even allies are viewed with suspicion. Hence, national security derives from factors both external and internal to the state. Protection from outside forces results from frontier defense and the ability to project national power. Internal threats stem from leftist subversives bent on overthrowing the organic state itself. Ultimately, in the thinking of many officers, safety results from military power, national economic development, and stable and conservative civilian leadership.

A "Feel" for Geopolitical Writing

Few South American geopolitical works are found in English translation, and some are difficult to locate even in Spanish or Portuguese in the United States. The style of these treatises reflects a simplicity and enthusiasm with, often, an emphasis on conventional viewpoints. In certain instances, for example, in the work of Juan Enrique Guglialmelli, Ramón Cañas Montalva, and Jorge Villacrés Moscoso, the prose becomes quite nationalist, emotional, and polemic. Many of the best-known publications, replete with English and German theories and general reviews of the traditional literature, serve also as textbooks, but with limited local application and little interest in testing theories that may not apply to contemporary South America. They deal primarily with frontier security, national development, and regional conflict and cooperation. (See chapter 3 for an inventory of the leading South American authorities.) The most favored foreign geopolitical authorities include Friedrich Ratzel, Rudolf Kjellén, Alfred Thayer Mahan, Halford Mackinder, Nicholas John Spykman, Karl Haushofer, and Saul Cohen.

At present, the major South American geopolitical journals are *Geosur* (Uruguay), *Geopolítica* (Argentina), and *A Defesa Nacional* and *Política e Estratégia* (Brazil). Four other journals, *Estrategia* (Argentina), *Geopolítica* (Uruguay), *Estudios Geopolíticos y Estratégicos* (Peru), and *Revista Geográfica de Chile "Terra Australis"* (Chile), merit our attention, although the first three are no longer published and the fourth has shifted its focus to political geography and away from foreign policy. The better general texts on the subject come from Atencio (1986); Badía Malagrida (1919); Briano (1977); Child (1985); Kelly and Child (1988); Londoño (1978); Marini (1982); Meira Mattos (1977a); Pinochet Ugarte (1984); Pittman (1981a); and Quagliotti de Bellis (1979a). Editorial Pleamar of Argentina is a leading publisher of geopolitical books.

New Directions in Geopolitical Theory

A "critical geopolitics" has emerged among a group of British and North American scholars who are attempting to reconceptualize traditional geopolitics. According to Klaus Dodds and James Sidaway (1994: 516):

> The concepts of power, knowledge, and geopolitics are . . .
> bound together in a provocative way. What is suggested is that
> forms of power / knowledge operate geopolitically: a certain
> spatialization of knowledge, a demarcation of a field of
> knowledge and the establishment of subjects, objects, rituals,

and boundaries by which a field (and the world) is to be known . . . [b]y examining the various narratives, concepts, and signifying practices that reside within geopolitical discoveries, it would be possible to understand something of the power of these discoveries to shape international politics.

This reconceptualization is important because it shows how geopolitical words and expressions — especially when these become biased, ethnocentric, and ideologically motivated — can affect policy. South American geopolitical writers frequently use metaphor, for example, to legitimize their policy recommendations: organic, or "living," frontiers to justify Brazil's occupation of the Amazon valley or Argentina's settlement of Patagonia; "cancerous cells" to describe the internal subversion that destroys the state's health; or the "disease" of communism, which destroys the health of national development (Hepple 1990: 13 – 20).

Accordingly, the new school aims to point out and correct such distortions when they appear (see Dodds 1994; Ó Tuathail and Agnew 1992; Dalby 1990; Ó Tuathail 1986). Except for occasional articles that apply these features to Latin America, the South American writers appear not to have taken up these directions themselves. Of much greater importance to them is the "dependency thesis," a charge of northern abuse of southern nations and a demand for compensation.

Geopolitical Concepts and Theories

"Concept" implies ideas, objects, symbols, or actions; "theory" indicates connections or relationships between concepts that can describe, explain, and predict specific events. For example, "distance" represents a geopolitical concept: the extent of space or territory from one location to another. "Voting for peacekeeping measures in the United Nations" signifies another. A theory links concepts, in this case, the anticipation of a possible tie between distance and U.N. voting and attempts to determine whether explanations of such associations can be found by way of these theoretical connections.

I have found a strong statistical association between the distance of Latin American countries from the United States and General Assembly voting in the 1950s and 1960s on peacekeeping issues. The Latin American republics farthest from the United States voted more frequently for these measures than those closest to the United States (Kelly and Boardman 1977). Hence, both variables interrelate to reveal the existence of a geopolitical theory that ties distance to General Assembly voting.

The study of South American geopolitics must grapple with concepts and theories, since writers pay significant attention to both, and both are vital to interpreting important national and regional events. Following is a series of important concepts and theories that are central to an understanding of South American geopolitics.

Strategic Concepts and Theories

Something that is "strategic" represents a continental or an extra-continental relationship in which an event in one location will affect another, distant, event. For example, a U.S. president makes a speech in which he appears to favor Brazil over other Latin American states. This speech reverberates throughout Argentine and Peruvian policy. Or Brazil's new superhighways stimulate construction of canals in the Plata valley. Or the Malvinas/Falklands war of the South Atlantic increases Guyanan-Venezuelan frontier tensions. Or the cold war's end further isolates South America in world affairs. These four strategic examples exist within a geopolitical context also, since they embody position, space, terrain, and resources, albeit at great distance.

The Core-Periphery Thesis
A good assortment of strategic examples fall within the "core-periphery" format, in which certain world areas have become important core regions, and other spaces are relegated to less-vital peripheral locations. Many depictions of this dichotomy exist in the geopolitical literature.

The Hundred-Year Cycle Thesis
Two cyclical suppositions, also strategic in nature, offer other variations on the core-periphery format. Modelski's "hundred-year cycles" hypothesis, for instance, locates a regular technology- and maritime power–based rise and fall of western empires over the past five centuries (1982; 1978). Although these leadership cycles have bypassed the southern lands, competition and destructiveness among core nations could lead to the ascendancy of a peripheral nation. Brazil could achieve higher world status as a result (Kelly 1992c; 1989).

The Pan-Regional Thesis

A more specific core-periphery model occurs in the "pan-regions" design (map 13), also a concept one sees in the geopolitical literature of South America. This Orwellian structure compartmentalizes the globe into three or four self-reliant longitudinal sectors in which the placement of technology and industrialization guarantees continued northern hegemony. Many Latin Americans see in the permanent members of the U.N. Security Council (China, Russia, France, Great Britain, and the United States) potential for pan-regional leadership. A more blatant conspiracy definition for pan-regionalism appears in the "condominium" concept.

The Key-Countries Thesis

The key-countries concept adds to the North-versus-South configuration of struggle and conspiracy (map 14). Here, the United States allegedly has chosen certain pivotally located periphery nations (Brazil, Iran, Zaire, and West Germany, for instance) that, with military and economic assistance, will be directed to pacify surrounding regions. President Richard Nixon and his security advisor and secretary of state, Henry Kissinger, advocated this strategy and made statements backing Brazil as the natural leader of South America, much to the distaste and alarm of its neighbors. In the early 1970s, for instance, leftist groups in Chile and Uruguay feared attack from Brazilian "sepoyan" (mercenary) armies, allegedly supported by U.S. assistance (Mutto 1971).

The Heartland Thesis

The most prominent core-periphery structure springs from Halford Mackinder's "heartland" thesis. Here, heartlands emerge as rather isolated compact regions embedded within continents and that occupy interior and strategically important positions, contain the resources to support industry and larger populations, compete in various ways with coastal areas, and exert an impact beyond their immediate boundaries (Kelly 1991). Mackinder focused on the vast space from eastern Europe to Siberia and from Persia and Tibet to the Arctic Ocean (map 15). He posited that possession of a "pivotal" zone, or heartland, gave an advantage to nations or alliances bent on domination of outlying regions. Countries in this continental position could exploit the resources of Eurasia by means of improved land transportation. If the holders of Eurasia strengthened

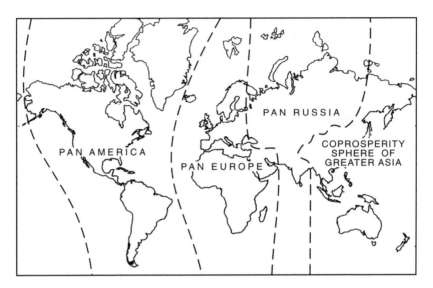

Map 13. The Pan-Regionalism Concept (after Marini 1982, p. 350)

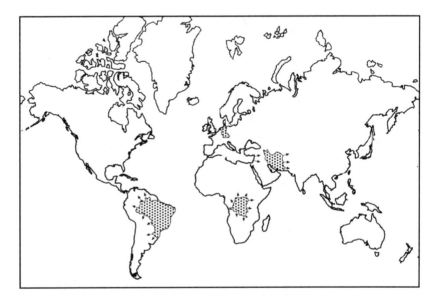

Map 14. The Key Countries Concept (after Marini 1982, p. 416)

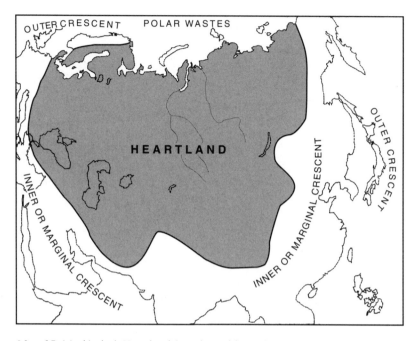

Map 15. Mackinder's Heartland (as adapted from Gray 1977, p. 24)

their military capacity by also developing a significant naval power, they could eventually encircle and defeat the great maritime nations, including the United States, and thus dominate the globe. Mackinder's thesis greatly influenced South American geopolitics, particularly Brazilian strategic thinking.

Three South American regions have received attention as centrally positioned heartland territories. Mario Travassos (1947), for instance, designated the Charcas triangle of Bolivia a heartland, as it links the towns of Sucre, Cochabamba, and Santa Cruz de la Sierra (map 16). In Mackinder-like terms, U.S. diplomat and strategist Lewis Tambs asserted that the Bolivian "heartland power center" and its "political epicentrum," Santa Cruz, could someday govern the continent (1965: 36, 42–43). Tambs alleged that Brazil's trans-Amazonian highways and the moving of Brasilia, its capital, to the interior derived from the nation's intention of dominating South America and gaining Pacific Ocean ports by absorbing the Charcas triangle.

Map 16. The Charcas Triangle of Bolivia (after Mario Travassos' "Charcas Heartland of South America" from Pittman 1983, p. 36)

The Sea and Land Power Thesis

The designations "sea power" and "land power" likewise come from Mackinder and the heartland thesis. Both Eurasia, primarily a land-power focus, and the United States, part of the maritime world, allegedly struggle to control "rimlands," or peripheral Eurasian areas (western Europe, the Middle East, south and east Asia, for example). Nicholas Spykman (1942), a U.S. Mackinderisk theorist who is greatly respected in South American geopolitical circles, maintains that whichever bloc dominates the rimlands will eventually control Earth.

Latin America does not have maritime importance in this strategic geopolitical calculation. Although Chile is recognized as a modest sea power within the South American context, and Argentina and Venezuela to an even lesser degree, their navies resemble ill-equipped and politically weak forces designed primarily to guard the coast. Despite the primarily maritime continent within Mackinder's outer crescent, South America's geopolitics shows a clear land-power orientation in both policy and theory.

The URUPABOL Thesis

The URUPABOL configuration—Bolivia, Uruguay, and Paraguay—also lays claim to South American heartland status, as suggested by several Southern Cone writers (Dallanegra Pedraza 1983; Velilla de Arréllaga 1982; Quagliotti de Bellis 1976b). Centered in Paraguay, and more specifically at the giant binational hydroelectric power station at Itaipú, this strategic axis is visualized as stabilizing continental politics by separating the two prime antagonists, Brazil and Argentina, and thus preventing an escalation of tension aimed at the Andean states and beyond and by providing access to regional economic integration.

The Continental Welding Zone Thesis

Golbery do Couto e Silva's "continental welding zone" (map 3), like the URUPABOL pivot, encompasses a region that includes Bolivia, most of Paraguay, and the Mato Grosso and Rondônia provinces of Brazil. He envisioned the possibility of Brazilian control of the continent and the South Atlantic if the country became more integrated and developed(1981). According to U.S. geopolitical writer Howard Pittman (1981a: 347–348), the general specified approaches for realizing this expansion of territory:

> 1. Link the Northeast and the South [of Brazil] to the central nucleus [the heartland] to provide the economic base for continental projection and at the same time guarantee the inviolability of the unpopulated interior by closing off routes of penetration. 2. Starting from the central nucleus, stimulate colonization to the northwest in order to integrate the "central west peninsula" into the Brazilian ecumene. 3. Starting from an advanced base of the central west and under cover of frontier nodules (defense points) flood the Amazon basin with civilization, coordinating this movement with an East-West progression along the axis of the river.

Thus, central location means protection, maneuverability, access to resources, and the ability to use military force, all factors within the geopolitical perspective.

The Pentagonal Thesis

An expanded version of Mackinder's original heartland awards global dominance to a "pentagonal" alignment of world areas (Japan, China, Russia, Europe, and North America). What counts originates within this core, and other regions, including South America, are left behind on slower and less-important tracks. The marginal areas simply lack relevance; globally significant events, particularly positive and productive ones, seldom transpire there. Many South American geopolitical writers and practitioners have accepted this thesis of peripheral inferiority, which may have retarded the continent's participation in global affairs and limited its geopolitics more to the regional than to the strategic.

The Dependency Thesis

Several other theories arise from this strategic core-periphery juxtaposition. The "dependency" thesis, for example, which attracts wide notice in South America, alleges northern capitalist domination, which has created a southern subservience and exploitation. Northerners beget wealth at the expense of southerners because of superior location, resources, and technology. The solution, in the form of a "new international economic order," may lie in negotiation and the core's voluntary relinquishing of power and resources.

A violent remedy to this wealth imbalance takes place in the imperialist claim that only urban and rural insurrection can rectify the inequality among world peoples and continents. Uruguay's Abrán Guillén (1967:123–146) advised urban terrorism against capitalist enclaves in South America. If U.S. companies were weakened by armed attacks, he alleged, their "super profits" could no longer help pay higher wages to the "internal proletariat" of the United States, which would eventually prompt socialist revolution in North America. With the "colonial" ties between North and South thus broken, prosperity and independence would end the periphery's marginality.

The Ocean Cycle Thesis

An "ocean cycles" conjecture, supported primarily by Chilean and Colombian geopolitical writers, links world control or hegemony to certain bodies of water, formerly the Mediterranean, currently the North Atlantic, and possibly a prosperous and commanding Pacific Rim in the future. Enthusiasts of this idea claim that such ocean bodies are strategically located adjacent to population centers, significant sources of wealth, and pivotal communication routes. These basins transmit a seafaring mentality to surrounding peoples, promote cultural and commercial unity, and provide a strong advantage for an eventual expansion of power. In the case of South American geopolitics, the Pacific Ocean holds promise from the standpoint of its great expanse and wealth, the rich technologies of Japan and the United States, and the immense economic markets of Asia and North America.

The Imperial Thesis

The "imperial thesis," another South American theory, applies best to the larger American states, particularly Peru, Chile, Brazil, and Argentina. According to this theory, "imperial" countries originally filled small, compact areas that early on began a territorial expansion to satisfy defense and material needs. Peripheral lands became incorporated into the older and commanding middle, although the newly incorporated territories and inhabitants differed in many ways from the core. Thus, a spatial division based on distance and central-versus-outlying position was established. Such an environment encourages frontier tensions, authoritarian rule, regional rebellion, and national disunity, suffered to some extent by all of the aforementioned countries.

The Manifest Destiny Thesis

The "manifest destiny" thesis resembles the imperial thesis. Under this canon, certain nations, originally small and limited to coastal enclaves, felt a right or mission to extend their territory across continents and to other oceans. The need to spread civilization and religion frequently provided additional motivation.

Because western portions of North America were perceived as largely vacant and available, the United States fulfilled its "manifest destiny" by expanding to the Pacific. Because Brazil, Chile, and Argentina could not project their power over larger continental areas, for reasons of distance, climate, terrain, limited resources, and other countries' settlement in desired areas, South America has not experienced the higher unity of the United States. The failure of a South American manifest destiny—of a Brazil or Argentina as two-ocean nations and clear leaders—has meant not only a divided continent and checkerboard diplomacy but also a geopolitics of regional and not strategic impact.

The Realpolitik Thesis

A pejorative term, "realpolitik" connotes a sinister, Machiavellian "power politics," an amoral, pragmatic, secretive, manipulative diplomacy that some writers mistakenly equate with geopolitics. In the case of South America, many place Brazilian statesman and general Golbery do Couto e Silva under this rubric. Other leaders sometimes associated with realpolitik include the United States' Henry Kissinger, Germany's Otto von Bismarck, and nineteenth-century Brazil's Baron of Rio Branco. But, to me, realpolitik contrasts starkly with geopolitics in that, where realpolitik centers on power and exploitation, geopolitics pertains to position, resources, and adaptation.

The Monroe Doctrine

Strategic concepts apply to inter-American geopolitics as well, and for these one must begin with the Monroe Doctrine of 1823. President James Monroe pronounced three themes in his declaration (Bemis 1943: 63–64): "(1) [T]hat the American continents . . . are henceforth not to be considered as subjects for further colonization by any European powers. (2) We should consider any attempt on their part to extend their system to any portion of this hemisphere as dangerous to our peace and security. (3) Our policy in regards to Europe . . . is, not to interfere in the internal concerns of any of its powers." A variety of protocols and corollaries, some of which tended to contradict the original document, amended these statements in later decades. But Monroe's purpose has remained a constant feature of strategy: to prevent the spread of Eurasian conflict and intrigue to Latin America, which could jeopardize U.S. security.

The Western Hemisphere Thesis

The Western Hemisphere thesis, another geopolitical premise, suggests a common heritage and cooperation among all American countries (Whittaker 1954: 1): "The . . . peoples of this hemisphere stand in a special relationship to one another . . . [which] sets them apart from the rest of the world." But, a close-knit America clearly has not risen; wars, neglect, tensions, interventions, and broken regional economic ventures instead have proved commonplace.

A strong momentum for "regionalism," or cooperation within both Latin American and hemispheric contexts, seems evident in present American diplomacy, however (Hurrell 1992). Rapprochement since 1980 between Brazil and Argentina, a clear signal of South American regionalism, has paved the way for economic accommodation in MERCOSUR's Plata integration. The North American Free Trade Agreement (NAFTA) offers another example of an integration that could spread farther south in the future.

Geopolitical Regional Categories

Within a geopolitical world system, six categories of regions and subregions also provide insight for interpreting South American geopolitics (Kelly 1986a):

- "Strategic countries": great-power states, such as the United States and the former Soviet Union, that possess transcontinental economic, political, and military impact. None of the South American countries fit this designation; the best, but still quite distant candidate is Brazil.

- "Allied regions": independent regional states more or less supportive of strategic countries' policies, for example, Western Europe during the cold war. Again, this type is not found in South America.

- "Independent areas": relatively neutral or uninvolved areas in a strategic sense and not tightly aligned to any strategic country. South America is the best contemporary example of this category.

- "Spheres of influence": regions more or less under the control of one strategic country or its allies, for instance, cold war Eastern Europe under Soviet dominance and contemporary Central America under the thumb of the United States. In the past, although not at present, South America was part of Spanish, Portuguese, and English spheres of influence.

- "Shatterbelts": regions in which two strategically important countries compete for control, with a resulting two-tiered structure of interrelated regional and strategic conflict. Shatterbelts pose a danger of escalation, of wars that might spread elsewhere, and of smaller countries' prompting serious confrontation between their larger, strategically important sponsors. This happened in the Cuban missile crisis of 1962. Shatterbelts no longer exist in South America, although they were evident during the Spanish and Portuguese competition for the continent.

▪ "Buffers": strategically neutral states or regions that help
prevent contact between belligerent countries and a spreading
of conflict. Middle America, comprising the Caribbean and
Central America, serves this function between North and
South America; the URUPABOL buffer countries plus Ecuador
help contain strategic South American conflict among the
larger states.

In this constellation, South America figures as an independent area
and not as a strategic world force nor part of a strategic alliance,
sphere of influence, or shatterbelt. Middle America, in contrast, has
alternated between sphere-of-influence, buffer, and shatterbelt status.

Geographic Locations

The identification of certain important geographic locations forms
another vital part of the continent's geopolitics (map 17). For instance, surrounding oceans demonstrate differing policy perspectives. The Caribbean, labeled by some geopolitical writers as the
"American Mediterranean" because it separates the northern and
southern continents and is controlled by a northern power, has ro-
tated historically between shatterbelt and sphere of influence. Only
Venezuela of the South American states possesses geopolitical interest in the Caribbean. Interestingly, the rimland of the American
Mediterranean includes a large portion of South America, for the
countries of Guyana, Suriname, Colombia, and Venezuela and the
French colony of Guiana are located adjacent to the sea (see map 1).
Uplands, jungles, and distance close off the Caribbean from the
Amazonian, Plata, and Andean-Pacific sectors of South America and
prevent a longitudinal unity that would connect the northern tier of
South America more closely to Southern Hemisphere affairs.

Areas of strategic concern in the Caribbean include the Panama
Canal, once a part of Colombia and still valuable to the nearby
South American states and the United States; the oil-producing
Maracaibo basin and the minerals-rich Guajira peninsula, both
occupying tense frontiers between Colombia and Venezuela; the
mouth of the Orinoco River, where several territorial disputes are
ongoing among Guyana, Venezuela, and Trinidad-Tobago; and the
offshore islands and "choke points," or straits, along the southern
Caribbean edge through which oil and other traffic passes.

In this strategically relevant sectional configuration, a second
portion of South America, the "Southern Cone," begins at the

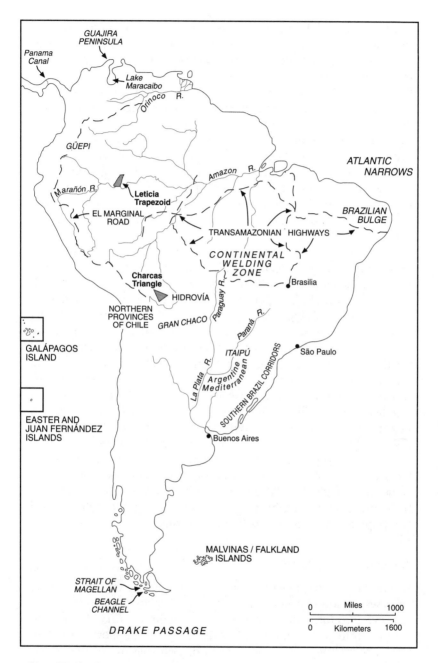

Map 17. The Strategic Areas of South America

southern edge of the Amazon watershed and extends to the Antarctic. The most dynamic and prosperous part of South America, particularly along the South Atlantic coast of Brazil and Argentina, this region encompasses the Plata River system for the most part, although the Andean Pacific states of Chile and Peru belong to the Southern Cone as well. The most vital strategic areas happen at the Brazilian and Argentine industrial ecumenes (São Paulo and Buenos Aires); the great hydroelectric power station at Itaipú on the Paraná River; the Argentine "Mesopotamia," or interior provinces of Formosa, Corrientes, and Misiones, which separate Argentina from Brazil; the overland truck "corridors" passing across southern Brazil from Bolivia and Paraguay; and the strategic northern provinces of Chile, a "triple-point" area that has been tense since the War of the Pacific in the 1870s.

Southern Cone maritime choke points likewise are strategically important South American areas. The Atlantic Narrows between the northeast salient of Brazil and the west African coast, through which pass Middle East petroleum and other vital cargoes, gained distinction as a strategic passageway in World War II and also during the cold war. Hostile submarines and coastal batteries allegedly could have prevented these products from reaching Europe and North America. In addition, if freight through the Panama Canal was sabotaged, the significance of several "southern passages" between Antarctica and the lower extremes of Chile and Argentina (the Beagle Channel, the Strait of Magellan, and the Drake Passage) might increase. Adjacent islands as well, including the Malvinas/Falklands, Easter, and Galápagos, would share the strategic relevance of the southern passages. Finally, the two most dominant river systems of South America, the Amazon and Plata, likewise assume value in strategic calculations because they access the resources of the continent's geographic interior and they flank the technological and population cores of Brazil and Argentina.

The Equilibrium Model

Several balance-of-power configurations require description for later analyses of South American geopolitics. "Balance of power" connotes various formations or structures of major-country alignments, ranging from an "equilibrium," or the fairly equal apportionment of influence among a particular system of countries, to a "preponderance," or the absorption of most power into one nation or bloc.

Structures can also reveal various constellations or poles, for instance, bipolar or multipolar. Such distributions conform to a regional and a strategic perspective. The United States enjoys preponderance in North America, which enables it to project authority beyond its region, but it shared strategic equilibrium with the Soviet Union during the cold war.

The South American balance of power fits the equilibrium mode in that no country or alliance dominates the whole continent, although the larger republics overshadow and often make demands on the weaker states. The fact that Brazil or the other great nations of South America could not individually establish continental mastery, and thus extracontinental projection, has defined the continent's past and present geopolitics.

Within the equilibrium model, the historical pattern in South American geopolitics has resembled a "checkerboard" balance of power, in which neighbors appear as enemies, neighbors of neighbors as friends (Child 1988a; Seckinger 1976; Burr 1955). A "mandala" of concentric and alternating cycles of hostility and alliance offers a variation on this design (map 18).

South America's checkerboard and mandala structures correspond to a "multipolar" balance of power, a fragmented design in which the necessity of two-border defense probably has restricted conflict escalation. Because of its peculiar mix of climates, its isolation, topographies, country positions, and heritage of Spanish, Portuguese, and English competition, among other factors, the continent seems a natural for this checkerboard motif. As depicted on map 18, Brazil, Chile, and Colombia at times appeared in opposition to Peru, Argentina, and Venezuela. This multipolar balance-of-power framework has influenced regional diplomacy since the 1820s.

Checkerboards bring advantages and disadvantages to the region's politics. The alignment seems to have encouraged more peace than warfare among the republics, although often in the form of a wary, armed, and strained composure rather than the deeper harmony of trust and relaxation of tensions. Checkerboards share credit for power equilibrium (and thus a continuity of relations) among the larger countries, checkmate major regional shifts of power and territorial conquests, and guarantee the independence of the weaker buffer states.

The mandala system presents the possibility of escalation or a heightening of conflict, and even war, among opponents. These patterns foster frontier tension, force participants to plan two-front

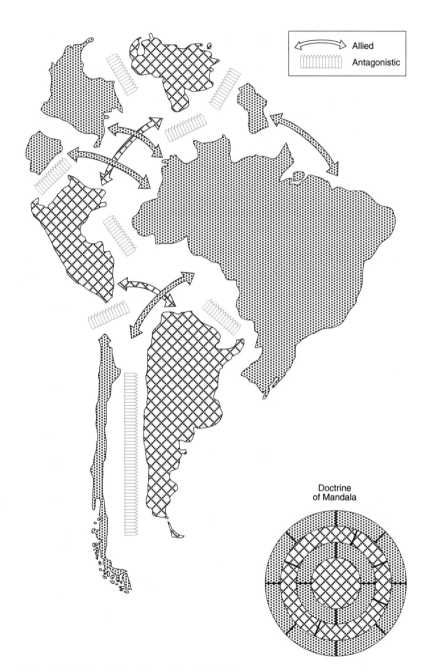

Map 18. The South American Checkerboard

defenses (and thus detract from national development), allow the United States and other outside nations to manipulate regional affairs, and prevent productive cooperation among states by prolonging the status quo.

One of the remarkable evolutions in South American geopolitics, nevertheless, has come about since the 1970s in the apparent transition from the traditional checkerboard to a more cordial state of affairs, anchored in the Brazil-Argentine rapprochement. Will this dynamic expand into extensive regional cooperation, even confederation, or revert again to mandalas or some other balance-of-power mode? We shall analyze these possibilities in later chapters.

A number of South American countries fit the "buffer state" designation: Ecuador, Bolivia, Uruguay, and Paraguay, with the recent additions of Guyana and Suriname. These smaller countries are located between larger republics, and their value lies in preventing direct contact between nearby states, which could escalate into high tension and warfare.

These pivotal nations, although protected to some degree by checkerboards as well as by regional cooperation, have not fared well throughout South American history. All have lost territory to larger neighbors; they have been the site of the continent's major wars; and their foreign policies have been manipulated by outsiders. But, probably the medial position of the buffers has helped deter continentwide escalation of conflict, and the buffers have guaranteed their own survival by virtue of being buffers. They may, in fact, play a central role in future regional integration.

Smaller republics centrally positioned among more powerful states frequently exhibit "pendulum foreign policies"; that is, they balance, for security and economic reasons, one stronger neighbor against another. This process relies on several criteria pertinent for the buffer state (Kelly and Whigham 1990): (1) competition among larger neighbors for the buffer's resources (and access to resources); (2) neighbors' awareness that buffers may prevent checkerboard-driven escalation of conflict; (3) larger states' guarantee of the buffers' independence, although one sponsor may have greater influence in the buffer than other sponsors; and hence, (4) reactive and not assertive foreign policy in buffer nations, with, normally, a penchant for regional integration and cooperation.

In sum, the pendular approach seems a reaction to the threats of the surrounding larger powers, which enjoy greater geopolitical maneuverability. Such a policy reflects relative weakness and clearly not the international status accorded a normally functioning state in contemporary world society.

Some commentators find "domino" formations common to Latin America. Jerome Slater describes this pattern as follows (1987: 107): "In its most familiar form, [domino] theory holds that the United States must take decisive action to prevent a communist victory in small country A, in itself of little or no economic or strategic significance to American interests, for the fall of that country would set in motion a chain of events that would lead inexorably to communist takeovers in geographically contiguous countries B, C, D and so on throughout the entire region." Sen. Jesse Helms claimed the existence of falling dominoes in Central America (Schoultz 1987: 66): "Cuba's already gone. If we sit out, Guatemala, Honduras, Costa Rica—bam, bam, bam."

In contrast to checkerboards and buffers, however, dominoes appear alien to a study of South American geopolitics. The domino concept reflects an anti-Communist fervor that distances the thesis from geopolitics, which likewise exhibits a spatial dimension but attempts to avoid ideological tainting. Lack of a clear case of falling dominoes in contemporary South America also presents further evidence. Hence, except in cases of a contagion of political events (riots, subversion, democracy), which does occur in South America from time to time (Govea and West 1981), the domino phenomenon seems an inappropriate interpreter of South American affairs, although the theory remains important because U.S. policymakers continue to imagine its potential for harm.

Regional Concepts and Theories

The Frontier Theory

An assortment of regional qualities merit attention in our review of South American geopolitics. A majority of these concern frontiers. The term "frontier" encompasses not only specific boundary demarcations but also the larger territories within a transnational setting.

Frontiers represent a prime focus of geopolitical writers for a variety of reasons. First, South America contains a multitude of border areas, and these sometimes fall near disputed positions or resources. Second, some boundaries appear poorly drawn because of faulty colonial cartography or difficult terrain, which precluded accurate surveying. Third, the German influence on South American writers, with its emphasis on frontier concepts, maintains this characteristic because Europe, like South America, contains a multitude of frontiers. Finally, the territorial ambitions of some states, Brazil being the most noteworthy, prompt focus on frontier tensions as well.

All major South American territorial conflicts and wars relate somehow to frontiers. In the 1820s Cisplatine contest between Brazil and Argentina for control of Uruguay, access to the Plata River mouth underlay the struggle. The Triple Alliance War in the 1860s sprang from Paraguay's violation of the Argentine frontier. The War of the Pacific involved Chile's quest for nitrates on the Peruvian and Bolivian borders. Twentieth-century wars for the Leticia, Chaco, and Marañón territories were all frontier disputes, and the Malvinas/ Falklands conflict of 1982 between Argentina and Great Britain likewise centered on disputed ownership of territory. (Discussion of these conflicts appears in chapter 4.) Interestingly, the growing South American movement toward common markets and integration seeks to remove frontier pressures and to substitute regional cooperation across international boundaries.

Because of the apparent correlation between borders and conflict in South America, some geopolitical thinkers (primarily Carlos de Meira Mattos and Julio Londoño) have proposed types of frontiers that might impede disputes. Some encourage "natural frontiers," where mountain crescents, jungles and deserts, river thalwegs, or some other geographic distinction clearly separate one nation from another. Artificially drawn borders (along lines of latitude or longitude, for example) that surround densely populated areas might encourage aggression because of their lack of clarity. Another conjecture describes "satisfied" and "imperialist" states (Meira Mattos 1990a), wherein the former accepts existing territorial ownership and the latter strives to expand national domain.

The Organic Theory

"Organic" theories appear in the geopolitical writings of South Americans as a reflection of the German impact on the republics' foreign affairs. As described earlier in this chapter, countries are made "human" in South American geopolitical writing; they begin life, mature, age, and then die, as would a person. Hence, as nations grow and die, frontiers naturally expand and contract to reflect the life cycle. This organic cycling resembles the concept of *lebensraum*, so notorious in fascism before the Second World War, in which "youthful" and therefore vigorous and expanding countries, that is, the fascist bloc, possessed the "right" to take territories and resources belonging to others. Common sketches of "dead" and "live" frontiers receive their inspiration from this format. The former are endangered by frailty, the latter by anticipating expansion. In South America, particularly in Brazil, this assumption of territorial expansion as a right of "growing" nations frequently appears in geopolitical discourse.

The Spatial Theory

Spatial theories are also common in South American geopolitics. The premise is that territorial space somehow affects foreign policy. Proponents of "space consciousness" argue, for instance, that a people's awareness of space and position will advance their national destiny. An expansive consciousness, which larger nations seem to possess, underlies the concept; a lack of spatial perception has hindered the weaker. Hence, states should strive for "space mastery," in which governments endeavor to fully populate and develop peripheral spaces to avoid absorption by neighbors. Along with the notion of space, or "raum" struggle, state survival depends on territorial growth, with the more secure countries assembling greater expanses of land.

"Autarky," or national self-sufficiency, commonly surfaces in the literature, often in the guise of "economic nationalism" or plans for national development. If countries modernize sufficiently to enable a high degree of autonomy, national defense and economic security allegedly follow.

Finally, those who favor the "law of valuable areas" claim that precious but unpopulated and underdeveloped spaces run the danger of seizure by stronger neighbors (Pittman 1981a). Neglect of and weakness in territorial policy may cause partition, which is feared by the menaced buffer states but endorsed by the Peruvians and Brazilians.

The Balkanization Theory

A fear of "Balkanization," or "Polandization," observed particularly in the geopolitical treatises of buffer state authors, derives from historical fact (all of the weaker nations of South America have lost territories to larger neighbors) and from the emphasis given the organic state theses (map 19). Frequently, the areas most susceptible to this dismemberment are in the "hinterlands," or interior regions

Map 19. The "Polandization" of Buffer States

COLOMBIA

ECUADOR

Ecuador to
Brazil, 1904

Ecuador to
Peru, 1942

Bolivia to
Brazil, 1903

PERU

BRAZIL

Bolivia to
Peru, 1909

Bolivia to
Brazil, 1907

Bolivia
to Peru,
1929

BOLIVIA

Paraguay to
Brazil, 1872

Bolivia
to Chile,
1883-1884

PARAGUAY

Paraguay to
Argentina, 1870

Uruguay to
Brazil, 1851

CHILE

URUGUAY

ARGENTINA

distant and isolated from coastal population and industrial centers, and in the "Mediterranean," or landlocked, spaces.

The Geographic Opportunity Theory

Frontiers are closely associated with war and conflict in South America. James Wesley (1962) promotes the geographic opportunity axiom whereby the more borders a country possesses, the more wars a nation will be involved in. Hence, centrally positioned states suffer more warfare than countries of the periphery, as is frequently noted in the political science literature (Richardson 1960). I tested this proposition exclusively for South America by comparing the number of international frontiers with the frequency of war (Kelly 1992a: 47) and found a high association between the two variables.

The Fluvial Laws Theory

A variety of fluvial "laws" are enunciated within geopolitics: (1) Mediterranean countries inherently strive for an ocean outlet; (2) centripetally flowing rivers unify nations; (3) states naturally expand to dominate entire river watersheds; (4) major river estuaries embody strategic and sometimes shatterbelt zones where larger countries compete for control; (5) states that occupy estuaries tend to expand along adjacent seacoast lines; and (6) the direction of a river's flow reveals the regional directions in a country's foreign policy. None of these theories has ever been systematically tested by their pronouncers, so there is no proof that these geopolitical phenomena consistently occur.

Most authors normally see waterways as acceptable natural boundary lines, although rivers are best utilized as unifiers of nations and regions. Nonetheless, for the most part, South America's rivers have not played a significant role in the region's foreign affairs. The Amazon, Orinoco, and Plata Rivers access a largely deserted continental core where the development of resources has proved expensive. Indeed, it is uncertain whether the South American hinterland holds exploitable wealth that would make fluvial traffic profitable.

Antarctica and the South American territorial seas are growing in importance in geopolitical thinking as a result of recent technological advances. Although the 1961 U.N. Antarctic Treaty, which froze territorial claims to the subcontinent, continues in force, Chile, Brazil, and Argentina remain in competition for their claimed Antarctic areas, making this issue divisive and potentially conflictual. Brazilian theoretician Therezinha de Castro advocates the *defrontação* thesis, in which Antarctic ownership is determined by longitudinal lines that flow from a South American claimant's ocean frontage to the Antarctic pole (see map 20). Other sources assert common or national ownership of the southern continent.

Coastal states have come to recognize the strategic and, particularly, the economic value of adjacent ocean waters. Bolivia's quest for a port, Peru's and Ecuador's fishing demands, the Beagle Channel dispute, and the Malvinas/Falklands war are examples of the increasing strife currently associated with the territorial zones. Traditionally, just ocean straits, or choke points, and sea lines of communication figured in maritime geopolitics as pivotal transit zones. But with the new fishing and seabed exploitation technologies, the seas have grown in importance (Morris 1990; Glassner 1985). Continued technological advances and growing scarcities in natural resources could convert the coastal frontiers into a major concern in South American geopolitics.

The Climatological Theory

Some South Americans assert a link between climate and political behavior. Temperate regions allegedly invigorate, for instance, whereas the tropics sap the energy. General Londoño links topography and elevation to certain democratic and governmental behaviors. He also laments the disadvantages caused by South America's harsh environments and theorizes that northern "world power centers" benefit from lower average temperatures (1965; 1948).

Sometimes racial overtones intrude into these comparisons, as one can observe in Riesco's "White-Temperate" and "Dark-Tropical" South American depiction (map 10). But General Meira Mattos of Brazil contests the premise that the tropical impact constrains national power (1980a). Indeed, he sees a "challenge and response" feature in Brazil that will stimulate the nation toward higher international status once his people face and overcome the obstacles of the Amazonian jungles.

The Regional Integration Theory

Despite Simón Bolívar's widely accepted declaration for continental confederation, little has happened to help South America reach this goal until recently. Now, regional "integration," or an economic and political collaboration among the South American republics, receives significant support from geopolitical writers, indicating that

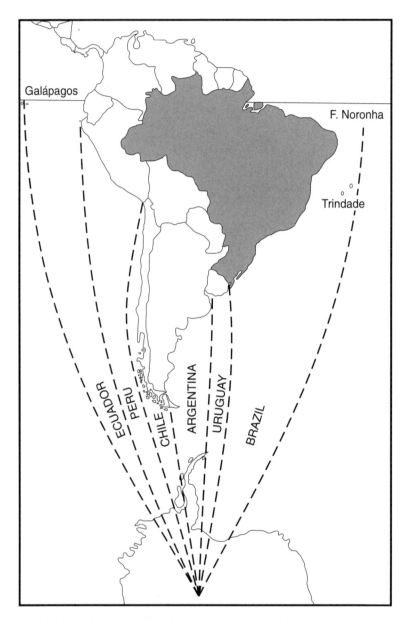

Map 20. The *Defrontação* of the Antarctic (after Castro 1982b, p. 83)

South American geopolitics now encompasses harmony as well as competition. The momentum for integration, especially in the Southern Cone's MERCOSUR treaty, merits our close attention.

As will be shown in chapter 4, the transition in the 1970s from rivalry to regional cooperation occurred in both geopolitical writing and foreign affairs. This change seems to symbolize a significant shift in the continent's balance of power, one that many will follow with interest. If integration succeeds, will it expand into some sort of South American or hemispheric common market? Will the checkerboard power rivalries completely disappear? Might some type of political federation someday rise? How would federation influence relations with North America? What happens if integration does not take place?

The definitions, characteristics, concepts, and theories described in this chapter introduce South America's geopolitical milieu. They will appear again throughout the book. Now we turn to national geopolitics, regional and international issues, and an account of the South America – United States geopolitical relationship.

T his chapter and the next examine the geopolitics of each South American country. Here I discuss the primary geopolitical themes or concerns of each of the thirteen nations. Chapter 3 focuses on the writings of major South American geopolitical authors.

I begin with Brazil because its power and position usually dominate the continent's international relations. Brazil's looming, at times threatening, presence seems to imprint strongly on the foreign policy of the other republics. Argentina, Brazil's traditional rival, and the buffers Uruguay and Paraguay, come next. I then move west and north to cover the other states' geopolitical perspectives and their consequent foreign policies. I first give a brief geographic background for each nation, followed by a study of its most prominent geopolitical themes.

The Geopolitics of Brazil

Brazil, with its population of 150 million, about half of all South Americans, its pivotal position in the continent's center, and its significant national wealth, overshadows the geopolitics of South America. The country's vastness, nearly half of South America and fifth-largest country in the world (behind Russia, China, Canada, and the United States), also contributes to its geopolitical preponderance. Brazil rates as the only South American state poised for world status.

Yet, problems impede Brazil's authority on the continent. Human resources, for example, are divided very unevenly, and national unity—social, political, and spatial—appears rather weak. Despite impressive technological achievements, which by themselves place the country among the ten top industrial economies, great pockets of poverty and neglect affect its world leadership position and reduce its regional geopolitical impact. In addition, most citizens reside along the Atlantic coast; little development reaches far inland. Another problem facing Brazil is its imperialist reputation; neighbors often distrust its intentions (see chapter 3).

The nation divides geographically and culturally into five distinct subregions (map 21): the Amazonian North, the Northeast, the Southeast, the South, and the Central-West.

The Amazonian North

Largest of the five subregions, with 42 percent of Brazil's area, but sparsest in population and in political influence, the Amazon basin exhibits low plateaus and rolling hills of tropical rain forests, or *selva*. Lacking in economic development and not well integrated with the rest of the country, this potentially rich area started attracting new settlement and government involvement in the 1970s. Development has prompted international charges of serious ecological damage to this great watershed and of resumed frontier expansion against the surrounding states. General Meira Mattos and other commentators (1980a; also Sternberg 1987) fear the Amazon region could separate from Brazil if lags persist in population growth and integration with the other subregions. Modern mineral prospecting techniques have uncovered huge amounts of iron ore, bauxite, tin, and gold in the *selva*; additional natural wealth may await discovery. Nonetheless, debate continues concerning the development of the Amazon.

The Northeast

The Northeast, a strip of tropical *selva* extending along the Brazilian "bulge" (or the peninsular protrusion into the Atlantic toward Africa) from Fortaleza to Salvador, changes in terrain and climate as one moves south, from a rain belt to a much drier interior woodland known as the Caatinga. Both areas are heavily populated (almost 30 percent of Brazilians), by mainly blacks of African slave origin. The primarily agricultural economic base suffers from persistent drought, which creates political unrest and forces migration to already-overpopulated southern cities. The federal government's attempts to encourage residents to establish settlements in the Northeast's Amazon basin have not met with great success, and the area, like the Amazon, remains loosely tied to the dominant Southeast.

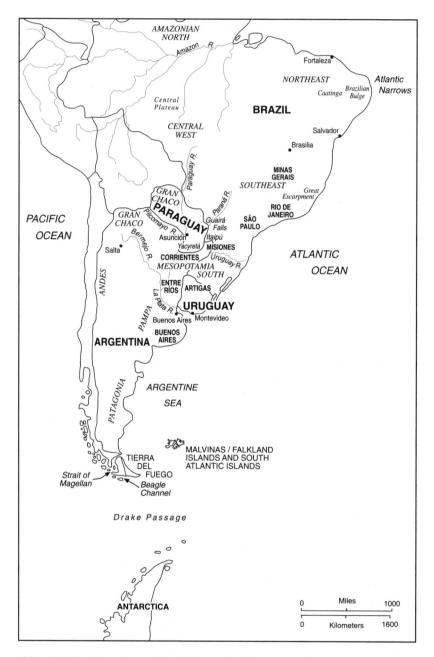

Map 21. The Subregions of Brazil, Argentina, Uruguay, and Paraguay

The Southeast

Another coastal space, the Southeast, runs south of Salvador to the state of São Paulo and dominates the entire length by the Great Escarpment, an abrupt natural wall set back from and paralleling the ocean. This ribbon of land eventually rises to sixty-five hundred feet above sea level, where the Central Plateau begins to reach westward. Significant mineral deposits have encouraged manufacturing in the states of Minas Gerais and Rio de Janeiro, but most of the nation's high tech industry is concentrated in São Paulo. The most advanced industrial zone in Latin America, São Paulo leads the country in the production of almost everything except certain tropical products and minerals. Despite having only 10 percent of the surface area of Brazil, the Southeast is home to 44 percent of its population. By a large margin, this geopolitical fulcrum dominates the country's economy and politics.

The South

The South, a semitropical tall-grass prairie, envelopes the southern extremity of the Great Escarpment and contains mostly people of Italian, Japanese, German, and Middle Eastern descent. Its products include rice, wine, and cattle, and it has a growing industrial potential. In national political impact, this region ranks second, but at some distance behind the Southeast.

The Central-West

The Central-West encloses the vast area of the Central Plateau, about three thousand feet above sea level. Despite an annual rainfall of forty inches, relatively level terrain, and the presence of Brasilia, the Central-West is sparsely inhabited and contributes little to national affairs except access to the great hydroelectric power complex at Itaipú on the Paraná River. This complex, shared with Paraguay, supplies much of the industrial energy needs of the southern coastal ecumenes.

Brazilian Geopolitical Themes

Seven important themes dominate Brazil's geopolitics. Most prominent among these, territorial expansion, stems from a long history of organic frontiers pushed steadily outward from the original coastal Portuguese colony. In fact, Brazil's manifest destiny very much resembles that of the United States: westward movement toward the Pacific. In Brazil's case, the movement is also toward the Plata River and the Caribbean. Such "imperial" growth originally came from pioneers and slaveholders reaching west for new lands and peoples to exploit; later, it arose from a conscious government policy of expansion, with the last great hiatus occurring during the time of the assertive Baron of Rio Branco one hundred years ago.

During this period, hinterlands were exposed to absorption by the Portuguese Americans, and growing industrialization provided a need for the natural resources of the Amazon and Central Plateau. Political turmoil and neglect of borderlands throughout Spanish America allowed Brazil to annex new spaces by force or formal annexation, although this growth has substantially slowed during the twentieth century.

A contemporary policy to renew aspirations to expand the country's territory forcibly likely would prompt considerable regional and international tension. Brazil's someday achieving by peaceful means an enclave on the Pacific or Caribbean appears doubtful. However, the mere potential of territorial growth maintains a wariness on the part of neighbors, something even the current diplomacy of accommodation cannot erase, and this possibility continues to stimulate the Spanish Americans to secure their own hinterlands as well as to move more rapidly toward regional integration in league with Brazil.

In light of this expansionist tendency, a second major theme of Brazilian geopolitics—fear of Spanish-speaking encirclement and of a hostile alliance against Brazil—deserves attention. In particular, rivalry between Brazil and Argentina for leadership of the Plata watershed and for control of the three buffer states, Bolivia, Uruguay, and Paraguay, embodies this historical competition and South American geopolitics in general. Argentina plays a necessary role in this geopolitical drama by having helped prevent Brazil from attaining a Pacific foothold, and by having created the possibility of a continentwide escalation of conflict through the South American checkerboard configuration. These aspects represent two essential keys to South American geopolitics.

In addition, the Brazil-Argentine contention preserved the buffer states' autonomy, restricted regional economic integration, allowed the United States' "divide-and-conquer" diplomacy toward South

America, and checkmated both Brazil's and Argentina's global participation. But the recent rapprochement between the two states, which could transform continental geopolitics, has relaxed tensions in the area, increased regional integration and development, kept U.S. influence at bay, and heightened international status for both Brazil and Argentina.

Brazil's central position on the continent brings a further dimension to national geopolitics. The country's pivotal location, positioned within the Amazonian, Plata, Andean, and Caribbean areas, facilitates access to continental communications and to most South American resources. It makes an anti-Brazilian bloc among the Spanish American states more difficult and puts Brazil in a leadership position in the continent's commerce, development, peacekeeping, and foreign affairs. Its focal position bestows on Brazil a strategic role in America second only to that of the United States.

Central position brings liabilities also, primary among these the apparent risk of imperial disintegration. Because it originated as a coastal enclave at Salvador, the nation absorbed dissimilar parts during expansion and thereby created several real or potential problems. Uneven development and lack of national integration plague the country's economy and politics, and distant frontiers tend toward rebellion. Unattended boundaries likewise encourage unauthorized Brazilian forays onto vacant neighboring territories and cause diplomatic embarrassment and tense borders. The gold miners' attack in Venezuela (see chapter 1) provides a good example. Smuggling and illegal colonization across frontiers, such as one sees along the Bolivian and Paraguayan borders, for example, also illustrates the point.

A stable Brazil tends to stabilize the continent, as is evident in the key-nation thesis and in the country's traditionally close ties to the United States. But if Brazil's disintegration seemed imminent as its several sections demanded autonomy, all of South America clearly could face similar levels of unrest. If Brazil indeed became unstable, a shatterbelt might arise, the checkerboard might erupt into warfare, older territorial disputes might resume, and boundary lawlessness might abound. Clearly, the geopolitical landscape of South America holds the potential for radical transformation should Brazilian authority collapse.

The growth of industrial power and national confidence has expanded Brazil's strategic interest in the South Atlantic, in Antarctica, and in African affairs. Brazil's position astride the Atlantic Narrows has spurred its interest in establishing a greater military presence in the area and a leadership position in the proposed South Atlantic Treaty Organization (SATO), which someday may link South American and African states in terms of naval security. Diplomatic ties to West African states have grown substantially recently, and Brazilian writers, most notably Therezinha de Castro, have formulated national claims to Antarctic territories and waters.

Since colonial times Brazil has sought *grandeza*—status as a great world power. The nation aspired to permanent membership on the League of Nations Council and United Nations Security Council only to be defeated by Spanish America. The United States has encouraged Brazil's aspirations. But Brazil's interest in greater world status rose particularly during the 1970s after its significant spurt in industrial growth relative to Argentina's economic and political stagnation. At present, however, calls for *grandeza* appear less often because of Brazil's recession and political turmoil and its decision to weaken its ties with the United States and to foment stronger linkages within the continent.

Will its South American neighbors support or continue to fear a greater world role for Brazil? Could the United States work harmoniously with Brazil as a great power? How assertively might Brazil perform on the world stage?

Last, Brazil's foreign policy is the clearest geopolitically oriented example among the South American states and reflects the importance given geopolitics by leaders and the influence exerted by the major geopolitical writers. Its geopolitical orientation also reflects the country's geographic position and the need to carefully consider the advantages and liabilities relative to its heritage of spatial expansion, its encirclement by Spanish neighbors, its imperial composition and potential for national fragmentation and frontier unrest, its internal resources and maritime concerns in the Atlantic, and its historical objective of international status. There is consensus in domestic policy because the country's geopolitical framework is widely accepted, partly because of its past successes in attaining bordering territories and economic concessions and because of the ability of prominent geopolitical theorists to occupy important leadership positions. In addition, Brazil's position within a regional environment of strategic isolation, U.S. sponsorship, smaller surrounding states, and economic and political opportunity also seems to encourage a coherent vision of policy needs and approaches.

The Geopolitics of Argentina

Among Latin American states Argentina ranks second in territorial size to Brazil, with one third the territory of its northern neighbor, and third behind Brazil and Mexico in population, with only 20 percent of the Brazilian figure. Argentina, noted for its climatic, topographic, and historical variations, stretches two thousand miles from the northern *selva* along the frontiers with Brazil and Uruguay to the Antarctic climates of southern Patagonia. In its broadest latitudinal expanse, from the massive Andean range on the west to the Atlantic, the country spans eight hundred miles, tapering to fewer than three hundred miles in the extreme south. The Province of Buenos Aires dominates Argentina; distance from this province correlates with political significance and development. As with Brazil, the republic has distinct subregions: the Andes, the Chaco, Mesopotamia, and the Pampa (map 21).

The Andean Area

Bordering Chile, the Andes Mountains of Argentina constitute a formidable barrier of single and parallel ranges that attract sparse settlement and contain few valuable mineral or energy resources (the main exception is the natural gas deposits near the Bolivian border at Salta). Most contact with the Pacific comes through several mountain passes in the northwest section and through the Beagle Channel in Patagonia and below by way of the Drake Passage.

The Chaco

The Argentine Chaco, a large portion of which belonged to Paraguay before the Triple Alliance War in the past century, consists of monotonous flat lowland terrain isolated from the rest of the country. It has a harsh semitropical climate of extreme wetness alternating with dryness. This sparsely inhabited region exhibits little economic activity beyond livestock grazing and seems to be ignored by the rest of the country.

Mesopotamia

Mesopotamia, a humid lowland area between the Paraná and Uruguay Rivers and including the three northeastern provinces of Entre

Ríos, Corrientes, and Misiones (the last also taken from Paraguay), although also sparsely populated and with few minerals, does have significant strategic value: it is the country's only land frontier with Brazil and its access to the hydroelectric power facilities at Itaipú and Yacyretá on the Paraná River. Thus, Mesopotamia frequently receives notice by geopolitical writers.

Patagonia

Patagonia lies in the southernmost third of the country, with 25 percent of national territory but only 2 percent of the population. It extends one thousand miles in longitude from the Colorado River to the Beagle Channel, south of Tierra del Fuego. Patagonia, with its cool, dry, windswept, rolling plateau, is populated only in several of its northern valleys. Despite its distance from Buenos Aires and its historical isolation, this area has experienced recent economic growth, more integration with the north, and increasing strategic importance, given its proximity to the South Atlantic islands, Antarctica, and the southern maritime passages. Suspicions of Chilean interest in Patagonia and in the southern passages continues to hamper relations between the two nations.

The Pampa

Last and most important, the Pampa region, which includes Buenos Aires, embodies the nation's agricultural and manufacturing heart, with grain-growing areas in the west and pasture grazing and significant industry in the east. Gilbert Butland writes this about the Pampa (1960: 260):

> In no other part of Latin America has there been such a comparable transformation of an apparently valueless region to one of the premier economically developed zones of the continent within much less than a century. It is a story more reminiscent of the settlement of the interior lowlands of North America where much of the development followed similar lines and for broadly comparable reasons.

To this zone came the great surge of European immigrants between 1880 and 1930, giving Buenos Aires its distinctive Italian and Spanish flavor. The slowness in integrating these masses provides one explanation for the persistent political instability and economic uncertainty during much of this century. Today, over 70 percent of Argentina's population resides in this province. A railroad network, the best in Latin America, extends from the coastal hub to link the periphery to this ruling ecumene, and 80 percent of national exports pass through Buenos Aires. More than in any other South American republic, the capital and its surrounding hinterlands dominate the political, economic, and cultural arenas of the nation. Most national attention and resources are focused on this sector, which makes the country's overall development more difficult.

Jack Child (1988a: 47–50; 1979: 95–102) and Howard Pittman (1983: 58–72) characterize Argentine geopolitics as lacking consensus and direction, "obsessed" with perceived Brazilian expansionism, fearful of Brazil–United States intrusions in the Southern Cone, feeling deprived of its rightful place of leadership in South America, feeling "geopolitically dissatisfied," and "mutilated" and "humiliated" by past aggressions. In this perspective, Child writes (1988a: 47):

> As Brazil's geopoliticians plot her moves toward great-power status with self-confidence, Argentina's geopoliticians focus on a more sterile and bitter analysis of why Argentina's path to greatness has been frustrated by her adversaries. Argentina is a country, geopolitically dissatisfied, whose geopolitical analyses tend to concentrate on this dissatisfaction. . . . [A]mong Argentine geopoliticians there are also deep divisions and polemics, as well as a sense of hostility toward their two geopolitically important neighbors, Brazil and Chile. There is general agreement among Argentine geopoliticians that Argentina has been cheated of her rightful greatness and place in the world and that some sort of national project has to be devised to restore that place and greatness. But there is little agreement on just what the project should be. There is also a profound sense of frustration over the country's inability to unite and function as a unit.

My reading of these characteristics differs. I see more vigor, creativity, pragmatism, and experimentation in recent geopolitical writings, particularly those of Marini and Boscovich. What Child and Pittman describe seems to reflect earlier disillusionment with national progress. The problem appeared to be a policy and power imbalance, the former exaggerated and the latter insufficient. The solution that I feel the new generation of writers discerns turns on

adjustment and retrenchment, which frequently create disappoint-
ment at first.

Argentine Geopolitical Themes

The most basic of the Argentine geopolitical themes—control of
the Plata watershed—describes a sphere of influence over the economies and politics of Bolivia, Uruguay, and Paraguay. Child (1979:
97) describes the "Camino de la Naranja" ("Path of the Orange")
thesis of Argentina's natural ascendancy over the region. This thesis
claims that "an orange (or anything else) dropped anywhere in the
River Plata basin must sooner or later float past Buenos Aires, and
thus be subject to Argentine control." It appears natural to me that
Argentine aspirations would first center at the Plata estuary, then
point across its north and northwest frontiers, for in these distant
areas lie its viceregal sphere of influence, its contemporary regional
markets and sources of energy and unprocessed materials, and its
cultural and political connectedness with Southern Cone neighbors,
friends or foes. Chile's and Brazil's position on the Plata's two extended flanks only intensifies the importance of this northern area.

A second theme, countering perceived Brazilian expansionism,
derives from the first. For centuries, Argentina has seen itself as responsible for maintaining a Spanish dike against Portuguese hegemony on the continent, for neutralizing Brazil–United States intrigue in the Southern Cone, for safeguarding the buffer states'
sovereignty, and for blocking Brazil's and Chile's territorial and maritime encirclement. Because Brazil's power now figures so much
greater than Argentina's, unilateral intervention against its neighbor's expansionist ambitions appears nearly futile and is recognized
as such by the Argentines. Fortunately, rapprochement between
Brazil and Argentina is steadily growing. Multinational integration
of policies and goals within the Southern Cone, a process that
promises to continue, not only helps remove the two conflictual
geopolitical themes from continued tension but also raises the relationship to a higher dimension of cooperation.

The problem of national integration offers a third geopolitical
perspective. Most large nations, including Argentina, have overpow-
ering national capitals and provinces and peripheral regions that
lack resources and population. The disunity has led to a variety of
difficulties: isolation and neglect of frontier lands; borderlands exposed to neighbors' territorial appetites, as possibly exhibited by

Chile's interest in Patagonia and Brazil's coveting of Mesopotamia; missed opportunities for erecting more comprehensive national development plans for exploiting potential wealth in the provinces; overpopulation, unemployment, and economic and political uncertainty pressed onto Buenos Aires; and limited ability to project regional interests beyond the country's borders. Nevertheless, one sees a persistent focus in Argentinean writing on resolving the problems of integration by, for instance, proposing frontier development and colonization, improved communications and transportation, moving the capital to Patagonia, and constructing a national integrationist project.

A fourth theme points our geopolitical focus toward Antarctica and the South Atlantic islands, passages, and resources. In these environs, geopoliticians envision the resources of these spaces fulfilling Argentine goals of Southern Cone leadership and national integration. Again, Child writes on this perspective (1988a: 74, 77): "At stake are not merely economic resources and strategic assets, but something of the soul of the nation itself. The argument is frequently made that (with the possible exception of Chile) no other nation gives such a high priority to the South Atlantic and Antarctic interests . . . that Argentine greatness and influence in the world would flow from control of this geopolitical space." Within these themes fit the South Atlantic as an "Argentinean Sea" and a tricontinental Argentina, or "Atlantártida," composed of the South American mainland, the Argentinean Sea, and the Antarctic possessions. Such visions caused the nation in 1982 to attempt to regain the Malvinas/Falkland Islands. Competition for control of southern resources and strategic passages, particularly with Chile and Great Britain, has kept the region tense, although negotiations with Chile apparently have resolved the Beagle Channel question for the present.

Last, for much of its history Argentina has asserted a neutralist and nationalist "third force" foreign policy that distanced the country from Brazil and the United States. During the 1980s, nevertheless, the republic swung toward integration with Brazil and accommodation with the North Americans. In this geopolitical oscillation, Argentina seems caught in the dilemma of a semiperipheral position in space and wealth. It no longer can block the expanding influence of Brazil as it seeks Southern Cone leadership, but Argentina's available resources and technology still place the country far ahead of the other Spanish-speaking South American nations in terms of power and influence. Argentina is continually isolated and frustrated because it cannot sustain a leadership position in the region. And alignment with Brazil could spell subservience. Perhaps the best alternative lies in working actively with Brazil for Southern Cone integration. This choice may offer the nation greater markets and accumulations of technology, better access to natural and energy resources, a heightened leadership position in the Southern Cone, and reduced security requirements while still checkmating the threats of Brazilian expansion and U.S. interference. Hence, status, stability, and prosperity could come through prudence.

The Geopolitics of Uruguay

The Oriental Republic of Uruguay is located on the east bank of the Uruguay River and marked the shatterbelt meeting ground of Portuguese and Spanish expansion during colonial days. As a result, it became the scene of struggle for regional hegemony between the two great imperial powers during the seventeenth and eighteenth centuries. This rivalry lessened by 1828, after Brazil and Argentina agreed, at British insistence, to guarantee Uruguay's sovereignty. Nevertheless, since that time, Uruguay's location has represented a classic example of buffer status, in which a neutral and much weaker state owes its existence as a country to the desire of larger neighbors to set themselves territorially apart from each other. This cushioning function largely defines Uruguayan geopolitics and foreign policy.

As the topographical transition between the Argentinean Pampa and the hilly Brazilian uplands, Uruguay is a geographically compact country of level, gently rolling terrain, broken by narrow river valleys. The climate is normally temperate, and fertile soils provide pastureland in the north and agriculture in the south. The people, almost totally of southern European origin, reside primarily in the southern regions, with 45 percent in the capital, Montevideo. Although the smallest of the original South American republics, the nation boasts the continent's most educated citizenry and democratic institutions, despite limited industry and natural resources.

Uruguay's geopolitics evolves primarily around its buffer status. Joseph Tulchin (1986: 213) describes this perspective thus:

> The nation's identity is built around the inescapable fact that it is virtually surrounded by two vastly larger and more powerful neighbors, both of which have stated and reiterated their

concern over their internal affairs within Uruguay, and both of which have shown themselves eager, on more than one occasion, to intervene directly in those internal affairs or to exercise influence over them in less direct ways. It is hardly surprising, therefore, that so much of Uruguay's national energy has been spent in establishing a national identity that is separate from those neighbors and in assuming international postures independent of them, nor is it surprising that those efforts have been only partially successful.

Distance from Brazil and differences in European origins facilitated Uruguay's separating itself from its northern neighbor. But these qualities were unimportant when the country tried to detach itself from Argentinean territorial ambitions, since both countries share a similar heritage and are located at the Plata's mouth. Yet, gradually autonomy came, after skillful diplomatic efforts that balanced the larger neighbors against Uruguay's will for national independence.

Frontier pressures from Brazil still endanger Uruguay. Unlike the republic's southern and western border areas, which have more inhabitants and more clearly defined river and coastlines, Uruguay's artificially defined northern frontier contains few people and boasts less development than do the adjacent Brazilian territories.

Some of Brazil's recent colonization and economic energy has spilled into Uruguay, creating new regional tensions. One statistic (D'Adesky 1979: 55) reveals that, in 1972, Brazilians owned 40 percent of the land in Uruguay's Artigas Province and 20 percent of the land in the other frontier provinces. One would assume that these figures have risen. Although in most cases Brazilian expansionism appears dormant, the specter of past aggrandizement persists and current examples threaten South American stability.

Some advantage derives from buffer states' ability to play one larger neighbor against another in a pendular foreign policy of gaining concessions and protection from the source currently most pertinent to national security and prosperity. Yet, the balancing also creates dangers, requires caution because the diplomacy expected of Uruguay has tended to disrupt national affairs, and invites intervention to deal with local instability. The Colorado Party of the southern and more urban regions historically has sided with Brazil, for example; the northern and agrarian Blanco Party normally aligns with Argentina.

This scene resembles the continental checkerboard pattern in miniature. Such divisions have intensified partisan struggle and exposed the country to greater international permeability. One instance of outside threat came during the early 1970s with rumors of invasion by Brazil to quell terrorism and partisan turmoil in Montevideo (D'Adesky 1979: 54–55; Mutto 1971).

The recent suggestion that Uruguay serve as an integrationist "land bridge" could reduce the vulnerability of lying between Brazil and Argentina (Tulchin 1986: 227–228). In this case, the historical buffer role between its larger neighbors would diminish in importance with creation of an economic infrastructure based on regional transportation and communication improvements and Southern Cone integration. Such changes could enhance Uruguay's prosperity and security as well as its autonomy and identity.

In addition, the country's internationalist foreign policy has sought support beyond the Southern Cone to counter the danger inherent in a subservient position by promoting a pro-British and U.S. alignment; strong advocacy of international law and international organizations; assertiveness in favor of democracy, human rights, and nonintervention; and leadership in the integration process for the southern region.

The Geopolitics of Paraguay

Rivers define Paraguay. The Paraná outlines the country's eastern edge; the Pilcomayo, its southwestern border; the Paraguay, its southeastern frontier. The northern and western areas remain isolated and unpopulated. Furthermore, the Paraguay River divides the land longitudinally into two distinct sections, the desolate Gran Chaco and the humid east, which contains 95 percent of the population. The Paraguay-Paraná system, flowing southeastwardly through Argentina, links the republic to Buenos Aires and the South Atlantic. These riparian sources strongly condition national geopolitics.

The lands east of the Paraguay River are fertile, rolling lowlands, with occasional swamps, plains, and hills. West of the river lies the Chaco, a vast plain of dense scrub woodlands and impenetrable thorn thickets and brush. Paraguay lives basically on agriculture and has no significant industry or mineral resources, a semitropical and often inhospitable climate, and a population fluent in both Spanish and Guaraní. In general, Paraguay is poor, isolated, nationalist, not well integrated as a nation, but racially distinct, underdeveloped, and ill-governed.

Paraguay's relative weakness and small size distinguish its regional standing. Clearly, the country lacks the wealth necessary for establishing a strong industrial base, although more prosperity could emerge if national space were more effectively occupied, for example, in the Chaco and in other peripheral sections around the central core of Asunción. One major asset the country possesses in abundance is its hydroelectric power–generating capacity, with large complexes at Itaipú, Yacyretá, and elsewhere along the Paraná River. Because of the multinational nature of this energy source (shared by Brazil, Argentina, and Paraguay), the investment appears safe and not subject to outside manipulation by the larger powers. Hydroelectric power not only provides cheap domestic electricity, but on the international level, also solidifies Paraguay's participation in regional integration: it reduces subordination to neighbors because those involved, at least in theory, operate as equal partners and consumers; it compensates in part for Paraguay's lack of industrial production; it diminishes isolation in the Plata watershed by providing the nation with a vital and legitimate role in regional development; and it increases the importance of stability, prosperity, and development as a regional requirement for energy provision (Kelly and Whigham 1990).

Landlocked, isolated, and centrally located on the continent, Paraguay lacks physical access to a sea outlet, which restricts international trade and technological exchanges, hampers commerce, and encourages the country's subordinate status with regard to Brazil and Argentina, which provide Paraguay sea access.

Interior location renders certain advantages also. Isolation has intensified national unity and helped maintain a dependable agricultural base. Distance from Brazil and Argentina has increased security and independence. And being positioned midway between Brazil and Argentina (an advantage not enjoyed by the more exposed Bolivia and Uruguay) gives the country additional maneuverability.

Several geopolitical writers consider Paraguay's position within the Plata basin pivotal to South America. The writings of Bernardo Quagliotti de Bellis and Julia Velilla de Arréllaga, for example, urge the formation of URUPABOL by Uruguay, Paraguay, and Bolivia for coordinated economic development as well as for protection from outside hegemony. They reason that the Plata area merits a strategic designation because it possesses natural resources, hydroelectric power, and central access to the Plata, Pacific, and Amazonian export corridors.

The country enjoys neither protection nor autonomy from Brazil and Argentina; rather, it endures persistent outside interference. Its primary wealth, from agriculture and hydroelectric power, is coveted and increasingly dominated by Brazil, in particular, and Argentina. Apparently, Paraguay's diplomatic balancing of its two large neighbors, so long utilized for security, has become less effective because of Brazil's recent surge to Southern Cone supremacy and its promotion of regional integration.

The Brazilians realize the importance of hydroelectric power from Itaipú to their industrial centers in the southern provinces and will use military force against Paraguay, as they did in 1965 at the Guaira Falls to guarantee control over the energy source (Da Rosa 1983: 82). Likewise, illegal immigration of Brazilians into eastern Paraguay figures as an immediate threat to national sovereignty, resembling as it does the historical pattern of Brazilian expansion westward at the expense of its smaller neighbors. In contrast, Argentina currently represents a wedge against Brazil's possible expansion into Paraguay and another source of access, balance, integration, and diversification for Paraguay.

The Geopolitics of Chile

One of the most unusually shaped countries in the world, Chile occupies a narrow strip of land on the west coast of South America and stretches over 2,000 miles from Peru to the continent's end at Tierra del Fuego, with an average width of 130 miles (map 22). The geography of Chile divides along a north-south axis: the eastern Andes Mountains border Bolivia and Argentina; the Central Valley and the plateaus terminate in steep cliffs along the Pacific coast. Climate, however, presents a clearer divisor of national space by separating Chile latitudinally into three geopolitically significant natural regions: Middle Chile, the Desert North, and South Chile.

Middle Chile

Located between the Bío Bío River on the south and the city of Coquimbo on the north, and known as the Mediterranean sector, Middle Chile contains over 60 percent of the population but only

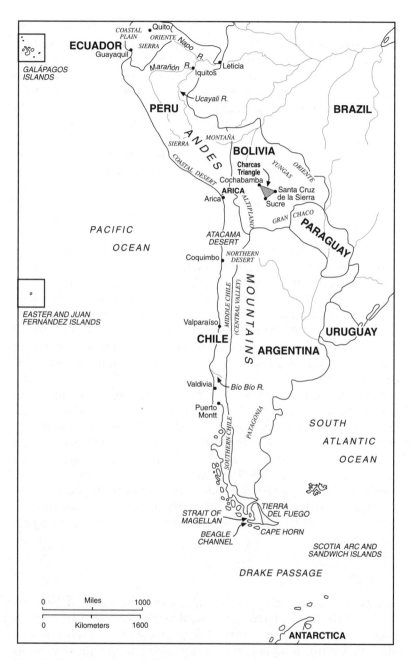

Map 22. The Subregions of Chile, Bolivia, Peru, and Ecuador

12 percent of national territory. Although occasionally whacked by destructive earthquakes, this sector dominates the nation in agriculture, industry and commerce, culture and education, and government administration. Similar to Argentina in that it resembles a European environment, Chile hosts a strong contingent of German and English immigrants mixed with colonial settlers. A mild climate, fertile soil, natural irrigation from steady Andean snow melt, and a good ocean harbor at Valparaíso further characterize Middle Chile. Isolated from other nations, the area has depended on the other two national sectors for deflecting pressures from neighboring Peru, Bolivia, and Argentina.

The Desert North

The eight hundred–mile Chilean segment of the Atacama Desert covers over 40 percent of the national territory, but only 10 percent of Chile's population lives there. Very forbidding, dry, and barren, this region draws its wealth from minerals, copper ores, the now less-important sodium chloride, sodium nitrate, and iodine salts from the dry basins. As a consequence of its success in the War of the Pacific (1879–1884), Chile took much of the Desert North from Peru and Bolivia, leading to an era of great national prosperity based on nitrate exports.

Unfortunately, the profits also created uneven development, favoring the upper-income classes and contributing to excessive dependence on foreign markets and persistent inflation. Today, Bolivia's bitterness toward Chile at the loss of its maritime outlet still festers, and this tension, in addition to the area's strategic location between the Amazon and Plata watersheds with their outlets to the Pacific, makes the Desert North of focal interest to the surrounding countries. The desert zone of Chile, and particularly the seaport of Arica, is one of the most geopolitically sensitive areas in South America.

South Chile

Forests, mountains, plateaus, and deep and narrow river valleys typify South Chile. Scattered agricultural settlements of German heritage colonists on the northern fringe give way to seven hundred miles of almost uninhabited territory with strong winds, frequent storms, and excessive rainfall at Valdivia and Puerto Montt, tapering off to scant precipitation at the Strait of Magellan and on the island of Tierra del Fuego.

Like the Desert North, southern Chile is geopolitically significant. Historically, Chile and Argentina sought control over Patagonia, the territory skirting the Atlantic coast of southern Argentina. Early in the original colonization effort, Chile probably possessed stronger title to the region than did Argentina, although its failure to solidify its claim caused it to diminish. Rivalry for possession continues, nevertheless, and occasional disputes arise over mining and border delineation. More recently, the Beagle Channel conflict between the two states almost erupted into warfare in 1987, signifying the importance of national involvement in the Antarctic and the southern oceans, a predominant theme in the geopolitics of Chile.

Chilean Geopolitical Themes

A sense of isolation determined by its peripheral location in the southwestern portion of the continent, by rather hostile topographic and climatic environments, and by distance from neighboring states, characterizes Chile's geopolitics. Isolation does not translate into security, however, for the Desert North and the southern passages and the country's Antarctic claims face the territorial ambitions of other nations. Hence, protecting itself from encirclement by Peru, Bolivia, and Argentina represents a second prominent geopolitical theme.

Chile maintains an efficient army and air force for patrolling mountain and desert passes on its eastern and northern frontiers, and a strong navy for impeding a maritime attack by Peru or Argentina. In 1987, for instance, Chile was willing to enlist force against Argentina to preserve its ownership of the Beagle Channel.

Like Uruguay, Chile has used international organizations and a democratic image (prior to 1973) to undergird its independence. After Gen. Augusto Pinochet's coup, Chile was seen as a pariah in world affairs, which weakened its progressive reputation and endangered its autonomy.

It has also used the de facto alliance with Brazil (and to a much lesser extent with Ecuador and Venezuela) to strengthen its security. This strategy reflects the traditional checkerboard pattern of South American geopolitics. Ties to Brazil have probably stabilized the several tension zones encircling Chile—in the northern desert, in Patagonia, and in the southern passages—although an escalation to continentwide violence erupting from these areas has never appeared imminent.

A final geopolitical theme centers on Chile's maritime projection. This oceanic orientation has secured the country against possible Peruvian and Argentine encroachments, in particular, the Argentine threat to the Drake and Beagle passages and the Antarctic. Likewise, with the country possessing a tricontinental vision of itself (the South American mainland core, the Easter and Juan Fernández Islands, and its Antarctic claims) Chilean geopolitical writers urge a new national emphasis toward the Pacific Rim, as Child describes (1988: 53): "Chilean geopoliticians also emphasize a geopolitical theory that argues that human civilization and development have been shifting westward over the centuries, that the era of the Pacific Basin is imminent, and that Chile has a rightful destiny of greatness as a major Pacific power. An essential part of this role is to make the southeast Pacific a Chilean sea."

We find another instance of the maritime thrust in the controversial "bioceanic" approach, a proposal whereby Chile exercises dominance in the South Pacific and Argentina controls the South Atlantic. How to define the border between the two oceans, unfortunately, has represented a heated source of dispute. Argentina wanted to place the boundary on the meridian of Cape Horn south to the Antarctic pole; Chile favored the Arc of the Southern Antilles, a string of islands that curve eastward into the South Atlantic (map 11). After years of negotiation, the two countries agreed to the bioceanic line as defined by Argentina, and the war scare of 1987 was averted. But Chile continues to asserts a vital interest in its role as "guardian of the doorway" between the two southern oceans.

The Geopolitics of Bolivia

Often described as "the rooftop of the world" because of its high elevation, Bolivia is a land of contrasts and extremes: frigid and tropical, barren and fertile, endowed with ample natural resources, yet providing only bare subsistence to most inhabitants. Landlocked and isolated, topographically and demographically fragmented, and lacking clearly defined international boundaries, Bolivia thus lives amid a dominant subregionalism that characterizes its national politics. Deficient in consensus and integration, the country dreads regional secession, which would threaten further territorial dismemberment because neighboring states, particularly Brazil, apparently still covet certain portions of the country.

Bolivia's mountains separate the country into three main regions: the Altiplano, the Oriente, and the Yungas.

The Altiplano

The upland plateau, known as the Altiplano, accounts for about 30 percent of national territory and 58 percent of the population. A cold, semiarid environment from twelve thousand to fourteen thousand feet above sea level, and surrounded by Andean peaks reaching twenty thousand feet, the Altiplano averages 85 miles in width, basically on an east-west axis, and 520 miles long. This plateau is the political, educational, and economic center of the country.

The Oriente

To the east and north of the mountains lies a lowland, tropical area, the Oriente, connecting the Amazon and Plata Valleys. Much of it unexplored and uninhabited jungle, this subregion includes 58 percent of the nation's land but only 15 percent of its people. But construction of new roads and the discovery of oil and natural gas in the Oriente have attracted new settlement. South of Santa Cruz, the province's main city, the plains become drier and merge into Bolivia's Gran Chaco.

The Yungas

The Yungas, semitropical valleys, lie between the Altiplano and the lowlands. Here 27 percent of the population lives on 13 percent of the total land area. Precipitous slopes and isolated basins and canyons characterize this region, which extends south two hundred miles from the Peruvian border on the northwest frontier to the city of Cochabamba. The Yungas enjoy a mild climate, fertile soil, and abundant rainfall, and they could support more people if there were better access through the rugged terrain.

Bolivian Geopolitical Themes

Bolivia has lost over half of its original territory through wars and forced negotiations with its more powerful neighbors (map 19). This persistent threat of Polandization expresses the country's primary concern: whether it should live as an independent nation or be divided among its five neighbors. Clearly, the potential for further dismemberment exists, augmented by the slowness of population growth and development on the eastern and northern frontiers, by an absence of national integration and unity, and by the inability of leaders to stabilize the republic's politics and lessen its regionalism.

Martin Glassner (1988: 156) reflects on this separatism:

> The lowlands of the Oriente are utterly foreign to most highland dwellers, as remote as Brazil or Europe. The southern part of Bolivia is clearly oriented toward Argentina, with only reluctant ties northward toward the political and economic centers of power. The eastern lowlands have no strong orientation in any direction, though the magnetic attraction of Brazil on the north and east is certainly influential. It has frequently been suggested that the ultimate solution to Bolivia's problems is simply to divide it among its neighbors. While that is unlikely to happen in this era of general territorial stability of states, a separatist movement in the Oriente could well develop, led by the ambitious, hard-driving, independent people of Santa Cruz de la Sierra.

To protect Bolivia's sovereignty, Mariano Baptista Gumucio argues (1983), his nation must colonize frontier regions and tie these more firmly to the Altiplano; erect a neutral, nonaggressive, internationalist foreign policy; integrate the national economy more closely with neighboring states; prevent entry of international enterprises that favor Polandization; and mobilize recognition in South America that Bolivia's central position can perform a vital balancing and harmonizing role in continental peace and economic integration.

Another important geopolitical theme centers around the Charcas triangle (map 16), a sought-after area formed by the towns of Sucre, Cochabamba, and Santa Cruz de la Sierra, or a South American heartland resembling that of Mackinder in Eurasia (map 13). In addition to being a site of conflicting continental forces, the Charcas triangle likewise signals regional integration, a harmonization of national and regional interests that could move continental peace and stability forward. Bolivia's geopolitical role, instead, may become that of regional contact for enabling closer communications and coordination among its neighbors. But Glassner (1988: 167) refutes this role as continental stabilizer by arguing that the country's basic challenge comes in simply surviving as a nation, and that "in conflicts between neighbors, Bolivia is simply bypassed; Bolivia is simply irrelevant." Nevertheless, the heartland theme remains a popular one among Southern Cone theorists and, therefore, merits our attention as a geopolitical theme.

An outlet to the Pacific ranks as a third important geopolitical theme. This passionate issue was created by Bolivia's loss of its outlet to the ocean in the War of the Pacific. It is a separate topic from dismemberment because the loss has never been recognized as irretrievable; manifesting its inherent right to this "salida al mar," or sea outlet, continues to preoccupy Bolivia's foreign policy, and sometimes its domestic politics as well, although the Plata's Hidrovía river network now at least affords eastern Bolivia a facility for reaching the Atlantic. I feel that a good chance exists for a negotiated partial recovery of Bolivia's former coast, because international law seems to be moving toward favoring sea-access rights for landlocked states. Whatever eventually transpires, Bolivians seem determined to press for a solution. And for reasons of terrain, nearness to the sea, and historical orientation to the west (Glassner 1988), that solution, for the Bolivians, translates into an eventual Pacific Ocean access.

The Geopolitics of Peru

In a geopolitical sense, one can visualize in Peru three separate nations coexisting uneasily: the desert coastal strip; the sierra, or Andes highlands; and the *montaña*, or eastern Andean slopes and Amazon plains. Each possesses a distinctive climate, terrain, economy, and culture; none appears well-integrated with the other sectors. Unifying these diverse areas into a functioning national whole has remained a major problem since colonial times. In addition, most frontier areas, including the maritime expanses, face potential conflict with neighboring states, although, because of the long distances and formidable topography encircling the nation, Peru's security against outside attack seems less threatened for the moment.

Because it is a large centrally located South American country that has fought two regional wars and won and lost territory as a result, Peru's geopolitics in part exudes a broader strategic perspective. But, simultaneous with this greater projection, the factors of disunity, isolation, and encirclement seem also to guide the country's foreign policy toward a parochialism in which domestic and frontier concerns often become paramount.

The Desert Coastal Strip

The narrow desert coast (between 10 and 40 miles wide) extends 1,410 miles from the country's northern to its southern border; it is erased at intervals where Andean slopes reach the sea. This very dry zone remains fairly cool because of the cold Peruvian, or Humboldt, ocean current from the Antarctic. In this subregion reside 27 percent of the population, mostly of Spanish descent, on only 12 percent of the national territory. However, this desert area incorporates the commercial and industrial center of Peru, and most of the nation's leading export products originate in the river-fed oases of the coastal desert.

The Sierra Highlands

Predominantly inhabited by Quechua and Aymara Indians, the sierra highlands extend 200 – 250 miles across and occupy about one third of Peru's land. The eastern foothills of the sierra, although lower than the central range's towering peaks, have deeply carved canyons and V-shaped valleys, which pose great obstacles to trans-Andean travel between the interior and the coast. Despite holding 60 percent of the nation's population, for the most part the sierra remains isolated from the main flow of national politics and commerce, with the exception of minerals exploitation in the highlands that tie the area to international markets and provide an important source of national revenue.

The sierra's indigenous peoples are historically hostile toward the coastal Europeans, which translates today into a resentful passivity and into support of the Shining Path terrorists and drug-related insurgency.

The *Montaña* Region

Peru's eastern *montaña* region comprises the lower Andean slopes and the jungle-covered plains of the upper Amazon basin, with 61 percent of the total area of Peru but only 13 percent of population. This sector is defined by rivers that originate in the Amazon— the Ucayali, the Marañón, and the Napo—all of which link eastern

Peru closely to Brazil. The most important city in the *montaña*, Iquitos, is a strategic port that has become the trading and financial center of the entire upper Amazon valley.

Peruvian Geopolitical Themes

As one might note from this brief overview, a great urgency about building a stronger national integration figures as a geopolitical theme in Peru. But a limited, if improving, transportation system, while attacking the harsh terrain, has not yet proved successful in unifying the diverse national sectors. Peru also requires a cultural consensus and a diminishing of the highland peoples' isolation from and hostility to the coastal Spanish. In the eastern sector, the uninhabited and potentially rich *montaña* is exposed to the enterprising Brazilians. Integration requires ample resources, which the country does not have because of disruptive climate and difficult terrain.

None of Peru's land boundaries are delineated by natural features; the result is the encirclement of disputed and ill-defined frontiers (Gorman 1982). The eastern march covers unexplored jungle expanse, and the Brazilians appear to be developing their side of the Amazon more quickly than the Peruvians are developing theirs, a sign of possible tension in future. This eastern vulnerability prompts the government's call for "la marcha para la selva," an opening toward the *selva* rain forest.

Likewise, Peru's northern and southern borders exude tensions with neighbors Ecuador and Bolivia. In the 1820s and 1830s, the country's armed forces tried to annex Guayaquil and the southern provinces of Ecuador and Colombia. These expansionist designs returned a century later as military clashes at Leticia and full-scale war against Ecuador in 1941. Peru emerged from the latter conflict with 100,000 square miles of disputed territory, almost 40 percent of Ecuador, including its only access to the Amazon through the Marañón River. Despite the Brazilian and U.S.-imposed Protocol of Rio de Janeiro, which ended the war and awarded Peru the territory, the Ecuadorans have continued to press for restoration of the Marañón, with the dispute flaring up in 1981 and again in 1995.

The 1879–1882 War of the Pacific between Peru and Bolivia on one side and Chile on the other destabilized Peru's southern frontier and created animosity with both Chile and Bolivia. As a consequence of that war, Chile annexed Peru's nitrates-rich coastal Province of

Arica, and Bolivia completely lost its former seacoast on the Pacific. According to the Treaty of Ancón (1929), which settled the territorial dispute between Peru and Chile, Chile could not grant an outlet to the sea to Bolivia through formerly Peruvian territory without Peru's approval. This provision prevented a possible agreement in the mid-1980s between Chile and Bolivia for a Bolivian coastal port when Peru refused to have a portion of Arica ceded to the Bolivians. The centennial of the War of the Pacific brought new concerns that Peru, armed with an arsenal of Soviet weapons, and Chile, then an isolated pariah under the Pinochet dictatorship, could once more enter armed conflict over the disputed coastal zone (Child 1988a: 55). Although there was no war, the area is still disputed and will someday require settlement, perhaps in the form of some type of an international access servitude, or agreement.

Although not as contentious as its territorial frontiers, Peru's geopolitical interests in the Pacific have also influenced the nation's foreign policy. After World War II, Peru and its Pacific neighbors declared their territorial waters to extend two hundred miles beyond the coast, and in the late 1960s, the country began excluding foreign fishing ships from these waters (Gorman 1982: 72). No serious international confrontation ensued because several declarations of the United Nations Conferences of the Law of the Sea did not preclude the two hundred–mile extension. The United States chose not to contest Peru's restrictions, and Peru's overfishing has reduced the issue's international significance.

Peru suffers from a serious guerrilla insurgency, the Shining Path movement in the sierra and *montaña*. It now controls substantial interior spaces and has recently linked itself with international cocaine trafficking. The guerrillas take advantage of the isolation, impenetrable terrain, large vacant land areas, and apathy of the indigenous peoples. This threat has distracted national politics, weakened the country's ability to develop the *montaña* and integrate the sierra, and may expose all frontiers to boundary adjustments with neighboring states. However, the capture of the Shining Path's leader has weakened the guerrillas' capacity to disrupt relations with other countries.

The Geopolitics of Ecuador

To a large degree, Ecuador owes its continued independence to isolation and to its buffer status, and not to a strong domestic cohesion and identity. Like Peru, mainland Ecuador divides into a narrow coastal plain, an uplands sierra, and a sparsely populated eastern jungle, or Oriente. None is closely associated with the others. This national disconnectedness prompted these remarks by Harry Kantor (1969:427):

> Ecuador emerged as an independent state in 1830. Since in its previous history it had never been an integrated political unit, it did not become one by assuming the status of an independent republic. Split by its mountains into varied geographical sections, populated by groups of people who had never had any unifying factor to knit them together, Ecuador grew continuously smaller as its neighbors took control of parts of the territory it claimed, and at least half the population lived a self-sufficient life untouched by Ecuadoran nationality. Since World War I great strides have been taken, but Ecuador still has a long way to go before it becomes an integrated nation-state.

Regionalism normally contributes to national insecurity, and this seems particularly true for Ecuador, for the republic's territories have attracted the strategic attention of larger states, including Peru, Brazil, and the United States. This coveting of territory by outsiders continues to condition national geopolitics and in time could threaten Ecuador's national survival.

The Coastal Plain

In the most practical sense, Ecuador consists only of coast and sierra. Forty-seven percent of the population lives on a narrow twelve to one hundred mile–wide strip of Pacific coastal plain, 25 percent of the national territory. Crops for domestic and international markets grow in this fertile and semitropical fringe, and the leading city, Guayaquil, is here also. It is Ecuador's economic capital, major market, and principal seaport. Less isolated and more prosperous, and thus the most advanced sector of the country, the coast exerts a greater impact on national politics than does its historical uplands rival, the national political capital, Quito.

The Sierra

The Sierra, of Andes highlands and plateaus, supports 52 percent of the national population on 30 percent of the land. Indians and mestizos are its primary inhabitants, and the economy features traditional and subsistence agriculture. The region subdivides into numerous basins that contain nearly self-sufficient and inwardly directed communities weakly linked to the coast.

The Oriente

The Oriente, sparsely populated by Indians, covers nearly half of Ecuador and consists of Amazonian rain forests. Except for large deposits of petroleum, the Oriente has little economic importance.

A fourth part of the country, the archipelago of Colón, or the Galápagos Islands, lies almost six hundred miles off the coast, with a total area of three thousand square miles but with very little population. The Galápagos account for little economic activity but have been the subject of strategic interest from nations interested in potential Pacific naval ports close to the Panama Canal.

Ecuadoran Geopolitical Themes

National integration attracts significant attention from writers and leaders. The Sierra is largely separated from the coast; the two sectors reveal vastly different worlds apparently disinterested in the welfare of the other. One wonders whether Ecuador indeed can stay an independent state, lacking as it does the resources and political maturity to attain higher levels of national unity. If Ecuador were merely a province of a larger state, little attention would probably accrue to its space.

Tied to the liability of few resources and political immaturity is the emotional issue of restoration of the Marañón region, once part of the Oriente but lost to Peru during the 1941 war. Border warfare in 1981 ended in defeat, and future efforts by Ecuador against its stronger southern neighbor probably would end the same way. The Peruvians allegedly sought the isolated *selva* from Ecuador for its oil potential and for access to the Amazon, and some suspect that Peru continues to covet total absorption of Ecuador.

The best chance for recovery of the Marañón territory may rest with the Brazilians and Chileans, traditionally the republic's allies within the South American checkerboard. Brazil envisions the Marañón valley as a good land corridor to the Pacific. Added evidence of Ecuador's importance to Brazil also comes from Brazilian attempts to purchase the Galápagos as a Pacific naval port. Utilization of the Galápagos and mainland coastal areas likewise has appeared in U.S. plans for continental defense.

Ecuador represents a classic example of a buffer state, juxtaposed as it is between Colombia, Peru, and, at greater distance, Brazil. Its potential to provide an Amazon-to-Pacific passageway and valuable deposits of oil complicates its buffer status, however, and increases its relevance and its insecurity.

Finally, the republic has a maritime bearing on geopolitics that reflects the importance of its Pacific islands, although this example would appear minor in comparison to the maritime devotion of the Chileans.

The Geopolitics of Colombia

Despite the loss of Panama at the turn of this century, Colombia sees itself as a geopolitically "satisfied" country, without ambitions for additional space, serious border disputes, or fear of territorial dismemberment. It is not a buffer state or within the sphere of influence of a larger country, nor does it own a particularly valuable natural resource. Its primary regional and strategic significance lies in its position, near Panama and between the Atlantic and the Pacific Oceans. Despite its location, its impact on the Panama area remains minimal, in part because it simply lacks influence beyond its frontiers. With the country's main population cores isolated in central mountain valleys, it has no diplomatic impact on the Caribbean and Pacific, nor does the republic exert leadership in Latin American affairs. It has taken an active stand in favor of Central American peace and regional integration and against international narcotics trafficking.

The Eastern Plain

A diamond-shaped country that takes up a large portion of northwest South America, Colombia consists of two distinct sections (map 23). An eastern plain covers two thirds of the republic. It is largely unpopulated and not developed but potentially wealthy. The northern part of this sector, the Llanos, or a usually dry plain, focuses on cattle raising; the southern half is Orinoco and Amazon River basin rain forest jungle. Because of the isolation of these

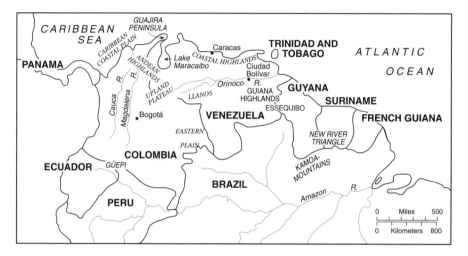

Map 23. The Subregions of Colombia, Venezuela, Guyana, Suriname, and French Guiana

periphery areas, threats of territorial seizure by neighbors appear remote for the moment, although the possibility of dismemberment could emerge.

The Western Third

The western third of Colombia separates into a narrow Caribbean and Pacific coastal plain, an upland plateau and series of valleys, and three very rugged mountain ranges that form the extended Magdalena and Cauca River Valleys, where most of the population resides. Because of the difficult terrain, most people live in fourteen main clusters of "city-states," each with a distinct economy and social character. Livestock and tropical crops predominate; a variety of agricultural and mineral products come from the uplands. Colombia possesses a significant potential for producing hydroelectric power in the western sector, and large amounts of valuable minerals may await discovery throughout the country.

In sum, geography has largely determined a national isolation and fragmentation, this tending to create a foreign policy of reaction, moderation, and some reliance on the United States.

Colombian Geopolitical Themes

In large part, Colombia is an internally focused, centripetally oriented country (*país centrípeto*). Its geopolitical center is Bogotá, and its main valleys are more vital to the country than are the peripheral eastern and coastal areas. The country's internal preoccupation runs the danger of exposing neglected frontier lands to absorption by neighboring states, particularly Brazil and Venezuela, and frontier conflict already exists between Colombia and Venezuela over illegal immigration and the disputed border of the resources-rich Guajira Peninsula. Colombia has seldom feared territorial dismemberment (it has lost only its Panamanian province); its advocacy of regional integration, peaceful settlement of disputes, participation in international organizations, and warm relations with the United States has strengthened its national security.

The "doctrine of the polar star," a looking north to the United States for foreign policy focus (Randall 1992; Bushnell 1975: 406), represents a second geopolitical theme. Colombia has maintained close trading ties with the United States, and its proximity to Panama guarantees a military linkage with the Unites States. Cooperation with the United States in controlling the illegal narcotics trade, a crisis of internal security, further solidifies the polar star connection.

In the opposite direction, the nation's location between the Pacific and the Caribbean gives it an important role in Andean integration as well as an American window toward the Pacific basin and its rimlands that may increase potential for development and heightened significance.

The Geopolitics of Venezuela

In comparison with the geopolitics of Colombia, those of Venezuela show a greater regional and strategic thrust, reflective perhaps of the nation's position as a pivotal area among South America's subregions, its more level terrain, and its abundant natural resources. Despite the lack of consensus within the country's geopolitical thinking (Ewell 1982), Venezuela's geopolitics is fervent and assured, with intellectual depth and connectedness to the national policy-making elite. Venezuela's diplomats firmly recognize the primacy of the Caribbean basin to the country's national destiny.

Various of its geopolitical writers bemoan territorial losses and charge contemporary leaders with preventing further dismemberment and establishing Venezuela's leadership as a regional voice. A general consensus seems to exist about favoring regional integration, instituting more effective petroleum-related policies, and protecting against U.S. interference.

Five distinct regions compose Venezuela, each unique in climate, topography, and economy.

The Coastal Highlands

The country's most important agricultural area and its manufacturing and political center lie in the Coastal Highlands, which account for only 9 percent of the territory but support 53 percent of the population. Paralleling the Caribbean coast from Lake Maracaibo to nearly the mouth of the Orinoco River, this territorial fringe begins to rise in elevation close to the sea, which tempers the climate. Caracas, the capital, with one fifth of the population, lies in the highlands.

The Andean Highlands

To the extreme west, the Andean Highlands border Colombia; here, 13 percent of the population lives on 3 percent of the national territory. The scattered and isolated farming communities of the Highlands open more naturally to Colombia than to Venezuela, and they support many of the estimated one million illegal Colombian aliens.

The Lake Maracaibo Basin

The Lake Maracaibo basin, with only 7 percent of the country's land surface but 15 percent of its population, also flanks Colombia. It contains two thirds of the national oil reserves and is involved in a territorial dispute with Colombia over the Guajira Peninsula.

South of Lake Maracaibo and the coastal mountains, the eastward flowing Orinoco River separates the two remaining geographic areas of the republic.

The Llanos

North of the river the Llanos roll gently toward the Orinoco delta on the Caribbean coast. They make up about one third of the country and support 18 percent of the population. Heavy tropical rains from May to November inundate the plains; a very dry winter prevents abundant agriculture but does support cattle grazing. An increasing proportion of the nation's oil production, above 30 percent, now comes from the Llanos, and growing industry suggests that this interior region may expand in commercial and political importance.

The Guiana Highlands

The Guiana Highlands, south of the Orinoco in the southeastern half of the country, border both Brazil and Guayana. They are the country's least-populated and -exploited area; some parts of the area have not yet been fully explored. Ciudad Bolívar's iron ore deposits represent this region's main economic activity, but extensive discoveries of other mineral wealth add to the attractiveness of the Guiana plateau.

Venezuelan Geopolitical Themes

Among major geopolitical themes, the perceived foreign threat to the nation's resources seems most prominent, because most resources lie near frontiers. Unlike Colombia, Venezuela fears encirclement from all directions: Brazil and Peru on the south; Colombia on the west; Guyana and Great Britain on the east; and the United States on the north. The petroleum in the Maracaibo basin and the Llanos, the largely untapped wealth of the Guiana Highlands, the country's Amazon territory, and the Caribbean coastal resources all appear exposed. In addition, the Orinoco River links the Caribbean to the Amazon and the continent's interior, offering another attraction to outsiders. Urgent calls for national integration frequently come from leading geopolitical writers, bent on protecting the nation's domain.

Attempts toward regional leadership also reflect the republic's pivotal location and its sense of vulnerability to encirclement. For this reason, Venezuela helped found the Organization of Petroleum Exporting Countries, opposed Cuban ties to the Soviet Union, participates in collective peacekeeping, and advocates democracy in Latin America. According to Sheldon Liss (1975: 424, 429), the republic "seeks to build an image as the Caribbean counterpart of Mexico . . . Caracas enjoys excellent rapport with Mexico, watches Mexican foreign policy closely, and tries to emulate it by conducting her relations with similar tact." Both nations possess substantial oil, a potential for internal fragmentation, and a close proximity to the United States; policies advocating balance, moderation, and international status may thus seem justified.

The Geopolitics of Guyana

An independent state since 1966, Guyana is isolated from the mainstream of the Caribbean and South America. Demographically and geographically, the country suffers from disunity, commercial underdevelopment, and a weak agricultural base. But it assumes geopolitical importance in terms of its substantial mineral reserves and its position between Brazil and the Caribbean. Its population reflects diverse racial origins, primarily East Asian and African, and most dwell along the northern coast. In this land of tropical rivers and forests, two regions predominate: the Coastal Plain, varying in width from ten to forty miles and covering only 5 percent of the national territory; and the Guyana Plateau, or Highlands, sloping northward away from the Kamoa and the Acarai Mountains, which form the southern boundary with Brazil.

The most immediate problem facing Guyana comes from Venezuela, bent on claiming the Essequibo, an area covering the eastern half of the country. The Essequibo dispute over potentially rich mineral deposits is now dormant but could erupt if Venezuela presses for a solution.

Countering this pressure, Brazil seems protective of Guyanan autonomy, probably because it too covets Essequibo and likewise finds Guyana a possible route to the Caribbean. The United States has supported Guyana also because of the Essequibo and to secure maritime choke points close by in the Caribbean.

The Geopolitics of Suriname

Suriname, a poor, isolated, unintegrated country with a tropical and largely inhospitable terrain, gained independence from the Netherlands in 1975. Its people came originally from East India and Africa and today are separated socially, culturally, and politically. Population (around 400,000) stays low, which reflects outward emigration. Of note economically, bauxite exports rank third in the world, although the mineral is less important to the economy because of abundance elsewhere and substitution by other products.

The original Spanish owners never considered the territory of sufficient value for exploitation. Today, Brazil and the United States, as in the case of Guyana, extend their spheres of influence over the region because both are interested in potential natural wealth and nearby strategic passageways. Brazil successfully prevented the Desi Bouterse regime from establishing diplomatic ties with Cuba and the Soviet Union (Conde 1983). A low-key border dispute with Guyana, at the New River Triangle, poses a minimal threat of escalation.

THREE

An Inventory of Sixteen
South American Writers

I have chosen sixteen South American writers who I believe best represent contemporary geopolitical thinking. My list comes primarily from my own reflections, although I have also consulted various geopolitical theorists interested in South America, including Jack Child, Howard Pittman, Klaus Dodds, Gustavo Chacón, Andrés Alfonso Bravo, Carlos de Meira Mattos, and Bernardo Quagliotti de Bellis. Other criteria also helped me identify these authors: association with leading geopolitical institutes and periodicals; a reputation as an outstanding contributor to the field; frequent citation in the literature; and extensive authorship of geopolitical writings.

Beginning with representative writers from Brazil and Argentina, then moving through the Plata region to the Pacific and northward to the Caribbean, the following individuals emerge as my selections: Carlos de Meira Mattos (Brazil); Golbery do Couto e Silva (Brazil); Therezinha de Castro (Brazil); Juan Enrique Guglialmelli (Argentina); José Felipe Marini (Argentina); Nicolás Boscovich (Argentina); Bernardo Quagliotti de Bellis (Uruguay); Julia Velilla de Arréllaga (Paraguay); Alipio Valencia Vega (Bolivia); Augusto Pinochet Ugarte (Chile); Ramón Cañas Montalva (Chile); Emilio Meneses Ciuffardi (Chile); Edgardo Mercado Jarrín (Peru); Jorge Villacrés Moscoso (Ecuador); Julio Londoño Londoño (Colombia); and Rubén Carpio Castillo (Venezuela).

These authors frequently hold the following general viewpoints in common:

- For the most part, their geopolitics pertain to South American regional and subregional affairs. The strategic domain receives much less attention.

- All fear loss of national borderlands exposed to aggressive neighbors or outside forces.

- Many recommend regional and continental integration as an additional method for protecting frontiers and solidifying national development.

- Most find a solution to possible territorial dismemberment in national development that strengthens military and economic power and connects the peripheral areas to major population centers.

- Several describe a continental balance of power and its impact on national geopolitics. They warn of dangerous escalation of conflict were this equilibrium upset.

- Few visualize a positive U.S. presence in South America. The United States is viewed as an undependable ally and an unwelcome intruder in South American affairs.

- With certain exceptions, few see the former Soviet Union or other non-American states as significant to the continent's geopolitics.

Carlos de Meira Mattos (Brazil)

Most scholars in Europe and North America recognize Gen. Carlos de Meira Mattos of Brazil as South America's foremost contemporary geopolitical writer. His work spans a variety of topics, from military history to Amazonian development, from modern weaponry to Atlantic security, from geopolitical theorizing to policy recommendations for elevating Brazil's world status. His work has contributed to an understanding and application of geopolitics as an important element in national development and foreign policy (Kelly 1992a; 1988a; 1984). Meira Mattos has served as contact person among Southern Cone and U.S. researchers.

Meira Mattos was born in São Paulo in 1913 and graduated from the Agulhas Negras military academy in 1936. As a junior officer he served in a variety of posts before being sent to Italy during World War II with the Brazilian Expeditionary Force. This posting placed him among the influential Sorbonne faction of the armed forces. He would write later about his experiences in Italy (1983). Other army assignments included commander of the Latin American contingent of the Inter-American Peace Force sent to Santo Domingo in 1965, division chief of political affairs in the Escuela Superior de Guerra (ESG, Superior War College), vice-chief of staff of the armed forces, vice-director of the Inter-American Defense College in Washington, D.C., and commandant of the national military academy. Meira Mattos earned his doctoral degree in political science in 1983 from the Mackenzie University of São Paulo, and he currently teaches at that institution.

A prolific writer for over thirty-five years, Meira Mattos approaches geopolitics from the realist perspective of international relations (Kelly 1984) and from the geopolitical traditions of his country. He admits to being strongly influenced by Mario Travassos' *Projeção continental do Brasil* (1947), which advocated western expansion of roads and colonization to the Bolivian and Peruvian frontiers. Likewise, the perspectives of Lysias Rodrigues, Golbery do Couto e Silva, and Therezinha de Castro appear in his writings (Pittman 1983). Nevertheless, Meira Mattos presents an original geopolitics, and he justly deserves credit for expanding the horizons of Brazilian and South American geopolitical thinking.

National development represents a central focus in Meira Mattos' writing. Development creates power, and together these factors produce national security. Without power, "a society becomes an inert corpse, without will, incapable of satisfying its proper reason for being, [or] its continuing evolution" (1977a: 54–55, 102–103). Solutions to developmental problems, Meira Mattos asserts, originate in "geographic realities," (1975: 4–6), because geography so essentially contributes to national destiny. And the link between geography and attainment of security and development comes through the implementation of geopolitics, the "application of policy to geographic space" (1975: 4; 1977a: 15). Geopolitics itself becomes an engine of development and thus a solution to security difficulties.

The Amazon basin fits closely within the development theme. Meira Mattos believes the country's greatest security threat and its most vital national challenge originate in this region. Extracting resources from rain forests, he asserts, will strengthen national development and meld Brazilians into a great "tropical civilization" (1984a: 3–6, 129–137). But this scenario is restricted to an "Amazon problem," in which other peoples and international organizations may demand territorial autonomy within the basin; for example, they press for the migration of stateless Asian refugees or international monitoring of jungle ecology (1980a: 93, 136, 145–146): "It would be dangerous to leave the vast Amazon basin empty and underdeveloped when there are areas experiencing grave overpopulation—Bangladesh, Indochina, and Japan—[It would not be] desirable to the Amazonian countries to lose their sovereignty over this coveted region under the pretext of their inability to exploit it." The region's isolation could attract internal rebellion (1973; 1952) and also leave coastal populations exposed to maritime blockade in wartime without a hinterland to support them (1980a: 148, 161–166). For resolving these liabilities, Meira Mattos recommends more tightly integrating the continental core to both the Atlantic and the Pacific coasts.

Amazonian wealth, "the discovery of new riches, the amplification of a potential hardly suspected and its transformation into power," attracts the general's attention as well (1973: 67; 1984a; 1977a: 15). Not only the resources but also the central position of the basin place Brazil at the forefront of continental responsibility: "[T]he heart of the problem of awakening the continent is centered in the Amazon . . . Brazil is in a privileged position . . . because a major part of our territory is adjacent to the course of the ocean outlet" (1980a: 134; see also 126, 131–134; 1977a: 92). But Brazil must become a cooperative leader, and not the South American hegemon so feared by Spanish-speaking neighbors (1980a: 139):

> Our recent diplomacy has readjusted our strategic lines, placing more importance on the policy of closeness with our neighbors on the continent. In a short time this direction has been crowned with success. We have strengthened our ties with South American nations through regional and subregional organizations. We have begun, in a very short time, to mobilize the chief nations of the Amazon to a Treaty of Cooperation. And finally, we have motivated our neighbors who are members of the Andean Pact to understand the importance of readjustment with Brazil, to the benefit of all.

Elsewhere, he connects this cooperative aspect to his original thesis of security rendered through development (1980a: 2, 136–137; 1977a: 143–144).

The South Atlantic poses another threat to Brazil. Vital trade routes here are necessary to national security and prosperity, as are the resources of the continental shelf, the territorial seas, and the more distant Antarctic region as well as access to African markets and Middle Eastern oil (1988; 1977a: 199–123; 1975: 75–76; 1962; 1960). On the security of this realm, the general asserts these points (1977b: 8–9; also 1977a: 142): "At the present time there exists a fundamental threat to the South Atlantic, and this is Soviet blockade of oil supply lines to the United States and Europe and Brazil. Blockade of the South African Horn would paralyze NATO, the principal instrument against the Soviet Union." The general recommends a Brazil–United States naval presence in the area and a South Atlantic Treaty Organization of Brazil, Chile, Uruguay, Paraguay, and Argentina, with eventual African membership as well, for protecting southern maritime choke points (1977a: 122; 1977b: 8; 1975: 76).

Meira Mattos is also known for his confidence in the Brazilian people, in democratic institutions, and in the future status of his country as a great power (1977a: 16–17, 31, 54–55; 1975: 101–102). He writes that Brazil contains "all the conditions for aspiring to a place among the great powers of the world," and that this growth will transpire within a context of "democracy with authority" (1977a: 143; 1975: 71–73).

Unlike the Machiavellian image of General Golbery do Couto e Silva of Brazil, whose works we will examine shortly, Meira Mattos is recognized as a champion of Brazilian development and integration. His vision reflects a positive and nonbelligerent purpose in regional politics, according to Argentinean Nicolás Boscovich (1986: 40–41). To the general, Brazil merits international recognition because of its regional leadership, not its power, and he wants to promote continental development as well as heighten Brazil's security and prosperity through an amicable geopolitical model (1984b; 1982; 1980b; 1979).

Frontiers, a topic common to many of the South American geopolitical writers, represent a prominent theme for Meira Mattos. He is interested in expanding and contracting national boundaries, in "live" and "dead" frontiers, and in natural and artificial demarcations. In *Geopolítica e teoria de fronteiras: fronteiras do Brasil* (1990a: 5–6), he writes that borders require clear and precise delineation in order to avoid international conflict (see also 1989; Kelly 1992a). Because modern warfare seems "suicidal" and international law and organizations have not been effective in settling frontier disputes, regional peace happens through patient and skilled binational negotiation.

Golbery do Couto e Silva (Brazil)

Among my list of South American geopolitical writers, General Golbery do Couto e Silva attracts the most controversy. General Guglialmelli of Argentina, for instance, characterizes Golbery in this way (1976c: 16):

His analyses, especially when he refers to South America and Southwest Africa, are frankly tendentious. He focuses unilaterally on certain factors; he omits, does not mention, or magnifies others; finally, he attributes [others'] political attitudes according to a convergence of his own interests. Thus, General Golbery do Couto e Silva tries to present Brazil as the central nucleus of South America, an area where it ought to exercise a "manifest destiny" that does not conflict with North American interests . . . he argues in favor of [receiving] preferential treatment from Washington. For this he shows his country as the fundamental axis of North American defense because of its geographic position, power, and destiny, and, accordingly, in the immediate sense, its purpose is to guard [the U.S.] maritime flank (in the South Atlantic), its rear guard (South America), and the continuing frontier of southwest Africa.

Golbery particularly irritated his Spanish-speaking colleagues by claiming exclusive Brazilian leadership of South America. For example, both Boscovich (1986: 39 – 40) and Guglialmelli (1976c: 13) quote this statement as an example of "imperial" Brazil's aggressive intentions: "As geography gives the Brazilian coast and its northeast promontory almost a monopoly of domination of the South Atlantic, this monopoly is Brazilian, [and] it ought to be exercised exclusively by ourselves." Such statements have solidified Golbery's realpolitik reputation.

His military career is similar to that of Meira Mattos: a variety of major infantry commands, an active role in professional military education, contacts with the U.S. armed forces, participation in the Italian campaign of World War II, and membership in the Sorbonne group of officers. Even more influential in government circles than Meira Mattos, Golbery served as a key advisor to three of the five military presidents from 1964 until 1981 in his position as head of the Casa Civil, an equivalent to the U.S. White House staff. Robert Levine states that "he was so influential that it was broadly assumed that Golbery actually ran the government" (1982: 61; see also Stepan 1989: 7–8). William Hoge describes him as the "power behind the 17-year-old military stewardship of Brazil" (1981).

Accordingly, Golbery possessed the authority to implement geopolitics-related policies that he had earlier advocated in his writings. In this respect, Boscovich (1986: 39) credits him with

consolidating Brazil as an economic-industrial power and positioning itself for the great leap in its territorial integration—

the "interiorization of Brazil"—with the construction of extensive and strategic highways, dozens of hydroeconomic improvements, internal navigation, deepwater ports as terminals of the "export corridors," and the incorporation into the national economy of the immense [western territories]. He tied [the concept of] Brazilian leadership in the subcontinent to the U.S.' world projections with the theories of "loyal exchange," "ideological fronts," "living frontiers," [and] "privileged satellite."

Several maps best introduce the major tenets of the general's geopolitics. One depicts the "interior and exterior world hemicycles" (map 24) and shows the "Communist and materialist East" in an exterior hemicycle, and the "democratic and Christian west" in an opposing interior hemicycle, both gridlocked in "dominant antagonism" (1981: 75–87, 129–131). Caught in the middle of this Mackinder-like struggle, Brazil must opt for an anti-Communist partnership with the United States.

Map 25 shows a strategic and tactical role for Brazil as guarantor of the South American and the South Atlantic status quo (1981: 86). Brazil's mission, depicted in three interlocking circles, should be to protect the United States' maritime flank in case of a Soviet attack across the Atlantic Narrows (1981: 49–52). Ocean traffic to the North Atlantic likewise must be protected to assure raw materials and energy resources for allied factories. Golbery also makes Brazil responsible for safeguarding South America and Antarctica within the cold war alliance.

The general distrusts his Latin American neighbors in this cold war pattern, a fact that probably contributes to his reputation. Argentina shows "imperialist" tendencies (1981: 61), and Brazil finds itself encircled by "a belt of nations, of the same Hispanic origins, that have united around various dissensions" (1981: 53). Fortunately, Brazil's major opponents, Peru, Colombia, and Argentina, are separated by great distances and jungle-mountain buffers, and all neighboring frontiers appear "dead" or not challenged and scarcely populated, with the exception of those around Mato Grosso, which lies exposed to Argentinean attack (1981: 59).

Golbery faces the problem of Spanish encirclement in several ways. He calls for the "internal expansion" of his country by colonizing and integrating marginal and frontier regions to lessen their exposure to aggrandizing neighbors (1981: 43, 169). Brazil's possession of the pivotal "welding zone" (map 3) in the continent's core

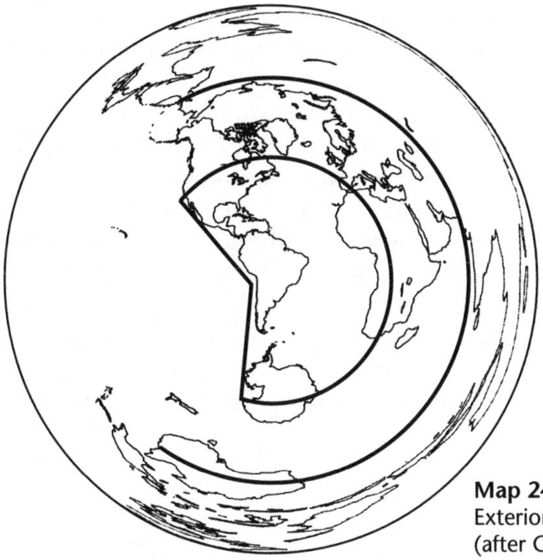

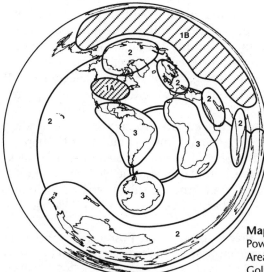

Map 24. The Interior and Exterior World Hemicycles (after Golbery 1981, p. 81)

Map 25. The Centers of Power: Esplanade and Interior Areas Hemicycles (after Golbery 1987, p. 86)

provides a further security advantage because river sources, mountain passes, and other communications routes intersect in this area (1981: 62, 128–129).

Golbery recommends an internal and coordinated strengthening of five Brazilian territorial sectors for security reasons. The "central nucleus" of São Paulo, Minas Gerais, and Rio de Janeiro would be secured by three flanking "peninsulas": the Northeast, the Central West, and the South. The "Amazon island" would also supply its resources to buffer the central "heartland" (1981: 38–47, 92–93, 112–126). Finally, he promises that Brazil will intervene to maintain the South American status quo, a "quick remedy" against "any revisionist tendencies or formation of regional political and economic blocs that could threaten the proper peace of the continent" (1981: 75, 134–135).

Therezinha de Castro (Brazil)

Therezinha de Castro's writings share parts of both Golbery's and Meira Mattos' perspectives. She is stridently anti-Communist but urges cooperation among the states of the South Atlantic. She sees Brazil and the western alliance threatened by Soviet-supported insurgency in the Third World and by the growth of Russian maritime strength in the southern oceans. Her solution resides in South America, in a regional maritime defense of the South Atlantic and economic integration among the Southern Cone republics.

A historian, cartographer, and geographer at the Colégio Pedro II in Rio de Janeiro, Castro has emerged as one of the most respected South American geopolitical authors. She has written more than ten books on the topic, and her many articles appear in the leading geopolitical journals of Argentina, Uruguay, and Brazil. Adept at applying the traditional works of Mahan, Mackinder, and Spykman, with frequent references to Ratzel and Kjéllen, she also builds her theses (1986a: 101-127) on other Brazilian writers, including Travassos, Meira Mattos, Golbery do Couto e Silva, and Delgado de Carvalho.

Castro characterizes Brazil's geopolitical position as inherently pivotal and strategic, made more so by the papal territorial divisions of the 1492 Treaty of Tordesillas (1986b: 1–9; 1984b: 17–27; 1983a: 21–49; 1982a: 17–20). This treaty brought shatterbelt-like "tension zones" to the South Atlantic, the Amazon, and the Plata systems at the northern and southern extremes of the original Portuguese colonial sector (map 26). As a consequence, a political "cantonization,"

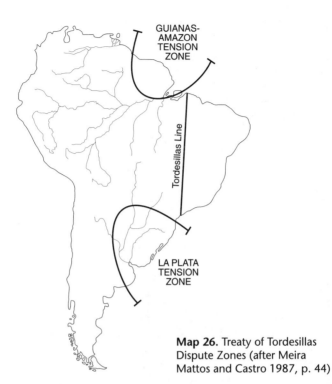

Map 26. Treaty of Tordesillas Dispute Zones (after Meira Mattos and Castro 1987, p. 44)

or Balkanization, of Spanish America prevented Portuguese colonization along the entire Atlantic seaboard of South America.

Visualizing Brazil within Mackinder's outer maritime crescent (in opposition to Russia's occupation of the Eurasian heartland), Castro labels the country as strategically vital to the defense of the Western Hemisphere and the North Atlantic Treaty Organization (1988: 91–93; 1986c: 16–20; 1983e: 41–42). Her concept of Brazil's "multiple vectors" (1986b: 17–20; 1981a: 39–41) shows the several directions of this foreign policy (map 27). For instance, in the South Atlantic, Brazil represents the "key point" between the Caribbean and the southern maritime passages because of the length of its coastline, because it faces the West African littoral, and because its northeast salient protects the Atlantic Narrows (1984b: 22; 1983e: 38–39). Two additional factors, the strategic raw materials, including Middle Eastern petroleum, that pass through the area to North America and to Europe, and a growing Soviet naval presence in the South Atlantic that threatens the security of this route, make Brazil's maritime dimension significant.

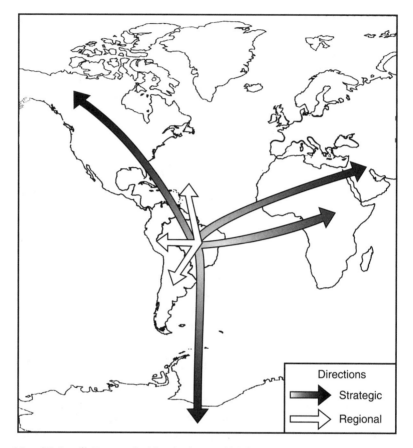

Map 27. Brazil's Present Position in the World (after Castro 1981b, p. 44)

Map 28 depicts this "strategic rear guard of the western bloc" (1984a: 94, 105–108; 1983b: 39–41; 1979: 69–71) under threat of Soviet submarines. Two triangles link actual or potential Russian maritime bases, each able to block choke-point access into the Atlantic. Castro's inclusion of possible Soviet Antarctic bases in this security scenario in the triangles shows her particular concern with a Soviet threat (1982b: 83–87). Her *defrontação* thesis (map 20), in which all Southern Cone states possess a portion of the glacial continent, could imply a tactic of unifying the region in defense of the South Atlantic (1977: 16–17; 1976: 116–118; 1972a: 116; 1972b: 140; 1968: 130–133).

The Plata basin receives wide coverage in Castro's writings (1985b; 1985c). She favors Brazil's playing a legitimate role in developing the continental hinterland, especially in league with Bolivia and Paraguay. Castro emphasizes the three overland rail and trucking export corridors that tie the Mediterranean republics to the southern Brazilian coast, in effect checkmating Plata River transport through Argentina and prompting Buenos Aires to compete with new schemes of river barge canal portages (also see Boscovich on this topic).

Brazil's strategic relationship with the United States frustrates Castro. Once an alliance of mutual respect between the two nations, since the 1970s diplomatic ties have weakened because of Jimmy Carter's distrust of Brazil's nuclear program and the Reagan administration's backing of Great Britain over Brazil and Argentina during the Malvinas war. Castro believes the United States possesses little interest in investing in South Atlantic security (1992: 290–304;

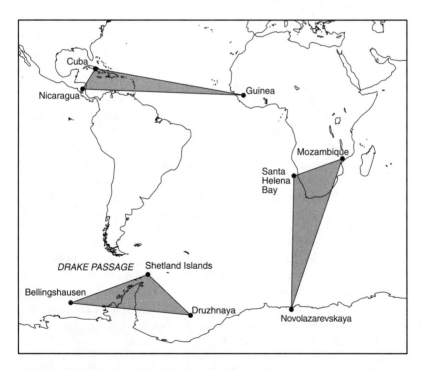

Map 28. Strategic Triangles of the South Atlantic Zones (after Meira Mattos and Castro 1987, p. 85)

1983b: 37–38; 1983c: 31–32). These and other disputes with the northern republic, she claims, moved Brazil's leaders to adopt a course of "constructive pragmatism" in foreign affairs, away from a strategic reliance on the United States and toward a regional commitment to South America.

In several of her articles, Castro ties Southern Cone integration to the strategic parameters of her geopolitics. Since the United States is no longer a dependable partner and NATO does not respond to the Soviet maritime threat in the South Atlantic, national survival may lie in part in the "continental" approach of regional self-sufficiency (1985a: 112; 1983b: 41; 1983c: 32–34; 1983d: 28–29).

Enrique Guglialmelli (Argentina)

Argentinean Gen. Juan Enrique Guglialmelli held a variety of important military and political appointments before his death in 1983. He headed the Escuela Superior de Guerra and the Centro de Altos Estudios (Center for Advanced Military Studies), commanded the Fifth Army Corps (a position that heightened his awareness of central government neglect of Patagonia and other frontier territories), and served as secretary to the Consejo Nacional de Desarrollo under the Juan Carlos Onganía military government (1966–1971). During his tenure with the Consejo Nacional de Desarrollo, he implanted his nationalist ideals on the country's development policy.

The dominant figure in contemporary Argentinean geopolitics, General Guglialmelli directed the Instituto Argentino de Estudios Estratégicos y de las Relaciones Internacionales (INSAR, Argentinean Institute of Strategic Studies and International Relations) and also served as editor of *Estrategia* (published from 1969 until 1984), a journal Jack Child calls "clearly Latin America's (and possibly the world's) most sophisticated and penetrating journal of geopolitics" (1979: 95). Guglialmelli wrote extensively in *Estrategia* about national and regional geopolitics, with a consistent and forceful emphasis on what he visualized as Brazil's expansionism and Argentina's inability to counter it.

Economic nationalism and national development and integration constituted his persistent recommendations for resolving Argentinean stagnation and encirclement by regional and international opponents. Not a theorist or a strong integrationist but a nationalist policy advocate, he ventured into topics not usually touched by the other writers considered here: the historical development of geopolitical writing in Argentina (1986; 1977b), the impact of indigenous nuclear weapons in the Southern Cone, and the proper role of the armed forces in national development. (The last two are discussed later.) Nevertheless, Brazilian and Argentinean nationalism are his major themes.

Argentina resembles a "peninsula," alleged General Guglialmelli, welded together of three parts: the continental northern interior and coast, the Atlantic extension (the "Argentinean" Sea), and the Patagonian and Antarctic peninsulas (map 29). This cartographic image cogently summarizes the essence of the general's geopolitical thinking. Here he rejected the idea of Argentinean internationalism as advocated by liberal trade partisans. Rather, he favored tariff protection and public subsidies of certain industries. Instead of having Buenos Aires as the sole focus of the nation, he supported a larger allotment of resources to the southern and northern frontiers so as to secure and integrate all national territory within a comprehensive development plan (1979c; 1979d; 1977b; and 1976b). The upper section of the map also shows the "geopolitical triangle" of Bolivia, through which Brazil traditionally has sought its "manifest destiny" of Pacific passage, thus thwarting Argentina in its quest for influencing the continental interior.

Guglialmelli described Brazilian expansionism in these terms (1979a: 13):

> Brazil, supported by Washington, has operated with clear objectives, tenaciously pursued and well equipped [and] spurred further today by the urgent need for primary materials and energy sources. It advances over the lesser countries [Bolivia, Uruguay, and Paraguay]; it searches for routes to the Pacific; it cooperates in the development of the smaller countries in the sectors that its own economy needs; it blocks Argentina's cooperation and projects; it gains a head start [over Argentina in Plata influence] by constructing great hydroelectric works [at Itaipú and elsewhere]; it lends technical and financial assistance; it opens, finally, its maritime coast at Santos, Paranaguá, and Rio Grande to interior access through highways, canals, and railroads in eastern Paraguay, Bolivia, Uruguay, and Argentina's Mesopotamia, openly challenging and competing with the [natural] portage system of the (Argentinean) Río de la Plata.

Despite the general's admission that Brazil and Argentina could cooperate for mutual betterment in the Southern Cone (1970: 52–55;

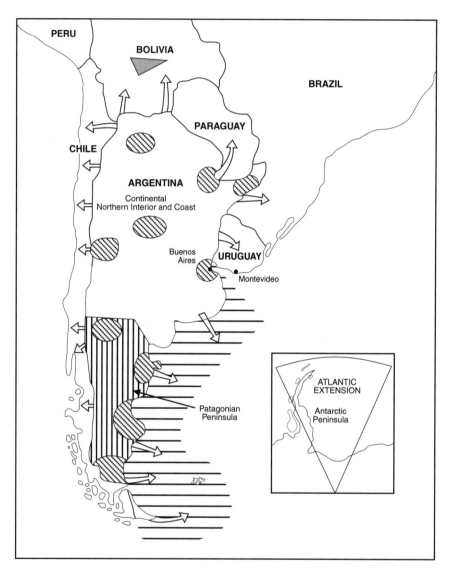

Map 29. Peninsular Argentina (after Guglialmelli 1979c, p. 26)

1975a: 21–26), Guglialmelli sees a threat from Brazil's historical geopolitical ambitions of absorbing the Mediterranean states of Bolivia and Paraguay and securing a land passage to the Pacific, both at the expense of Argentina's desired sphere of influence (see especially 1979–1980; also 1980a; 1980b; 1979d; 1977a; 1976c; 1975–1976; 1975a; 1975b; 1975c; 1973–1974; 1973a; and 1972–1973). According to Guglialmelli, Brazilian expansionism lessens Argentinean impact in the Plata valley and solidifies a threatening encirclement of the country by Chile in Patagonia and by Great Britain in the South Atlantic and Antarctic. He urged development and integration of marginal frontiers as the best guarantor of national security.

To reduce insecurity, the general recommended improvement and expansion of Plata River navigation (1979–1980: 24–25). He envisioned construction of canals at Bermejo and elsewhere as well as the establishment of other access and water flow facilities; migration to sparsely inhabited and threatened frontier areas, particularly Patagonia and Mesopotamia; and accelerated development and integration of the country's economy, preferably with heavy industry and economic expansion toward the nation's marginal territories over the traditional emphasis on agro-business.

The only one among our writers to explore the topic of nuclear weapons, Guglialmelli reluctantly advocated Argentina's construction of such weapons if Brazil first initiated an arms race (1982). He could not otherwise justify unilateral production of the atomic bomb (1982; 1978a; 1976a; 1975b; 1974; 1970–1971). Neither country could afford these weapons, he claimed, and worse still, the United States would enter the Southern Cone as Brazil's ally. Better to cooperate in peaceful uses of nuclear energy, and thus maintain regional separation from northern strategic involvement. Guglialmelli further advised Argentina's (and Brazil's) exclusion from the Non-Proliferation Treaty and its hemispheric equivalent, the Tlatelolco Pact, but continuation of indigenous energy programs and policies independent of the great powers.

Guglialmelli's antipathy toward traditional free-trade policies and his championing of nationalist protectionism represent a second major theme in his geopolitical writings. External "enemies" or "interests" (advocates of "comparative advantage" free-trade capitalism and Brazilian, British, and U.S. multinational corporations), collaborating with an internal "fifth column" of "liberal cosmopologists," had made Argentina dependent on international economic "imperialism." This aggression resembled a "bomb attack" against the nation

(1978b: 16–17; see also 1979b; 1978b; 1977c; 1976a; 1973a; 1973b; and 1972).

Particularly since the 1880s, national policies concentrated power in Buenos Aires to the neglect of the marginal territories. This fostered agro-business exporting over the development of advanced technology and heavy industry. The consequent dependency appeared dangerous to Guglialmelli because it bred national weakness and disunity (1979a: 255).

Economic weakness, social disunity, and neglect of frontiers seemed to him particularly worrisome because they exposed the country to the territorial encroachments of Brazil, Chile, and Great Britain, in addition to weakening Argentinean diplomacy, trade expansion, and leadership in the Plata region (1980–1981; 1975–1976).

Guglialmelli called for an "emancipator strategy," a "second revolution" for independence, to "retake the road of liberal integration" and regeneration (1973a: 51). The popular sectors—workers, clergy, business, cultural groups and the intelligentsia, and the armed forces—must unite to gain control of national planning. Efforts to devise an "internal frontier" would strengthen sovereignty based on national material and spiritual cohesion. He advocated protective tariffs, prevention of foreign corporate excesses, enhancement of heavy industry and advanced technology, improvement of internal communications and transportation, and integration of all marginal territories into national developmental. Because the armed forces reflected the popular sectors (1973b; 1972; 1969a; 1969b; 1969c), they also stood as sturdy proponents of nationalist strategies and as "vanguards" for asserting liberation.

José Felipe Marini (Argentina)

José Felipe Marini, a retired army colonel, has taught geopolitics at the Argentinean National War College, at the Foreign Service Institute, and at various regional universities, including those at Tucumán and Belgrano. Among his books on geopolitics available to readers in the United States, *El conocimiento geopolítico* (1982) is the best known and one of the better treatises on the topic. Marini is a scholar, a strategist, and an integrationist, a combination that creates a tightly reasoned but still flexible approach to Southern Cone policy suggestions based on geopolitical insights.

Marini laments the lack of an effective Argentinean frontier policy, which has led to neglected and disconnected borderlands. The policy is more positioned to cede than to sustain or increase the national domain (1980b: 146–147). "Our country lacks economic and geopolitical integration," he declares, a deficiency that has made it vulnerable, dependent, and insecure (1980b: 170).

Marini argues that Argentina has become so geopolitically fractionalized that it runs the risk of domination by "super monopolies," including the oil cartels and the Trilateral Commission (1987: 69; 1980b: 38–41, 56–62). "Our territory finds itself dangerously fragmented by climate, seas, and a powerful foreign nation [the United Kingdom]," he asserts, so exposed that an attack by the "territorial appetites" of Brazil and Chile very likely looms (1980a: 97, 108; 1980b: 97). The United States' association with Brazil, which has the latter performing a surrogate function as peace enforcer within a pan-region and key-nation format, also threatens the security of Argentina (1987: 57, 77–78).

According to Marini, the solution to the problem of vulnerability to foreign interests, as created by national fragmentation and neglect, lies in domestic consolidation and Southern Cone leadership. Whereas Argentina benefits from an "exceptional geopolitical position" (1980b: 170) and abundant national wealth, past governments have wrongly concentrated resources in Buenos Aires to the exclusion of other national areas, and they have mistakenly relied on a failed policy of "turning their backs on the [South American] continent" (1980a: 102). Now, the nation must reverse direction by developing its marginal territories, by becoming more involved with neighbors, and by promoting regional integration (1980b: 151). Argentina would grow stronger internally and externally if it tied itself more closely to the destinies of bordering states (1980a: 105–106).

In domestic geopolitics, Marini urges promotion of heavy industry and international trade; creation of energy self-sufficiency; construction of "development poles" in the Argentinean hinterland and a linking of these to an improved transportation system; doubling of national population every twenty-five or thirty years; maintenance of a stable and democratic political system; colonization of frontier and vacant regions; strengthening of sea power in the South Atlantic; and consolidation of Argentinean positions in Antarctica and the Malvinas (1990: 91–100; 1987: 40–42, 158; 1980a: 98–99, 109–113, 124; 1980b: 38, 56–62). Without these transformations, Marini believes the nation will not be able to project its influence beyond its borders, which it must do to achieve national security, prosperity, and leadership within the Southern Cone.

The bulk of Marini's design extends from this national consolidation and strengthening. He asserts that Argentina, although an "island," holds the most "vital," or pivotal, strategic position in South America, for it more than others controls the Plata River watershed (1988; 1987: 96–98, 130–135, 141; 1982: 105–107; 1980b: 142–145). This vital basin, the continent's wealthiest in terms of resources, industry, transport, and population, holds the key to South American integration and peace. It provides the best passage to the Pacific and the Amazon, as well as to the continental hinterland.

South American political stability also depends on amiable Buenos Aires–Brasilia diplomatic relations. Furthermore, Plata integration protects against dependency on outsiders and, in particular, neutralizes the United States' impact in the basin.

Plata integration advances because of the region's great distance from northern power centers (1987: 144; 1980a: 99), although the Brazil–United States partnership threatens this isolation and requires Argentina to "delicately balance" its relationship with the North American republic (1980b: 144–145). For successful regional consolidation, Marini believes the hinterland requires development and populating, and national economies need closer coordination to restrict dependence on outside markets, capital, and technology (1987: 35–36, 140–158; 1980a: 99–103).

Marini also favors loosening Brazil from its close ties to the United States and shifting its focus toward cooperating with Argentina in Plata integration (1987: 57, 77–78; 1982: 116, 374–375; 1980b: 143–152). He depicts Brazil as a surrogate "key nation," which performs as the police of South America in support of U.S. security interests. As a "junior partner" to the Yankees, Brazil could expand territorially and rely on U.S. military and economic support. From this strategic linkage, Marini sees a potential for serious escalation of conflict in the Southern Cone.

Yet, Marini never denies the possibility of Brazilian-Argentinean cooperation (1987: 147–150; 1980a: 100–101; 1980b: 152–153). He predicts a weakening of U.S. ties to Brazil as Middle America absorbs a larger portion of U.S. attention; thus, he encourages Brazil to take up the advantages of trade and joint ventures with its neighbors (1987: 29, 69–75; 1980b: 13, 142).

Recommendations of closer relations with Chile and the desirability of easier land passage to the Pacific through Peru, Chile, and Bolivia add important dimensions to Marini's geopolitics. He argues that Chile figures as "the natural ally of Argentina" (1980a: 100–

102; 1980b: 143) and that both nations ought to cooperate in security matters and in sharing each other's ocean fronts. Facilitating the Salta-Antofagasta cross-mountain passage would particularly serve both countries and prove profitable commercially, block excessive Brazilian impact in the area, and reduce the importance of the southern maritime passages.

Nicolás Boscovich (Argentina)

An accountant and businessman by trade, Boscovich has published articles, chapters, and books that consistently advocate the development and integration of Argentina's northern regions as a solution to the threats of Brazilian hegemony and national economic stagnation. He focuses primarily on establishing improved river and canal communications within Argentina, specifically in the Bermejo River basin, although he is generally concerned with the entire Plata watershed. His suggested construction projects and improvements aim toward barge transport in the region, flood control, swamp drainage, irrigation facilities, hydroelectric energy production, encouragement of colonization and industry, and strategic cooperation with Bolivia and Paraguay to protect against Brazil's territorial encroachments.

Boscovich highlights two security threats to Argentina, the first from Brazil, the second from global marginality. Brazil clearly aspires to continental hegemony, he argues, and its recent successes in economic growth and internal integration have propelled the nation toward Southern Cone dominance (1983a: 60 – 61; 1983b: 20 – 21; 1979: 20, 191 – 202). Argentinean "decadence" has strengthened this challenge and placed the region's independence at "grave risk" (1979: 26). Argentina must block Brazil's western surge to the Pacific and neutralize its neighbor's overland "export corridors," which connect Paraguay and Bolivia with the coastal "superports" of Santos and Rio Grande do Sul. Only through an equilibrium of power between the two nations will Argentina's national security be affirmed (1986: 37 – 43; 1983b: 20 – 22; 1974: 35 – 36).

In a 1990 article, Boscovich moderates his distrust of Brazil, finding instead an emerging common interest. He urges binational coordination in river traffic and hydroelectric projects and argues that Brazil's expansion seems not necessarily aimed at Argentinean interests (1990: 39). Cooperation between the two nations, he predicts, could project the Southern Cone into world competitiveness and away from global marginality (1991b: 25 – 26; 1990: 41).

Boscovich (a member of the Radical Party) has especially harsh words for the Peronists and their lack of a "consistent geopolitical conception" (1983a: 58). In a tone like that of Marini and Guglialmelli, Boscovich laments the slow progress toward constructing a national plan for development and integration of the national interior, particularly the northeastern and northwestern provinces. Without increasing the contribution of these abandoned territories, he thinks, national growth is seriously retarded and the country is exposed to world dependency and economic stagnation (1992: 24 – 26; 1983a: 58; 1974: 28 – 30; 1973: 19).

One solution to these problems lies in developing the sparsely populated Bermejo basin of the "savage" northern river that needs "governing" before its great potential can be utilized (1984: 35 – 43; 1979: 15 – 20, 55 – 58; 1974: 32 – 34, 40; 1973: 10 – 28; 1960: 95). Boscovich envisions canal routes of eighteen hundred kilometers (map 30) that will connect the Bermejo to Argentina's Paraná River at Resistencia and at Santa Fé and ensure the river's economic feasibility by providing less-expensive barge transport, hydroelectric power, flood control, and irrigation facilities. He sees in his plan the possibility of another Mississippi or Tennessee Valley, one supporting upwards of 92 million Argentineans (1984: 40 – 43; also 1990: 41; 1983b: 23). Argentina would benefit from the Plata valley's "natural competitive advantage" by enlisting the cheaper facilities of barge transport (in comparison to Brazil's more expensive trucking and rail corridors) (1990: 38 – 41; 1983b: 22; 1979: 21). Furthermore, if Argentina were to discard its current "disintegration," Boscovich anticipates a significant advantage to the country when the Plata system becomes connected to the Amazon and Orinoco waterways (1991a: 28) to create a future "Mediterranean" communications network within the continent's heart.

Boscovich concludes that the Bermejo project can help resolve the problems of threat from Brazil and marginality. Argentina's powerful northern neighbor would find itself checkmated or co-opted by Argentinean interior development, and the nation's expansion would project beyond its Southern Cone confines onto the world political and economic stage.

Bernardo Quagliotti de Bellis (Uruguay)

Quagliotti de Bellis contributes two special dimensions to geopolitics, first, as the outstanding promoter of South American geopolitics, and,

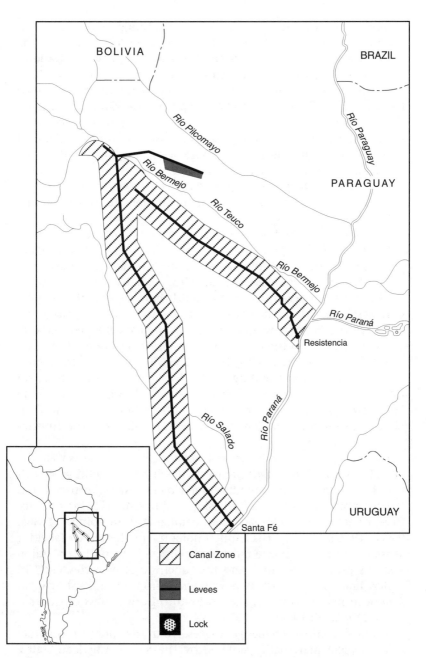

Map 30. Bermejo River Canal Plans (after Boscovich 1973, p. 66)

second, as the leading proponent of "integrationist" writing. By profession a journalist, with ties to the Uruguayan legislature and the armed forces, Quagliotti leads the Instituto Uruguayo de Estudios Geopolíticos (IUDEG, Uruguayan Institute of Geopolitical Studies), edits the influential journal *Geosur* (and previously the discontinued *Geopolítica*), and, according to Jack Child (1988a: 57), "is the driving force" behind the Asociación Sudamericana de Estudios Geopolíticos e Internacionales (South American Association of Geopolitical and International Studies), an umbrella organization that coordinates and encourages national strategic studies in the Southern Cone. Likewise, Quagliotti originated the URUPABOL concept, which advocates joint economic involvement among the three regional buffer states.

To understand the flow of Quagliotti's thinking, one must begin with the theme of Uruguay's territorial insecurity. Despite Quagliotti's eminence as an integrationist, he writes fervently about the perils of Brazil's aggrandizement and Uruguay's insecure position between Brazil and Argentina. He frequently cites comparative population statistics, which demonstrate that land pressures from the country's two larger neighbors threaten Uruguay's exposed "vacant" or "vulnerable" northern and western frontiers (1983: 173 – 177; 1982b: 19 – 20; 1981: 12 – 13; 1979a: 25 – 30). Quagliotti frequently cites the expansionist writings of Mario Travassos and Golbery do Couto e Silva as evidence of Brazil's desire to absorb bordering-state land and establish hegemony in the Southern Cone. Hence, to Quagliotti the security problem precedes and influences the integrationist theme.

Uruguay's current peril derives from a regional source as well: the unstable balance of power between Brazil and Argentina, which could escalate into continental-level violence. Quagliotti censures Brazil's ambitions for Plata leadership and British – U.S. interference in Southern Cone diplomacy as destabilizing Plata politics (1986a: 9 – 17; 1976a: 72 – 76). His "puncti dolenti," or shatterbelt label for sensitive escalation-prone territories, with the Paraná River – Itaipú area his primary example, and his "doctrine of encirclement," in which Brazil may thrust its power across frontiers against Spanish American insurrectionists, also speak to this awareness of external threat (1986a: 9; 1980: 16; 1976a: 84; 1975: 14 – 16).

A third security challenge comes from the global economic-technological marginality suffered by the South American states, coupled with a Balkanization, or political fragmentation, of the continent that weakens collective diplomacy (1990c: 7–8; 1986a: 5). The "crisis" of Southern Cone economic dependency, as dangerous as an imminent military attack, invites continued Plata disunity and northern interference. On this note, Quagliotti writes: "[With] Uruguay [acting] alone, no solution can exist." On the larger scale, without a "concerted integration" of resources, South America will remain stagnant and controlled by outsiders (1982b: 5).

Uruguay's geographic position also renders it important security advantages and solutions in addition to liabilities. Quagliotti avoids the term "buffer state," probably because it reflects Uruguay's inherent vulnerability, and instead uses "key" or "hinge" state to depict his country's location at the Plata River outlet as providing potential authority and opportunity. This possibility of "geopolitical metamorphosis" (1982b: 26) shows "Uruguay as a wedge, a romantic pad between 'two crystals' [Brazil and Argentina], a vital space for maintaining a harmonic integration and equilibrium in the Plata valley" (1986a: 19).

Four primary themes, central to Quagliotti's geopolitics, emerge from this transformation: the great necessity for nationwide development; the feasibility of South American integration; a significant connection between the success of regional economic cooperation and Uruguay's national security; and Uruguay's position as vital to Southern Cone stability (1981: 12–13; 1979b: 18; 1976a: 155).

Quagliotti believes his "nationalist-integrationist" approach will lead to effective governance, on both the national and the regional plane, that will construct "a modern nation-state interrelated within a greater regional-economic space" (1979b: 15). He suggests several steps, first on the national level, later on the regional, that will make economic growth in one sphere eventually complement and stimulate growth in the other. Within a coordinated process of national and regional integration, Uruguay becomes more secure, regional stability ensues, and South America exerts more impact on world affairs.

His plan for the Tacuarembó basin in north-central Uruguay typifies his strategy (1990a: 27–30; 1983: 177–196; 1982b: 9–19, 27–64; 1976c): a detailed examination of likely transportation improvements; hydroelectric power generation; industrial and agricultural growth; attainment of new technologies; and the like. In the Laguna de Rocha superport design, he envisions construction of a major deepwater port facility that not only would service all Plata River traffic that connects to the Atlantic but also would stimulate the Uruguayan hinterland around Laguna de Rocha (1989: 13–16; 1982b; 1981: 18–23).

Four additional national projects affect the remaining provinces (map 31). Development foci, in circles on map 31, coordinate and link provinces in national "project" zones. Here resources are collected, communications ties forged, local leadership tapped, and industrial cooperation made possible. Again, frontier security and the continued possession of exposed territories represent primary objectives of such national integration.

Regional integration among the states of the Plata River basin and beyond has created a "historic convergence of interests" (1976a: 156). Quagliotti finds an international economic trend toward regional cooperation, which causes a global division of labor that could place the southern areas in perpetually subordinate status unless they pool resources and declare an economic and diplomatic common front (1979a: 1–14, 37).

Although he falls short of suggesting a comprehensive regional plan, he has emphasized continental road and rail systems (map 32) that have had some impact on national policies. On map 32, Quagliotti again draws primary and secondary development poles that are composed of power projections, geopolitical axes, population clusters or cohesive nuclei, and exit ports. His Laguna de Rocha, Paysandá, La Plata Hidrovías, and URUPABOL proposals likewise depict a regional intent (1990b; 1982b; 1981; 1975).

The South Atlantic security perspective draws some attention from the standpoint of possible Russian interdiction of Middle Eastern oil traffic to the North Atlantic Treaty nations (1986b; 1982a; 1981; 1978; 1977; 1976b). Quagliotti does little other than describe this threat. But more clearly than the other authors we are discussing, Quagliotti expresses fear of a potential shatterbelt in the Southern Cone (1988; 1990c). Competing states outside the Southern Cone could align themselves with Brazil or Argentina, prompting an escalation of tensions that would threaten national security and regional integration.

Julia Velilla de Arréllaga (Paraguay)

Julia Velilla de Arréllaga best represents Paraguay's contribution to South American geopolitics. She is a historian and director of the

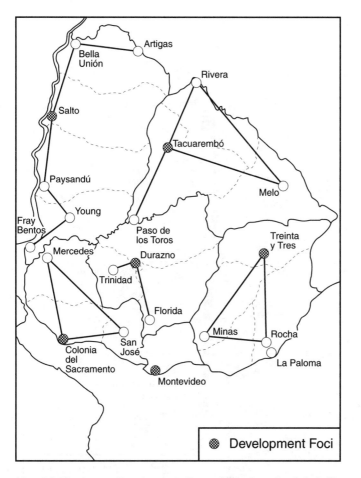

Map 31. Uruguayan Development Zones (after Quagliotti de Bellis 1982b, p. 29)

Instituto Paraguayo de Estudios Geopolíticos e Internacionales (Paraguayan Institute of Geopolitical and International Studies) and has maintained close ties with the proponents of Southern Cone integration, in particular with Quagliotti de Bellis and other URUPABOL enthusiasts. Her *Paraguay: un destino geopolítico* (1982) and articles in *Geosur* and *Geopolítica* (Uruguay) present a consistent and systematic geopolitical perspective of Paraguay's space, position, and resources nestled as it is within the heart of the Plata River valley.

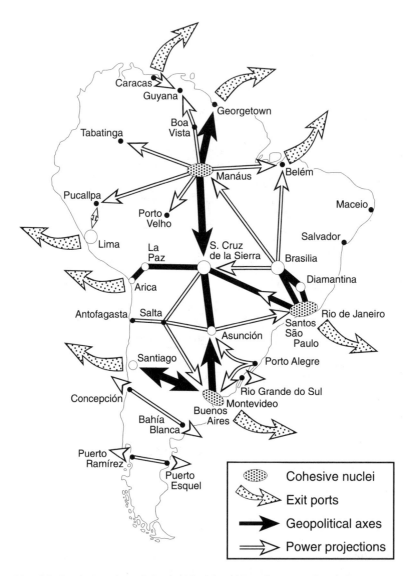

Map 32. South American Cohesive Nuclei and Development Center Zones (after Quagliotti de Bellis 1979a, p. 41)

The Instituto Paraguayo de Estudios Geopolíticos e Internacionales

Before examining Velilla de Arréllaga's primary ideas, I should first describe the Instituto Paraguayo de Estudios Geopolíticos e Internacionales, because it typifies the depth and activism of geopolitics in South America. The Instituto, established by political and intellectual activists, has sponsored a wide range of seminars on international and domestic matters. It copublishes, with the German-sponsored Fundación Friedrich Naumann, seminar proceedings and other materials, administers an Asunción office and library (partly funded by the U.S. embassy), and functions in a wide variety of other civic areas, for example, voter education and hosting of international election observers.

The Instituto plays a largely nonpartisan role in local politics (although it was one of the few groups to meet regularly and without censorship during the Alfredo Stroessner dictatorship). Unlike many other geopolitical associations (particularly those in Peru, Chile, Brazil, and Argentina), the Paraguayan organization has primarily civilian and scholarly members and purposes, although it cooperates with the Defense Ministry's Oficina de Geográfica Militar (Office of Military Geography), which teaches geopolitics in the armed forces academies and staff schools. During a 1986 visit to Paraguay, I attended several meetings of the group in Velilla de Arréllaga's home and once presented a geopolitical topic for discussion (see Kelly 1990b, 1989). I always found those in attendance open and enthusiastic, intellectually inquisitive, and dedicated to influencing national policy.

Velilla de Arréllaga's Geopolitics

Velilla de Arréllaga argues that Paraguay occupies a pivotal position on the continent and is destined for leadership in securing continental unity (1981; 1977). For instance, she describes Asunción as an "area of welding, a crossroads of encounter and union. It linked Atlantic with Pacific, united the Banda Oriental [Uruguay] with the ports of Upper Peru [Bolivia]. It is the meeting of the Amazon with the Plata, and it was union and equilibrium among Portuguese and Spanish powers in the Plata, impeding the *bandeirantes'* [Portuguese] advance" (1982: 255). Elsewhere, she envisions a larger arc of influence: "the Asunción, Montevideo, Cochabamba triangle is the true balance of continental equilibrium," a "key to continental domination," and a zone that plays a preponderant role in the continent. Paraguay and its "natural" allies, Bolivia and Uruguay, have become pivotal to regional and continental political and economic stability (1982: 135, 258 – 256).

Her most central geopolitical theme proposes an "energy and steel community" for linking the natural and energy resources of all Plata River states (1988; 1982: 229 – 248; 1977: 17 – 23). Initially, Bolivia and Paraguay would coordinate, where possible, their economies and communications networks, with the mineral wealth of the former tied to the agricultural, hydroelectric, and transit advantages of the latter. Later, this union could associate with the other Plata states. Reflecting on the "extraordinary geographic position held by Paraguay," she declares that the "key part of establishing economic integration and political integration in the region is [found in] Paraguay" (1982: 265).

Coordinating the resources of the URUPABOL group (Uruguay, Paraguay, and Bolivia), with Paraguay as the "hinge," would decrease Brazil's urge toward "imperial expansion" and Argentina's "zeal toward viceregal domination," for when the two interior countries are separated, they are exposed to exploitation (1982: 256 – 257): "Isolated, we are dominated, 'satellized,' but united, our powers of negotiation grow and we affirm our independence in interdependence." Once these "chains of colonialism" are lifted by regional and continental confederation, a new harmony and equilibrium will move South America toward peace and industrial progress.

Alipio Valencia Vega (Bolivia)

A historian and legal scholar as well as a geopolitical writer, Valencia Vega from the 1950s to the 1970s taught constitutional law at the Universidad Mayor de San Andrés and geopolitics at the Escuela de Altos Estudios Militares. He has written eighteen books on such topics as precolonial and colonial history, western capitalism and the nationalization of Bolivian mines, Bolivian political thought and constitutional law, and moral and civic education. Because he is not a theorist or a regional strategist, Valencia Vega's geopolitical works basically give a historical explanation for Bolivia's territorial losses to neighboring states, a process he labels "Polandization." To avoid further territorial losses, he offers historically derived policy proposals that he hopes will help safeguard his country's security.

Valencia Vega, like the Uruguayan and Paraguayan geopoliticans, stresses the point that his country deserves recognition as an authentic nation-state (1974a: 231–240). He sees Bolivia as composed of four interdependent geographic sections: the mountainous Cordillera and Altiplano, the valleys and *yungas*, the tropical eastern plains, and the Pacific coastal strip (despite the latter section's now being a part of Chile). Although other writers consider the country a strategic continental balancer, Valencia Vega brands this idea an "illusion" (1976: 46; 1974b: 239) and instead describes Bolivia as the "continental heart" and "divortia aquarum" (watershed) (1976: 45; 1975: 66–69; 1974a: 349–350) because its varied environments are so representative of the diversity of South America.

Bolivia's foremost danger derives from the potential of territorial dismemberment at the hands of neighbors, claims this author (1974b: 27):

> [Bolivia is a] country full of valuable natural resources, always having, on its frontiers, gold or silver or tin or oil or other metals and animal/vegetable riches of incalculable economic wealth. These frontiers, always deserted and destitute of Bolivian inhabitants capable of defending them and developing them, are largely the national weakness that, being visible externally, appears to authorize all attempts at deprivation and despoliation aimed at Bolivia.

Valencia Vega believes Bolivia's "permanent internal weakness" (1974b: 27) encouraged the greed of surrounding states and the resulting "economic wars" against Bolivian territory.

A solution to the problem of "abandoned" frontiers will come with an "internal conquest by the Bolivians themselves," with policies to attract migrants and economic growth to the borderlands. Systematic communications planning would link new development and colonies to Bolivian core regions (1975: 94–95; 1974b: 514, 546–557). Although benefits to Bolivia usually do not accrue from membership in regional integrative organizations, notes Valencia Vega, any continentwide movement that would guarantee Bolivia's access to the ocean must be encouraged (1975: 46–47, 58–59; 1974b: 537, 559).

Restoration of the Pacific littoral represents another important thesis. Valencia Vega enlists an assortment of anthropological and historical evidence showing a natural tie between ocean coast lands and Bolivian uplands, thus substantiating his argument that Bolivia possesses a more valid claim to the Atacama than does Chile (1976:

52–53; 1974a: 342–434; 1974b: 174–179, 543–547). Going beyond legal title, he claims that the Pacific provides "a truly indispensable respiratory organ" for the nation (1974b: 12) that, once returned, will assist in strengthening integration and resolving the threat of dismemberment.

Augusto Pinochet Ugarte (Chile)

General Augusto Pinochet is a prominent example in South America of what Howard Pittman labels "applied geopolitics" (1988a: 180–183). He based certain of his policies as president-dictator of Chile (1973–1990) on his teaching of and writing about geopolitics. A career army officer, Pinochet taught at war colleges in both Ecuador and Chile, thereby maintaining the strong involvement in military education so typical of the geopolitical authors examined in this chapter. He entered the armed forces in 1933 and attained the rank of colonel in 1966, general in 1973, after having served as commander of the 6th Army Division, as assistant to the undersecretary of war, and as member of the Chilean military mission to the United States. Pinochet led the ouster of Salvador Allende in 1973, and, after relinquishing direct control of the presidency in 1990, he remained as commander-in-chief of the armed forces.

As president, Pinochet initiated projects that he later characterized to Howard Pittman as "pure geopolitics" (1988a: 181). His Regionalization of Chile program recognized the tricontinental nature of the country—its Andean, Pacific, and Antarctic projections—with the intent of more closely integrating the core central valley to the geographically peripheral and less-developed areas. This plan stipulated redrawing provincial boundaries and constructing land and maritime highways to isolated southern territories; the latter was intended to avoid having to cross into Argentina to reach remote Chilean areas. Pinochet likewise confirmed the national interest in the oceans by establishing the Chilean Pacific Ocean Institute and related activities under the auspices of the National Oceanic Policy. A further example of this "applied geopolitics" appears in the coordination of geographic education, starting in elementary school, "that teaches geography in geopolitical terms and by the publication of news and magazine articles that publicize and disseminate geopolitical policies and plans. Official maps produced by the Instituto Geográfico Militar show the reorganization of Chile and include the Chilean Antarctic claim in the national territory" (Pittman 1988a: 181).

The impact of geopolitics on Pinochet's foreign policy surfaces in the Chilean presence in the Antarctic and the Beagle Channel, in negotiations for an access corridor for Bolivia to the Pacific (which advocated exchanging maritime for land space and guaranteeing a security zone in cooperation with Peru), and in the promotion of an independent foreign policy intent on preventing encirclement by Peru, Bolivia, and Argentina.

Geopolítica (1984) originated from Pinochet's teaching of geopolitics to military academy students. Frequently cited in South American geopolitical bibliographies, the book, like the Hennig and Körholz text (1977) and Atencio (1986), focuses on broader theoretical issues. The fourth "enlarged and corrected" edition contains more description of Chile than do the earlier versions.

The central argument in Pinochet's writing revolves around the state as a living organism (1984: 31, 35),

> constantly struggling for its existence. . . . This fact relates politics to space, with its own specific and constant rules, which permanently affect the peoples who act in a definite area, as they appear throughout history . . .
>
> The State is considered an unconscious but necessary process of human nature and is placed above free will or the fancies of individuals. The State is an organism; it is the highest personality of life . . . a superperson, as the highest form of social evolution.

Four elements compose a state: expanding and contracting frontiers; the hinterland, which normally lacks population and developed resources; the vital nucleus or heartland core, which will absorb the hinterland if the state is vibrant; and communications, the nerves of leadership. The "vital life cycle" of a nation's birth, growth and development, and death indicates the particular stage of a state's existence (1984: 187–232; 237–259; see also Pittman 1981a: 1216–1235). In all cases, geopolitics offers the format for the state's expansion and prosperity, and developmental policies under these organic directions will take Chile to its expected "greatness."

The general deplores the absence of a national center for geopolitical study in Chile similar to those in Brazil and Argentina, and he recommends certain areas of study should such an institution eventually arise: (1) development of a greater maritime role with a vigorous merchant marine, improved port and related facilities, and exploitation of oceans for food and mineral resources; (2) creation of a "mountain consciousness" among Chileans to stimulate development of the Chilean-Argentinean frontier; and (3) strengthening of an industrial economy by erecting "secondary manufacturing nuclei" in hinterland and peripheral zones (1984: 64, 73, 96, 138, 233–235).

Grateful that the Panama Canal has reduced Chile's isolation, Pinochet advocates construction of an improved trans-Isthmian passage. He believes the lack of will in the United States for containing communism may expose South America to Russian threat, and he advises an independent Third World bloc of nations to "muffle" great-power actions (1984: 89–92). Isolation fosters a nationalist spirit of self-reliance and an "entrepreneurial spirit" that allows for love of liberty and indigenous national development. Here, Pinochet characteristically attacks infiltration by dangerous "foreign doctrines whose consequences would be fatal for the cohesion of the State itself" (1984: 176, 156, 181).

Finally, an "Era of the Pacific" will bring wealth from Antarctica and the Orient, although the introduction of nuclear weapons into the Pacific basin (1984: 85–92) could endanger Chilean expansion.

Ramón Cañas Montalva (Chile)

While stationed in Punta Arenas at the continent's southern tip, during the early part of his career, then-colonel Cañas Montalva authored a series of newspaper articles urging increased national attention to Chile's southern territories, including Antarctica, and its claims to oceans adjacent to Chile's coasts. When he returned to command the southern military region a decade later, General Cañas Montalva continued to proclaim the importance of these territories. Specifically, he saw Argentina's coveting of the southern provinces, stimulated by international dynamics that had transformed the area into a "world geopolitical epicenter" of strategic importance and an integral sector in the coming "Age of the Pacific" (1955; see also Von Chrismar Escuti 1988; Pittman 1981a: 1195–1198).

Originating from the general's concern with such factors, the establishment in 1948 of the journal *Revista Geográfica de Chile "Terra Australis"* aimed to help "inspire the formulation of a national geographic consciousness" (1959b: 17). With Cañas Montalva as its initial editor, the journal carried the main thrust of his geopolitical thinking. In all, he published fourteen major articles in this journal that present his regional and strategic arguments for securing and developing the country's southern domains.

He claimed that the "universal epicenter" of power had shifted from the Mediterranean and the Atlantic to the Pacific basin. Technological improvements in aerial and maritime transport, augmented by the markets, resources, and populations of Asia, had brought about this shift in power centers (1981: 24–27; 1979: 89–90; 1955: 11–12; 1948: 29). Within the new configuration, Chile held a strategically vital position, since it commanded the South American and Antarctic littorals and maritime passages that opened into the Pacific (map 33) (1981: 27–31; 1979: 98–99; 1960: 6–8; 1959a; 1959b: 20–22; 1955: 11–16; 1953b: 11–14; 1948: 32–38). The general explains this importance (1948: 34): "Our country, after the annoying [depiction of it as] *corner* of the world in the past, is linked today through direct and expedient aerial and maritime routes across the swarming islands of Oceania to Australia and Asia, connecting itself with nations and territories that until yesterday appeared to us to form part of a distant and inaccessible system." Cañas Montalva decried the "blindness" and "myopia" of government leaders, which caused "inconceivable delays" in integrating and developing the southern frontiers (1959b: 20; 1956–1957a; 1953b: 14).

Within the context of hemispheric security, Chile had taken responsibility for defending the "Chileantarctic" littorals and passages, for these had become the major maritime choke points of the continent's southern sector (1948: 35): "It is enough to glance at a map of Central and South America to understand that, with respect to the Pacific Ocean, the western zone of the Panama Canal and our southern spur of America-Antarctica are the basic points for sustaining continental defense, much as the eastern portions of the Panama Canal and the Brazilian northeastern salient constitute this perspective in the Atlantic." Because the Panama Canal appeared vulnerable to attack, the southern passages had become even more important, alleged Cañas Montalva. To protect these choke areas, he advised strategic cooperation with Brazil and Great Britain (Von Chrismar Escuti 1988).

But Argentina also held an interest in the Pacific basin, and its involvement threatened Chilean security, particularly when land and

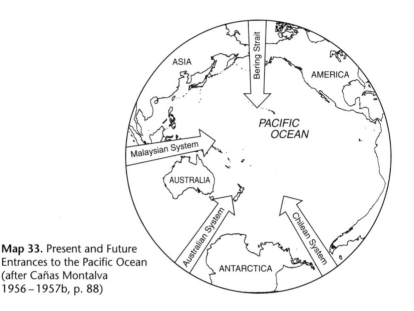

Map 33. Present and Future Entrances to the Pacific Ocean (after Cañas Montalva 1956–1957b, p. 88)

maritime passages through Chilean and Bolivian territories were taken into consideration (1960: 18; 1959b: 24–25; 1956–1957b: 77; 1953a: 13–14; 1953b: 10). Indeed, the "Nazionalism" or "neo-Nazi-Peronism" of Chile's eastern neighbor represented a conspiracy of aggrandizement against other Southern Cone states, as shown on map 34. The following quotation characterizes Argentina's "hegemonic" and "imperialist" expansionism (1953a: 10): "Argentinean foreign policy has shown a rare tenacity in its attainment of the objective of gaining passage to the Pacific. At bottom, the policy of the *cordillera libre* [Perón's Southern Cone free-trade proposal], revealed in the economic conspiracy within which it is disguised, aspires to a political ambition that is absolutely opposed to true Chilean interests and historical destiny as a central power of the South Pacific–Antarctic."

Cañas Montalva regretted the nineteenth-century loss of Patagonia to Argentina, and he drew on the historical Araucanian Indian occupation of both sides of the south Andean chain (1972–1973; 1970–1971: 51–52) to validate his claim that Chilean sovereignty should extend to Patagonia.

One of the first to oppose the doctrine of "Chile in the Pacific and Argentina in the Atlantic" (where the jurisdictional line between

Chile and Argentina extends immediately south of Tierra del Fuego), Cañas Montalva instead favored the "Arc of the Southern Antilles," or the Scotia Arc, which appeared much farther east and encompasses the Sandwich Islands (1956–1957b: 65–76). Argentina's endorsement of the Tierra del Fuego line, the general maintained, further illustrated its hegemonic aspirations.

A less-important theme subscribes to Chilean leadership over a "South Pacific Confederation" of Bolivia, Chile, Ecuador, and Peru (1979: 89; 1949; 1948: 29–30). The general argued that these republics in cooperation could more successfully exploit the possibilities of the coming Age of the Pacific. Furthermore, the four states working in unison could diminish the Argentinean threat.

Emilio Meneses Ciuffardi (Chile)

Howard Pittman writes about Emilio Meneses (1981a: 1284): "Emilio Meneses Ciuffardi, member of the faculty of the Catholic University of Chile, was the first civilian professor certified to teach geopolitics

Map 34. Colonial Pan-Germanism in South America (after Cañas Montalva 1956–1957b, p. 72)

by the Army War Academy. He has conducted courses and seminars at the University, lectures at the National Security Academy and the Naval War College, and specializes in seminars in geopolitics for officers of the Carabineros, the national police force."

In addition to teaching geopolitics, Meneses researches Chilean naval history and weapons acquisitions and contemporary Southern Cone diplomacy and makes recommendations for restructuring and integrating Chilean foreign policy (1989b; 1989c; 1989d; 1984; 1983; 1977). Not a theorist but, rather, a regional security strategist who prefers the maritime perspective, Meneses epitomizes a geopolitical scholar whose thinking is penetrating, creative, and still evolving.

Meneses describes Chile as geographically "marginal" to world affairs and as residing in an isolated and peripheral position—not Andean or even Southern Cone (1981a: 106–112, 132). This status could change if the Panama Canal ceases to function (thus raising the value of the southern passages) and if the South Pacific becomes more vital to global trade and manufacturing. Meneses, unlike Cañas Montalva, however, seems skeptical of a coming Pacific Age, and he focuses on the security of Chile within the Southern Cone context.

He warns that Chile faces serious threat from Peru, Brazil, Bolivia, and Argentina. Although he applauds certain of his country's security policies, he declares that others have not protected against regional encirclement. He argues against security policies that depend on a Southern Cone military balance of power with Peru, Brazil, and Argentina as simply not reliable (1989c: 20–25; 1989e: 33–34; 1982; 1981a: 139). Chile lacks sufficient resources for maintaining such an equilibrium, and alliances with Brazil and the United States cannot be trusted to prevail against Peru and Argentina.

Nonetheless, Meneses does advocate a stronger naval presence in the South Pacific (1991), especially for defending the southern and northern portions of the national domain. He doubts the efficacy of policies that depend on international goodwill toward Chile (as a democratic, peace-loving, and Third World nation) as a way to preserve national frontiers (1989a: 68–69; 1989e: 34–36; 1981b: 8–14). Reliance on indigenous sources for defense seems preferable to regional cooperation.

He asserts that Chile joined the Andean Free Trade Pact in part to contain Argentinean aggressiveness, and he believes Argentina's defeat in the Falklands/Malvinas war saved Chile from a likely invasion by its eastern neighbor during the Beagle Channel dispute

(1989a: 71–76; 1989e: 30–31; 1981a: 108–110). He favors establishing an international Commission of the South Pacific to extend Chile's influence into Asia. He also encourages "natural" international frontiers where possible and applauds the wisdom of previous leaders in not annexing the Argentinean territories of Mendoza and eastern Patagonia. Furthermore, he advocates peaceful settlement of border conflicts through negotiation (1989b: 6; 1981a: 112).

Map 35 provides a backdrop to Meneses' security strategy, as apparently influenced by Pinochet. A "vital, or heart, area" in the Central Valley, the country's "vital nucleus," is flanked on both north and south by sparsely populated and less-developed "hinterland" regions. At either territorial extreme, "secondary nuclei" appear (1981a: 126–145). Hence, Chile divides longitudinally according to three areas of national importance: (1) the northern zone of the Atacama Desert, the ports of Arica, Iquique, and Antofagasta, and the strategic land corridor into Bolivia, Argentina, and the continental "heartland"; (2) the central region, of historical, political, and economic significance; and (3) the southern sector, with three maritime passageways, the ports of Punta Arenas and Chacabuco, and ocean links to Chilean Antarctica and the southern oceans. The pivotal "southern welding zone," which connects Chile and Argentina, lies in this third region.

A significant danger comes from the lack of integration of the three nuclei, and securing the two peripheral sectors would significantly enhance national consolidation. With the flank areas exposed, Peru, Brazil, and Argentina threaten the northern part; the southern segment attracts the Argentineans.

Meneses' solution to the exposure of the peripheral regions is to establish a stronger navy and merchant marine, which could protect and improve national lines of communication (1981a: 145–160). Further, he recommends construction of two north-south highways in the Piedmont and coastal areas, exploitation of the continental shelf, and economic development of the hinterlands and the northern and southern territorial extremes. Consolidation of Antarctic claims and stronger linkages to Pacific islands offer added enhancements. Once these policies are instituted, the nation's increased geographic compactness will provide a higher level of security from the territorial ambitions of neighbors.

Edgardo Mercado Jarrín (Peru)

General Mercado Jarrín graduated from a number of Peruvian and foreign military colleges, including his country's military academy

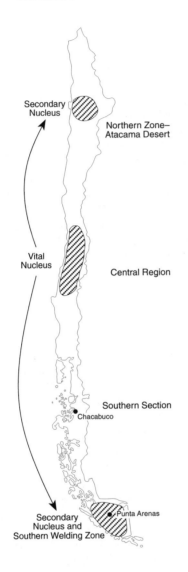

Map 35. Continental Chile's Primary and Secondary Structures (after Meneses Ciuffardi 1981a, p. 128)

and its Escuela Superior de Guerra and Centro de Altos Estudios Militares, as well as the General Staff School at Fort Leavenworth, Kansas, and the Inter-American Defense College in Washington, D.C. During the 1968–1975 period of military rule in Peru, he served in the influential roles of prime minister, minister of foreign affairs, minister of war, and commander of the armed forces. He has strongly supported world nonalignment.

Mercado Jarrín founded and helped lead the Instituto Peruano de Estudios Geopolíticos y Estratégicos (Peruvian Institute of Geopolitical and Strategic Studies), which has sponsored geopolitical conferences, books, and journals. With this record of accomplishment and his many publications on the subject, Mercado Jarrín qualifies as a major South American geopolitical authority.

Mercado Jarrín centers much of his geopolitics on the strategic position he sees in Peru as a "hinge," or "central pivot," location that links the Andean nation to the Amazon basin and the Atlantic (1985: 198–199; 1983: 29; 1981a: 4, 34; 1980a: 100). Because Peru's leadership on the continent offers a key to South American integration and peace, he advocates national policies that would establish this preeminence. For instance, he supports the MERCOSUR and Amazonian agreements and a revitalization of the Andean Pact; a rapprochement with traditional rivals Chile, Brazil, and Ecuador; a seaport for Bolivia; negotiation to settle territorial disputes; and South American disarmament (1991: 26–31, 41–42; 1989: 117–132; 1985: 198–199).

Extending his vision to the global arena, the general claims that Latin America is the most advanced area of the Third World; under Peruvian sponsorship, it could form a "bridge" between development in the nonaligned countries and First World economic assistance (1989: 18, 93–132; 1974: 22; 1972: 51). To encourage this intermediary role, Mercado Jarrín favors a "zone of peace" for South America, cooperation in regional development, peaceful settlement of conflict, and arms limitations to include nuclear weapons and extracontinental military bases. Peru figures importantly in this connection because of its independent "historical order," its Third World foreign policies, and its focal geographic position in South America.

Contemporary political trends have transformed the arena within which Peruvian leadership can now operate. The ending of the cold war, Mercado Jarrín believes, has provided South America an opportunity for resolving conflict and promoting regional integration (1991: 22–42; 1989: 117–132; 1980a: 85–86). The continent's "strategically marginal" location, without great-power interference, enhances this transition. While the United States will continue to demand of Latin America its traditional access to raw materials and political stability without extracontinental entanglements, the U.S. hegemon appears more economically vulnerable, and this "geoeconomic" factor represents a power relationship much more suited to a nonaligned Latin America.

New power transitions within South America expose Peru to diplomatic isolation and threats to its frontier. Foremost among these, according to Mercado Jarrín, is the current rapprochement between Brazil and Argentina. Such harmony may bring peace in certain areas, but it, unfortunately, erases the checkmating that Argentina provided against Brazilian threats to Peru. Accordingly, "Peru has lost its strategic significance for Argentina" (1991: 7). Settlement of the Beagle Channel dispute between Chile and Argentina and the rise of the MERCOSUR agreement further isolates Peru (1991: 26 – 42; 1989: 33, 117–132). To attain national integration and continental leadership, Peru must settle its traditional disputes with Chile and Ecuador and shore up its Amazonian territories against possible Brazilian encroachment.

Mercado Jarrín devotes the largest portion of his writings to Peruvian integration and development. He describes the country as an "untamed state" ("estado encabalgado"), with Lima its enormous "mushroom" head, detached from a feeble and neglected hinterland (1985: 199; 1981a: 4 – 18). A natural "pre-Columbian Inca unity," which demanded strong regional connectedness, seems to be missing, and the Andean sierra or upland, a "geopolitical axis," no longer links all territories (1981a: 5 – 6). To the general, the country's "historical mission" entails a refocusing on strengthening this integrative "geographic heart[land]," for "if Peru dominates the central sierra, it will come to dominate all national territory" (1981a: 27; 1980b: 18 – 25).

The existence of "dead," or exposed, Amazonian borders with Brazil and Ecuador threatens Peru, and these require closer attachment to the national domain (1981a: 5 – 11; 1981b: 25). Mercado Jarrín recommends construction of a "nucleus of central cohesion," formed by connecting the larger cities to common road and rail transport systems (1981a: 7–27). This plan would join the coast, sierra, and *selva* and help populate and extend development to the inland periphery. Not only the "expansionist aspirations" of neighbors would be challenged, but also the narcotics and internal subversion crisis (1991: 7, 44 – 48).

Jorge Villacrés Moscoso (Ecuador)

A diplomat, educator, journalist, and international law scholar as well as a geopolitical writer, Villacrés Moscoso brings to the South American political scene a bitter and vociferous protest against the steady territorial dismemberment his country has suffered since independence. His geopolitical perspective appears most focused on one topic: Peru's alleged conspiracy to absorb Ecuador's territory.

Whether it hopes to regain the glories of the Inca Empire or access to Amazonian oil or to the ports of Guayaquil and the Galápagos Islands, Villacrés Moscoso claims that Peru seeks dominion over Ecuador (1990b: 23 – 48, 105; 1975: 94 – 95; 1963: 108 –122). Brazil and Colombia, he declares, likewise have carved out large sections of territory from his vulnerable buffer nation. Constant treaty violations, frontier invasions, and illegal foreign colonization have reduced Ecuador to roughly 25 percent of its preindependence size.

With regard to the Galápagos, Peru, for instance, puts forth the claim that Inca navigators may have occupied the islands first, an assertion Villacrés Moscoso heatedly challenges. He also alleges that the proposed Vía Marginal de la Selva highway system, which someday may link the Amazon countries to Peru, is further evidence of imperialism directed against Ecuador. Illegal smuggling along the frontier and colonization in the tense Cordillera del Cóndor area provide additional examples of this conspiracy (1990a; 1990b: 11 – 23, 86 – 89; 1985: 67 –118; 1982: 86 –132).

Villacrés Moscoso suggests moves that could fortify Ecuador against further territorial encroachments, for example, more aggressive frontier colonization and more stable national government and leadership (1982: 22, 95 – 96; 1979: 140 –169; 1975: 5 – 21, 56 – 64). Alliances with Chile, Brazil, and Colombia could checkmate border pressures from Peru (1975: 9, 57, 68). Furthermore, Ecuador's membership in the Amazon Pact should be encouraged because this could counter Peru's expansionism, help restore lost Amazonian regions, develop the eastern provinces, and gain stronger recognition for Ecuador as an Amazonian nation (1979: 14 –27).

This author likewise recommends a "Great Interoceanic Highway" through southern Ecuador (map 36), which would link Guayaquil to the Amazon River (1979: 170 –190; 1962). Villacrés Moscoso believes that this passage offers a preferred continental route over those through Peru, Bolivia, or Colombia, and that the highway could strengthen Ecuador's security and prosperity.

In addition, he is wary of regional integrationist schemes, such as the Andean Pact, contending that these agreements place smaller states at a disadvantage to larger countries, and that Peru utilizes such pacts to legitimize its aggression against Ecuador (1982: 19 – 33, 77– 81).

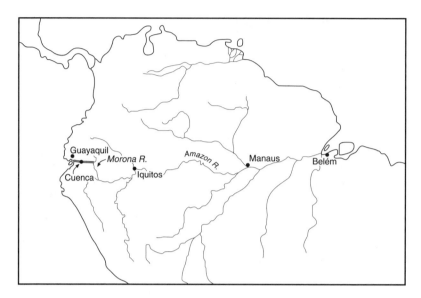

Map 36. Ecuador's Southern Interoceanic Route (after Villacrés Moscoso 1962, p. 2)

Julio Londoño Londoño (Colombia)

One could characterize the distinguished career of Gen. Julio Londoño Londoño (1901–1980) in a variety of ways (Kelly 1992b). As an army major, he led his nation's military in the Amazonian province of Leticia during the 1932–1934 territorial dispute with Peru. He steadily rose in rank and assumed command of the armed forces general staff from 1947 until his retirement from active service in 1949.

Throughout his life, he participated in the academic side of advanced military study, and was a professor of geopolitics at the national military academy at the time of his death. As a cartographer, Londoño assisted in negotiating border delineations along the Peruvian and Brazilian frontiers. He served as Colombia's ambassador to the Dominican Republic after his retirement, professor of history and geography at several of Colombia's civilian universities, president of the Academia Colombiana de Historia (Colombian Academy of History), member of numerous other scientific societies, and was the author of twenty-two books and sixty-seven articles.

Ten of Londoño's books and two articles pertain to his geopolitical vision of Colombia in Latin America; these writings span the years 1948 to 1979. His investigations include cultural, physical, and political geography in addition to geopolitics. A strong integrationist, the general also had an interest in theory and policymaking. He feared the "space consciousness" of allegedly expansionist neighbors Peru and Brazil, deplored Colombia's decision makers' lack of awareness of frontier dangers, and favored South American confederation as a method of achieving continental peace and prosperity and maintaining Colombia's security.

Londoño analyzes the United States' power advantage over South America (1977: 12–14; 1969: 6–7; 195?: 57, 73; 1948: 6, 45). For example, the greatest breadth of the northern continent extends mostly over zones of fertile soil and optimal climate, whereas barren jungle embodies the widest portion of South America. These differences translate into significant gaps in wealth that favor the north.

Londoño likewise sees for the northern regions a greater potential for sea power, with more natural harbors, better access to internal rivers, and nearness to the populated and prosperous seacoasts of Asia and Europe. Indeed, the United States clearly reflects the disparity in wealth that favors all northern portions of the globe, for four fifths of land surface lies above the equator.

This predominant northern power Londoño labels "el camino del sol" and contends that "it is not strange that the [wealthier, northern parts of the world] have established more powerful civilizations and that world history has had there its principal ascendancy" (1969: 1). Nowhere in his writings, however, does the general envision a threat to South America from the United States. Even though he occasionally criticizes northern materialism, commercialism, and cultural weakness, Londoño frequently refers to his support of Washington in its efforts to contain Soviet expansion (1973: 18–19; 1969: 7–8, 38, 78; 1949: 10).

South America's distance from northern power rivalries, according to Londoño, should allow continental unification and development. Likewise, the region enjoys a better position than most northern states for taking advantage of the coming "Pacific era" (1977: 28, 169–171; 195?: 27, 123–131).

But these regional objectives of confederation and opening to the Pacific, although not jeopardized by extracontinental forces, appear to be endangered by potential territorial aggrandizement and power rivalries within South America itself. Londoño's prediction of threatened continental stability, therefore, comes from the internal dynamics of the region's geopolitics; and the republic of Colombia, he claims, seems exposed to this onslaught.

Colombia is the most compartmentalized, dangerously fragmented, and disunited nation of South America, the general asserts. The country's terrain and compact shape encourage an inward-directed focus, particularly because the capital of Bogotá and other large cities are located in the center, in the "corazón nacional" (nation's heart), while the periphery is almost totally deserted jungle and mountain terrain (1979: 23–24; 1977: 33, 68–69; 1948: 20–43). Most rivers are "centrifugal" or insular in nature and do not contribute to a unifying or international tendency. Adding to this geographic complexity, a "biological archipelago," composed of many elevations and rainfall amounts, contains a wide variety of climates, cultures, and economies.

Londoño espouses five theories to warn of the impending danger of frontier dismemberment: the law of growth points, triple border points, the unifying characteristics of river watersheds, the geographic coefficient of population variance, and space consciousness and the imperial sense.

The Law of Growth Points

Growth points (*puntos de crecimiento*) (taken from Friedrich Ratzel and Ellsworth Huntington) are frontier sectors where one country's economic and demographic growth rates appear more expansive than those of its neighbors (1981: 7–13; 195?, 78–80; 1949, 60–63; 1948, 17–25). Accordingly, borders will expand or contract in response to these dynamic-static pressures (map 37). Colombia possesses "defensive," or static, nongrowth frontiers; its three large neighbors (Peru, Brazil, and Venezuela) have "offensive" borders with Colombia because their growth is more expansive than Colombia's along the frontiers. Londoño criticizes his country's neglect of frontiers and enlists the growth points thesis to show Colombia's vulnerability to the territorial pressures of neighbors.

Triple Border Points

Another of Londoño's geopolitical laws shows areas of probable tension where three national frontiers intersect (map 38). Such conver-

Map 37. South American Growth Points (after Londoño 1948, p. 19)

gences tend to protract escalating continental conflict, and disputes arising around these areas are difficult to resolve. Thirteen triple points (*puntos triples*) occur in South America: Brazil has nine; Bolivia, five; Argentina and Peru, four; and Paraguay and Colombia, three. (Londoño did not include the Guyanas in his triple points.) "The essence of South American diplomatic history," maintains the general, "has revolved about these thirteen points" (1949: 115), and Colombia's three translate to potential frontier tensions for the nation.

Map 38. South American Triple Border Points (after Londoño 1948, p. 19)

The Unifying Characteristics of River Watersheds

Because aggressive nations seek to dominate important river watersheds, Londoño frequently emphasizes the unifying characteristics of river systems (1981: 6 – 7; 1965: 133 – 142). Throughout his writings, he contends that most territorial disputes revolve around rivers used as international boundaries. When rivers as borders exist near triple-point areas and the growth points between neighboring states

wealthy and strategic areas belonging to smaller states or to states uninterested in safeguarding their frontiers. The general claims that Colombia fits this latter category.

In addition to vibrant national integration and development plans that would secure Colombia's peripheral territories, Londoño calls for a confederal system that would safeguard all of South America's borders (1969: 121–153; 1967; 1950; 1949: 104–106; 1948: 1–48). With confederation (in five sections: la Plata, Pacífico, Brasileña, Guayanesa and Grancolombiana), Brazil's propensity for expansion would be curtailed, territorial disputes would lose their significance, universal access to seaports would exist, and greater regional cooperation would arise.

Rubén Carpio Castillo (Venezuela)

Carpio Castillo brings a varied background to his geopolitical writings. He served as Venezuela's ambassador to Spain, Canada, and the United Nations, and as a frequent delegate to major international conferences, including those pertaining to the law of the sea. A political activist under the Partido Acción Democrática banner, he served in the national parliament where he specialized in foreign affairs. He studied geography in France, England, and the United States and has authored two books on regional geopolitics and several technical treatises dealing with Venezuelan frontiers and political and physical geography. Currently, Carpio Castillo is a professor of American geography at the Central University of Venezuela in Caracas.

Three clear and interconnected themes appear in Carpio Castillo's geopolitical thinking: Venezuela's generally secure and important regional position; its losses of territory to neighboring states and the potential for additional frontier dismemberment; and the disruptive impact of the United States in the Caribbean basin and, to a lesser extent, of Brazil in South America.

To Carpio Castillo, Venezuela holds a "unique," "important," and "strategic" geographic position as a "crossroads" and "transition" between North and South America, between the Caribbean Sea and the Atlantic Ocean, and between the Atlantic and the Pacific (1980: 1–38; 1961: 161–167). The country is part Andean, part Amazonian, part Atlantic, and part Caribbean, although the Caribbean aspect seems the most vital because the other sectors are isolated by distance and jungle.

Table 1. South American Security Quotients: Sepa

1. Brazil	
2. Chile	
3. Argentina	
4. Ecuador	
5. Colombia	
6. Peru	
7. Venezuela	
8. Bolivia	3
9. Uruguay	4
10. Paraguay	5
11. Guyana	15
12. Suriname	26
13. French Guiana	1,87

seem imbalanced, conflict is likely. The General sees
along Colombia's Amazonian and Putumayo littoral

Geographic Coefficient (Sepan Index) of Population

Utilizing the formula $A + B + C / P$, where $A + B$
summing of the populations of all neighboring states
the population of the country of interest (1969: 14
calculates relative vulnerabilities facing South Amer
(table 1). The lower the resultant quotient, the greate
rity. By some distance, Brazil appears the most prote
to this formula, as its enormous population depres
score. Colombia, ranked fifth, holds a middle positic
exposure. In a geopolitical format, the general enlists
warn Colombia of potential frontier dismemberment.

Space Consciousness and the Imperial Sense

Basing his judgment on Ratzel's seven points of terri
sion, General Londoño argues (1978: 31; 195?: 36 – 37
ing exacerbates the hunger for space so much as [availa
self" (195?: 31; 1948: 102), particularly when larger sta

Unlike Colombia, which is continental in geopolitical scope, Venezuela has both continental and maritime designs, as its access to the Caribbean and Atlantic is facilitated by accessible rivers and bays and by fewer mountains than its western neighbor has (1980: 53–54). Further, Venezuela's compact shape fosters national unity, and its topography of uninhabited frontiers and Caribbean coastal uplands and islands cushions it against threats across borders. Its size, between very large and very small, also brings advantages, as it is too large for neighbors to absorb but not large enough to become hegemonic (1980: 46–48). Generally, Carpio Castillo is optimistic about his country's geopolitical environment. It is not immediately threatened, and it possesses position and a natural resource base that might allow it to exert regional leadership.

But one senses a persistent frustration in Carpio Castillo that uninterested leaders have negotiated away too much of Venezuela's national territory and neglected its frontier (1981: 44; 1961: 178). In particular, the "disastrous" negotiated loss to Colombia of exclusive control of the Gulf of Venezuela and the Guajira Peninsula has weakened national sovereignty over the vital oil-producing region of Lake Maracaibo, an area "more important to Venezuela than to Colombia" (1980: 159–167). He sees similar failures to maintain ownership of the lands that now belong to Guiana and the continental shelf around Trinidad-Tobago.

The encirclement of Venezuela by other countries endangers the nation. Non-Spanish European colonies, some now independent, diminish Venezuela's security (1980: 25–34). For example, the English-speaking states of Guyana and Trinidad-Tobago reach almost to the Orinoco River's mouth and Venezuela's Atlantic seaboard, both areas of vital concern to the republic. Brazil's inroads and intrigue in Guyana and Trinidad-Tobago make this area even more sensitive. The Dutch islands of Aruba and Curaçao, situated near the Gulf of Venezuela's opening, offer another example of encirclement.

Despite Colombia's frontier being the most important to Venezuela, Carpio Castillo foresees more cooperation than conflict with its western neighbor. Brazil, however, represents a likely security problem. Its aggressive manifest destiny, to expand to both the Caribbean and the Pacific, is most apparent in its interest in Guyana and Trinidad-Tobago. Yet, Brazil's expansionism seems to worry Carpio Castillo little, for several reasons: the buffering effect of the vast frontier jungles of the northern Amazon; the Orinoco's greater

importance to Venezuela than to Brazil; Brazil's fear of Spanish encirclement; Brazil's preoccupation with the Plata River valley and
the South Atlantic; and the United States' likely negative reaction to
a Brazilian push into the Caribbean (1980: 21–22, 181–187, 220–
231; 1961: 167). Therefore, in foreign affairs Carpio Castillo advocates a Venezuelan-Colombian united front and an Andean Pact
ranged against an expansionist Brazil. He recommends maintaining
a jungle buffer and developing a national plan for populating the
hinterlands (1980: 168–192).

Carpio Castillo's harshest polemic focuses on U.S. "imperialism"
in Middle America, as seen particularly in *México, Cuba y Venezuela:
triángulo geopolítico del Caribe* (1961). The United States manipulates
the politics and economics of this central region, he charges; they
purposely impede Caribbean unity in order to maintain their own
sphere of influence, and they threaten to expand into South America as well. The northerners have "surrounded" Mexico and kept it
isolated from its Latin American roots, and the Yankees have used
economic and military intrusions to dominate Cuba (1981: 266;
1961: 17–18, 59–63, 140–144). The remedy lies in integrating the
Caribbean, the author contends, because Cuban, Mexican, Colombian, and Venezuelan cooperation could slow U.S. penetration of
the basin (1980: 256, 269–270; 1961: 82, 94).

He places strong emphasis on the tenets of international law. Carpio Castillo, the diplomat and boundary cartographer as well as
geopolitician, favors peaceful frontier negotiation above international threat and conflict (1980: 22, 32, 111–118; 1974). Like Londoño (whom he frequently cites), he advocates unilateral national
ownership of river watersheds, especially in the case of the western
Orinoco (1980: 130). However, unlike other South American writers,
Carpio Castillo believes the better borders arise as formally negotiated borders, not "natural" demarcations (1980: 117).

Finally, he urges more official attention to the northern coastal
"interior," or "enclosed," marginal sea of Venezuela. This "ante-
país" maritime belt, positioned between the outer Caribbean island
possessions of Venezuela and the mainland and including the
Dutch islands within this formation, rightfully belongs to Venezuela
(1980: 17–34), and its possession by Venezuela would greatly enhance the country's security and prosperity.

T his chapter treats disputed frontiers and territorial claims, illegal cross-border activities, revolution and democracy, Brazil-Argentina rapprochement, transportation and colonization, and development and free-trade associations.
Some issues span only the binational level, others, the subregional,
and a few, the continental. All cover the inherent qualities of geography—for instance, each country's relative position, topography,
resources, distance, or demography—that may condition foreign
policy. Thus, the interpretation of these regional topics in part becomes geopolitical.

Frontiers and Wars

Territorial disputes embody the essence of South American geopolitics. The unwillingness or inability of early administrators to draw
exact boundaries (often in isolated and distant areas) created great
potential for later conflict. Expansion of the larger states into vacant
land and water spaces amplified tensions throughout the continent.
New colonization and discoveries of resources have increased territorial pressures in the borderlands. Hence, frontier conflict represents the most common cause of South American foreign policy
dissension.

In fact, when quantified, frontiers and wars in South America
strongly correlate: the more international boundaries a nation possesses, the more warfare it suffers (Wesley 1962; Richardson 1960). I
used a Spearman Rho coefficient to test this geographic opportunity
thesis (1992a: 47) and found a strong statistical association between
borders and conflict (Rho of .71; significance level, .02) (see table 2).

Many South American geopolitical writers deal with expansion
and contraction of national frontiers. Brazilian writers are among

Table 2. Rankings by Number of Borders and by Number of Wars

Country	No. of Frontiers	Rank	No. of Wars*	Rank
Brazil	10	1	2	3.5
Argentina	5	3	2	3.5
Bolivia	5	3	2	3.5
Peru	5	3	3	1
Colombia	4	5	1	7.5
Chile	3	7	1	7.5
Paraguay	3	7	2	3.5
Venezuela	3	7	0	10
Ecuador	2	9.5	1	7.5
Uruguay	2	9.5	1	7.5

*Only the wars described in this book

the main proponents of "organic frontiers" and "harmonious boundaries," wherein the position of a country's borders reflect the growth needs of the state itself. These notions resemble the "uti possidentis actual" doctrine (in actual control or possession), in which claims to territory originate from de facto occupation (Pittman 1983: 21). In contrast, other South Americans, usually those most fearful of Brazil, argue for the "uti possidentis juris" doctrine (legal claim but not in actual possession), under which proper claim to frontiers rests on the limits of former colonial units, whether or not such areas are developed or populated.

Several theorists (Meira Mattos 1989; Pinochet 1984; Backheuser 1952) prefer "natural frontiers," as demarcated by rivers, oceans, deserts, mountains, over "political frontiers," drawn according to an arbitrary criterion (demographic, strategic, economic, or cartographic). They allege that the latter design tends toward more conflictual and destabilizing results, whereas natural boundaries are clearer, and hence more peaceful. This design also favors confederation of states into subregional blocs, because natural frontiers are more likely with greater expanses of space.

Seven wars (map 39), all caused in part by territorial competition, have occurred in South America since independence: the Cisplatine

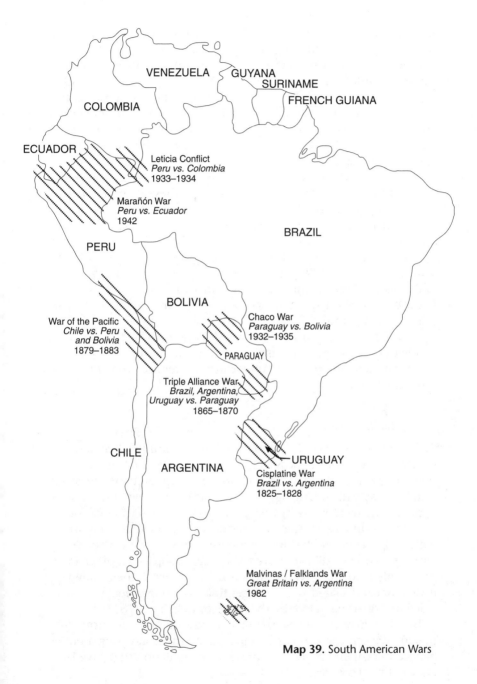

Map 39. South American Wars

War (Brazil and Argentina), 1825–1828; the Triple Alliance War (Brazil, Argentina, and Uruguay against Paraguay), 1865–1870; the War of the Pacific (Chile against Peru and Bolivia), 1879–1883; the Chaco War (Bolivia and Paraguay), 1932–1935; the Leticia conflict (Peru and Colombia), 1933–1934; the Marañón War (Peru and Ecuador), 1942; and the 1982 Malvinas-Falklands War (Argentina and Great Britain). Five of the seven wars directly engaged the buffer states (Ecuador, Bolivia, Uruguay, and Paraguay), but none seemed to measurably alter continental balance of power configurations.

That most warfare and territorial losses focused in the buffer states attests to the strategic importance of these neutral zones to continental peace. The buffers' central locations apparently helped limit violence among the larger South American powers. The buffers' territorial losses likewise may have satiated the immediate needs of larger neighbors for additional space. No South American state ceased to exist because of defeat in these wars, and only the Malvinas-Falklands conflict involved an extracontinental country, Great Britain. The Triple Alliance War added Paraguayan territory to Brazil and Argentina, Chile and Peru gained Bolivian land in the War of the Pacific, and Peru increased its domain in the Marañón conflict at the expense of Ecuador. With regard to ownership of territory, the remaining South American wars tended to reaffirm the *status quo ante bellum*.

The Cisplatine War

The Cisplatine War (1825–1828) revolved around Brazilian and Argentinean ambitions to possess the lands north of the Plata River estuary, the Banda Oriental, in the face of the inhabitants' quest for statehood as part of Uruguay. In 1817 Brazil occupied and in 1821 annexed the territory as its Cisplatine province, asserting its southernmost boundary as the Plata estuary and river. Buenos Aires, which also coveted the area, supported the resisting Uruguayan patriots, who in 1825 defeated Brazilian troops and proclaimed their independence. When Argentina recognized their independence, Brazil declared war on Argentina, which eventually was decided in Argentina's favor by the Battle of Ituzaingo (1827).

In subsequent peace negotiations, possession of the territory fluctuated between the two larger states until Britain, favoring a buffer between Brazil and Argentina, pressed a conciliation that gave Uruguay national sovereignty.

Threats to Uruguay's security as a neutral state occasionally have arisen, particularly from Brazil. Uruguay's focal position probably has helped contain its two great neighbors' rivalry for continental leadership, and the republic likewise stands to gain from Southern Cone economic integration because of its location near the Plata River system.

The Triple Alliance War

Scholars dispute the origins of the Triple Alliance War (1865 – 1870), whether from border disputes, civil war in Uruguay, the imperial ambitions of Paraguay's second López (Francisco Solano), or Brazilian and Argentinean intrigue (Abente 1987). From the Paraguayan perspective, the war was fought to maintain the Uruguayan buffer and free access to the sea. Benjamin Keen and Mark Wasserman (1984: 184 – 185) describe the war in balance-of-power terms:

> The younger López inherited a tradition of border disputes with Brazil that erupted into open war when Brazil sent an army into Uruguay in 1864 to insure the victory of a pro-Brazilian faction in that country's civil strife. López could not be indifferent to this action, which threatened the delicate balance of power in the basin of La Plata. López also feared that Brazilian control over Uruguay would end unrestricted Paraguayan access to the Port of Montevideo, which would make Paraguayan trade dependent entirely on the good will of Buenos Aires.

Uruguay protected its independence with a buffer's typical pendulum foreign policy. Brazil and Argentina, each interested in the Banda Oriental and Plata equilibrium, attacked jointly and later gained territorial concessions from a vanquished Paraguay.

Neither the extensive Polandization of Paraguay nor its disappearance into Brazil or Argentina followed. Exhaustion caused by war and the fanaticism of the Paraguayan defenders discouraged dismemberment. Had Paraguay been absorbed by the larger states, a transcontinental path to the Pacific might have opened, whetting ambitions between these great competitors for South American leadership. Instead, the war shows the checkerboard quality of the Brazil-Argentina relationship, a geopolitical checkmating formed not only by parity between the two states but also by the central position of the Southern Cone buffer states, which has tended to prevent westward expansionism.

The War of the Pacific

Similar geopolitical features appear during the War of the Pacific (1879 – 1883), fought by Chile against Peru and Bolivia. Two factors predominated: a disputed coastal boundary between Chile and Bolivia, and deposits of valuable nitrates in the contested areas and farther north in Peru. In the 1860s, Alfred Nobel had discovered a process for converting raw nitrates into explosives, making this mineral found in the bleak five hundred-mile-long Atacama Desert a very profitable resource. Backed by British capital, Chilean workers and businessmen began exploiting desert nitrates shortly after Nobel's discovery. Their rapid expansion into Bolivian and Peruvian territory prompted a need to clarify frontier lines, stabilize customs rates, maintain Chilean access to mines, and protect Peruvian and Bolivian ownership of their Atacama sectors. In the last instance, Peru and Bolivia secretly agreed to cooperate militarily in case the Chileans sought political control over all the nitrates regions. When Bolivia raised its customs demands and refused arbitration, Chile occupied the Bolivian port of Antofagasta, precipitating war. Naval engagements between Peru and Chile came first; shortly, Lima was occupied by the Chileans, as the allied forces were no match for those from the southern republic.

The war resulted in transfer of disputed lands to Chile, which completely cut off Bolivian access to the Pacific and raised international tensions in the area that have still not abated. Once synthetic materials were produced elsewhere, the economic importance of northern Chile diminished, but war during the 1870s, for reason of position and resources, seemed inevitable, and the area is still strategic by reason of its position as connector of the Pacific and the continental interior.

The Chaco War

The Chaco War (1932 – 1935) grew out of both the Triple Alliance War and the War of the Pacific. The first conflict so reduced Paraguay's territory that the additional loss of the Chaco might have risked national extinction; the second war closed off Bolivia's contact with the Pacific and transferred ocean access hopes to the Paraguay River on the eastern extreme of the Chaco wilderness. Of immediate relevance was the prediction of oil discoveries in the Bolivian Chaco, beyond the disputed region, which stirred up Bolivia's claims to Chaco lands adjacent to the Paraguay River. A river port, seen as the best export facility for the projected oil production, brought frontier clashes beginning in 1927. An arms race ensued, although both nations' economic resources were extremely limited.

A Paraguayan attack on Bolivian settlements in 1932 brought declared war, and, despite the superior numbers and equipment of the highlanders, the Paraguayans steadily moved the Bolivians back, forcing an armistice in 1935 and a peace agreement favorable to the Guaraní. But the Bolivians received a port on the Paraguay River that today is used in the Hidrovía river barge network, which ties Bolivia to Uruguayan Atlantic ports.

The Chaco War demonstrates the competition caused by mineral discoveries in disputed frontier areas. Again, the geopolitical issue of river and sea access arises. Likewise, we see conflict occurring once more in the buffer states, with the surrounding larger states, Chile and Argentina, manipulating these countries and seeking to advance their claims to regional leadership.

The Leticia Conflict

The Leticia conflict of 1933–1934, a remote but impassioned border conflict, involved more inter-American diplomacy and intrigue than actual armed struggle. Peru and Colombia had negotiated a territorial settlement in the Salomón-Lozano Treaty of 1922 in which Colombia gained a sixty-five-mile river frontage to the Amazon in exchange for a strip of land awarded to Peru along the border with Ecuador. The river port village of Leticia, on the Brazilian frontier and downstream from the major Peruvian port of Iquitos, provided "a cartographic point on the continent's greatest river and so gave to Colombia, however tenuously, the coveted status of an Amazonian power" (Wood 1966: 170, also 169–251). The Peruvians probably advocated the treaty initially because it removed direct contact between Colombia and Ecuador, and this exposed Ecuador's coveted Marañón Valley to later Peruvian expansionism. However, soon after the treaty, Peruvians protested their negotiated loss of Leticia.

In 1933, a filibustering group of Peruvian irregulars, apparently with their government's blessing, forcibly occupied now-Colombian Leticia. The following year a Colombian military flotilla sailed up the Amazon River and reestablished authority over the territory with minimal loss of life. Brazilian mediation shortly thereafter ended the conflict.

In a geopolitical sense, we remember the Leticia conflict for these reasons: the significance of access to rivers and oceans; the importance of the Amazon River to the eastern provinces of the Andean republics; the Peruvian plan to isolate Ecuador from Colombia in preparation for later movement into the Marañón Valley; and the continued notoriety of this location because of its pivotal placement among four countries, its role in the ongoing Marañón dispute, and its relevance to Brazil in developing the upper Amazon.

The Marañón War

The 1942 Marañón War originated from vaguely drawn colonial demarcations that led to unsuccessful attempts to mediate settlement and occasional border skirmishes. As in the Leticia conflict, access to the Amazon was one of the causes of this dispute. Battle locations, exclusively in Ecuador, again hit a buffer area hardest, and the buffer state again lost territory. Here, the South American checkerboard arose once again; Argentina backed Peru, Chile and Colombia favored Ecuador (Wood 1966: 255 – 342). The United States tended to side with Ecuador, at least symbolically, and played the outsider role of peace enforcer. Although the Ecuadorans continue to dispute the peace settlement, which gave Peru the Marañón, the war and its aftermath did not upset continental stability or change relationships among the larger South American powers.

Peruvian troops' rapid occupation of the disputed territories distinguished the war, with the occupiers remaining until the larger powers pressed a peace treaty on Ecuador. Peru won all of its demands from the Brazilian, Argentinean, and U.S. mediators, and Ecuador had to abandon its objective of being an Amazonian power when the mediators gave much of the Oriente to Peru.

The timing of the conflict fit Peruvian more than Ecuadoran purposes, for the United States had become preoccupied by threats from Japan and Europe and failed to recognize Ecuador's plight. Faced with a two-front war, the United States clearly desired a compliant and cooperative South America. Hence, Peru succeeded in annexing the Marañón despite possible injustice to Ecuador, although one could speculate that Brazilian and U.S. intervention might have saved Ecuador from extinction.

The Malvinas/Falklands War

Argentina's occupation of the Malvinas/Falkland Islands in 1982, precipitating war with Great Britain, reflects the recent geopolitical orientation toward Antarctica and the southern oceans. Argentina's ruling military junta faced serious difficulties at home, and its gamble to win popular support by invading the islands was the most immediate source of the conflict. But more important in the strategic sense was the belief that the Antarctic held large deposits of oil and other products and that strategic routes between oceans and to the Antarctic had become more vital. Maritime and territorial disputes with both Chile and Great Britain threatened this growing priority. Because the military dominated the government, geopolitical planning predominated, and taking the Malvinas became an inherent part of the government's strategy: "These geopolitical reappraisals significantly contributed to the political climate in Argentina in the years 1976 to 1982. They helped heighten interest in the recovery (or acquisition, from a British viewpoint) of the Falklands/ Malvinas and associated territory: not only were the islands of great symbolic and historic significance for Argentina, but they were now also a central location in the territorial space Argentina needed for future economic and political development, the 'New Frontier'" (Hepple 1988: 228).

Nine thousand Argentinean troops stormed the islands, but the junta miscalculated disastrously by assuming British acquiescence and U.S. neutrality. English forces soon dislodged their South American opponents after bloody land, sea, and air engagements.

War in the Falklands/Malvinas created tensions throughout Latin America, from the Beagle Channel between Chile and Argentina to the Essequibo between Guyana and Venezuela to Middle America between Belize and Guatemala and Colombia and Nicaragua. United South American backing of Argentina during the crisis did not materialize. Instead, the familiar checkerboard patterns emerged. Peru and Venezuela lent diplomatic support to Argentina; Chile collaborated with the British (Child 1988a: 89; Connell-Smith 1984: 81–85); Brazil played a cautious role. At first Washington sought closer ties to Buenos Aires, anticipating Argentinean mediation in Central America, but soon shifted its support to England after realizing that its primary interests lay in Europe and not South America. In addition, the war figures as a rare example of an American conflict affecting European security as NATO forces engaged a South American army, allegedly for establishing a strategic base in the South Atlantic (de Hoyos 1988; Hepple 1988: 228–235).

Contemporary South American Territorial Disputes

Several South American wars still smolder as contemporary territorial disputes: Bolivia's unwavering quest for a Pacific Ocean outlet after the Pacific and Chaco Wars; Ecuador's quest for Amazonian access through the Marañón basin; and Argentina's claim to the Malvinas. Potential strife also arises from several other conflicts over land or water (map 40): disputed claims to Antarctica; Chilean-Argentinean rivalry in the Beagle Channel; two Venezuelan frontier controversies, with Colombia and Guyana; and certain claims to territorial seas and the continental shelf (Child 1985). I will first focus on the Antarctic conflicts, then move north to the Beagle Channel rivalry, Bolivia's quest for an ocean outlet, and finish with the territorial sea conflicts that surround the continent.

The Antarctic Conflict

Antarctic conflict has a number of geopolitical ramifications (Child 1986). Substantial resource wealth could exist, and the continent flanks the strategic Drake Passage and Beagle Channel. But certain American and European claims compete, and this condition could stimulate international strife. The Antarctic Treaty System, ratified under United Nations auspices in 1961, locks in national claims to territory, controls minerals exploitation, prohibits military operations, and encourages scientific and ecological study. But other proposals have arisen as well: the "common heritage of humankind" concept, which would make Antarctica available to all nations; the "quadrant condominium," or "common heritage of the Americas," plan, which would give the South American nations joint and exclusive right to exploit the American-Antarctic frontage; and a "world ecological park" design, which would convert the region into a natural preserve and exclude all economic and developmental activities (Child 1988b: 201–202; Clark 1988; Pittman 1988h).

Brazilian involvement in Antarctica derives from the "frontage thesis," or *defrontação* (map 20), as described by Jack Child (1988a: 134): "Under this theory there would be a South American sector extending from longitude 24 to 90 west, which are the limits of the

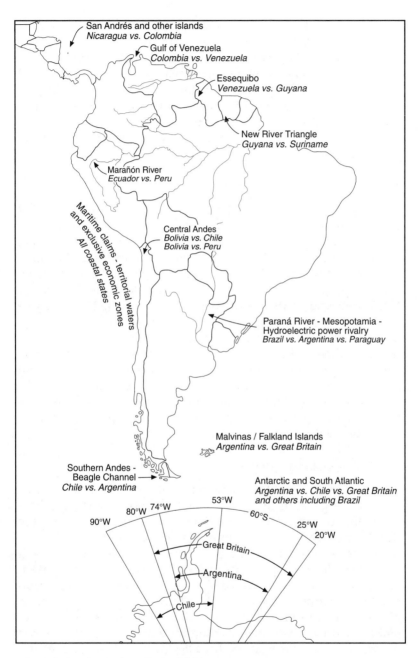

Map 40. South American Territorial Disputes

Rio Treaty of 1947. Within this sector, each nation with frontage to the Antarctic (that is, with an open sea exposure to the Antarctic that was not blocked by any other nation) would have rights to a subsector defined by the meridians of that exposure." This proposal gives Antarctic claims to Peru, Ecuador, Uruguay, Chile, and Argentina, with Brazil receiving the largest portion of all. Although it is not official policy, Brazilian geopolitical writers strongly promote *defrontação* (Castro 1976), which encourages the Antarctic appetites of other American republics as well.

The Malvinas-Falklands Conflict

The Malvinas-Falklands negotiations are deadlocked since the 1982 war. Despite renewal of diplomatic relations, the end of the 150-mile exclusive economic zone around the islands, and resumption of air and sea communications, the sides now appear farther apart than previously. Argentinean writers claim a British (and U.S.) "hidden conspiracy," a "Caribización," or an attack by the Normans or North-men against the south (Hepple 1988: 230–232). Rubén de Hoyos asserts the "Gibraltarization," or Britain's strategic absorption, of the South Atlantic (1988: 239–244). Both nations appear frozen in their earlier stands, and even the "lease-back" proposal, wherein the English would transfer sovereignty if Argentina would lease the islands back to Great Britain, no longer seems plausible. The resolution could rest on time and distance factors; serious negotiations may be postponed far into the future, and geographic closeness may eventually favor the Argentinean side.

The Beagle Channel Rivalry

Both Antarctica and interoceanic transit shape the Beagle Channel question. Negotiators in 1977 awarded Chile three small uninhabited islands (Lennox, Picton, and Nueva) at the eastern mouth of the strait. Argentina rejected the award and protested Chile's extension of its territorial waters two hundred miles into the Atlantic, which Argentina alleged could cut its mainland linkage (as well as invalidate its claim) to the Antarctic. Chile's victory appeared to Argentina to be a further tightening of the Chilean-Brazilian encirclement of Argentina; this fear has traditionally colored the republic's geopolitics (Pittman 1988a: 8). War almost erupted in 1978, but was prevented by papal mediation. The 1984 Treaty of Peace and Friendship, brought about by defeat in the Malvinas/Falklands War and by a return to democracy in Argentina, preserved the bioceanic ideal by confirming Argentina's position that Cape Horn is the Pacific-Atlantic divisor. Thus ended the quarrel (Child 1988a: 77–85) for the moment.

Bolivia's Quest for a Pacific Ocean Outlet

Bolivia's quest to regain its *salida al mar*, or opening to the sea, has not diminished since the 1879–1883 War of the Pacific. There have been diplomatic efforts throughout the intervening century; however, the best opportunity for attaining coastal access came during the mid-1970s, when domestic and regional conditions seemed favorable. For a short time, Gen. Hugo Banzar Suárez of Bolivia deflected domestic politics toward this diplomatic objective, and Gen. Augusto Pinochet of Chile, desiring a better international image, initiated in 1974 the Ayacucho Declaration, which recognized the desirability of an ocean outlet for Bolivia.

Although Chile promised in 1974 to cede Bolivia a narrow corridor to the coast, its demands for territorial compensation appeared excessive to Bolivia. Because of a 1929 protocol to the Treaty of Ancón, Peru likewise possessed veto power over transfer of lands once part of its territory. It likewise rejected the Chilean proposal, suggesting instead tripartite administration of an enlarged coastal corridor. This did not meet the approval of the Chileans, and negotiations had ended by 1980. Any solution may come through continental integration, wherein boundary lines become less vital and expansion of regional contact is encouraged. Bolivia's hope for the ocean thus may lie in broader structural change, something it lacks the power to influence alone.

The Marañón Conflict

The Peru-Ecuador Marañón border conflict continues to simmer. Border incidents have flared up, in 1980 and again in 1995, and both nations' militaries have suffered casualties. Despite its loss of river access, Ecuador remains an Amazonian power by virtue of official policy and its membership in the 1980 Amazon Pact. Brazil continues its interest in a transoceanic route through Ecuador (Meira Mattos 1980a: 141–158), and its sponsorship of the buffer state could help resolve the animosity. Indications point to a détente in Peru-Ecuador relations, for example, the Güepi incident described in chapter 1 and in a 1993 conference in Quito that recommended closer ties (Hurtado 1993). But the hostilities in 1995 obviously indicate a continued high level of border tension.

The Essequibo Conflict

The Essequibo dispute embodies the most important of the four northern South America conflicts. The controversy originated in 1899 arbitration between Venezuela and Great Britain over territory adjacent to the Orinoco River's mouth (Meislin 1982; Grabendorff 1982). At the insistence of the United States, the British agreed to submit the question to arbitration, and a five-member board was formed, chaired by a Russian. The board awarded the Venezuelans the mouth of the Orinoco, but Britain received the desired coastal zones to the east. Both sides apparently found the award acceptable. However, memoirs of the arbitration were published decades later by the lawyer who represented Venezuela, and these offered strong evidence that the British bribed the Russian chairman, who in turn gave the English a favorable award. This deception has encouraged the Venezuelans to resume demands for the Essequibo basin, now believed to contain significant gold, uranium, bauxite, diamond, and oil deposits. The disputed area includes fully five eighths of the former British colony and the newly independent country of Guyana.

The Treaty of Port of Spain, Trinidad (1970), proclaimed a twelve-year moratorium on the dispute. That period lapsed without extension, and Venezuela has since pressed its claim vigorously. There is some speculation that Venezuela's interest extends to the petroleum wealth lying below Guyana's territorial waters. Military tensions at the border peaked during the early 1980s, but when the Guyanese received Brazilian backing, the conflict diminished in intensity. Guyana, confident in its legal standing, favors taking the case before the World Court; Venezuela advocates direct negotiations. At last word, the United Nations seems intent on investigating the claims of both sides and is urging mediation.

The Guajira Peninsula and Monjes Islands Conflict

The Guajira Peninsula and Monjes Islands dispute between Colombia and Venezuela combines several sources of conflict. As drawn in the nineteenth century, the original border gave Venezuela a narrow strip of the peninsula facing the Gulf of Venezuela, which allowed the republic to claim the entire body of water. But discovery of oil in Lake Maracaibo and possibly in the open waters of the gulf and adjacent areas has caused Colombia to protest the earlier demarcation. Other natural wealth on the peninsula, coal and iron ore in particular, also figure in this competition over resources. Illegal immigration and drug smuggling between the two nations further intensifies the altercation.

The Territorial Seas Conflict

A final dimension of South American territorial conflict, involving the coastal republics, revolves around claims to territorial waters. This recent geopolitical component is based on the two hundred–mile territorial waters extension (Pittman 1981b: 166–167), although international law does not yet sanction this distance. Strife between Ecuador and the United States arose during the 1970s over fishing rights in the Pacific. As new technologies expand exploitation of ocean beds, one might expect competition in fishing and mining to escalate.

The Future of Conflict in South America

In describing South American conflict in the 1980s, several U.S. writers predicted increased strife among countries (Pittman 1986; Child 1985; Grabendorff 1982; English 1981; Gorman 1979). Child found an upturn in continental violence during the 1970s, despite relative peacefulness in the region since World War II (1985: 3):

> For many years it was possible to consider South America as a region of peace in comparison to so many other areas of the world. For a number of reasons, this state of affairs began to change markedly in the middle and late 1970s and reached a dramatic and bloody climax in the Anglo/Argentine Falklands/Malvinas conflict of 1982. There are few informed optimists today who would predict that the South Atlantic war was an isolated event that could not be repeated in some other battlefield of the Western Hemisphere.

Because it is "motivated by ideology and competition for influence and resources," Child sees "the conflict panorama of the next few years in Latin America [as] increasingly dangerous."

Pittman argues that "conflict has been a fact of life in this region since the discovery of America" and rejects the thesis that democratic governments will terminate this propensity for violence (1986: 67):

Governments in the Southern Cone will pursue their own national interests and their respective geopolitical goals whether their governments at a given time are democratic or authoritarian. This is why old continental disputes remain active and new ones can be expected to arise over sovereignty of the sea, the islands and Antarctica. So far, even if one credits the return of democracy in Argentina with a settlement in the Beagle Channel case, the impact of democratization on geopolitics and conflict in the Southern Cone has been minimal and its future impact, by implication, may not result in a lessening of tension, dispute and conflict in the region.

Unlike Child, Pittman notes a natural tendency toward violence among Latin Americans and assumes such contention will persist in hemispheric relations.

Both Pittman and Child affirm that geopolitical thinking contributes to South American conflict (Pittman 1986: 3–23; Child 1985: 10–12). They allege that geopolitics equals power politics and a competition for territory, security, status, and wealth that naturally encourages conflict among nations. Frontier disputes will persist, these writers believe, and their intensity will be heightened by ideological rivalry and the strong need to access resources for national development. Economic and political difficulties at home likewise could translate into aggressive foreign policies and regional strife. The possibility for conflict escalation in South America—one dispute giving rise to others—further enhances the potential for violence. Finally, U.S. retrenchment of power, they feel, opens the region to more conflict, with the larger republics better able to bully the weaker without U.S. interference.

My prediction differs from that of Child and Pittman. I envision a continent generally at peace and successful in conciliating disputes and subregional and perhaps hemispheric integration. Experience in the 1990s seems to support this forecast, for in no section of South America does international violence appear likely at present. The Beagle Channel question appears resolved, the Antarctic claims seem to be contained, and the Malvinas/Falklands conflict has taken the diplomatic route. The Chilean and Caribbean coast controversies are dormant at the moment. I may be an optimist, but I see eventual resolution of the northern Chile conflict, with river and seaports awarded Bolivia through arbitration. However, the Marañón, Malvinas and Essequibo dissension could persist for a longer period because of their deeper connections to national sensitivities and great wealth in terms of resources.

What generates the present calm? Will it last? Ten points may help answer these queries.

- The shift in Brazil's foreign policy toward more positive involvement in South America, linked to Argentina's apparent acceptance of rapprochement with its northern neighbor, to me is the strongest argument for continental peace. This conversion negates an escalation of violence caused by the South American checkerboard, it precludes a shatterbelt, it stabilizes frontiers, and it encourages economic and political integration—all of which support peace.

- Escalation of violence caused by the checkerboard structure seems less natural to the geopolitics of South America, even though certain diplomatic disputes continue. Distances and topography, weak economies, the high cost of maintaining the armed forces, similar national cultures, the buffer states' role in cushioning violence, among other factors, contribute to the avoidance of widespread warfare.

- Certain conflicts appear resolved, for example, over the Beagle Channel and along the Brazilian periphery. The status quo may have been accepted in Antarctica and on the Caribbean littoral.

- Negotiation and political maneuvering seem recognized by small and large republics as the most effective way to regain lost territories, in the Malvinas, northern Chile, and Essequibo disputes, for example.

- The high costs of developing hinterland areas, Antarctica, and territorial waters may inhibit competition for those areas.

- Access to resources appears to be most easily attained through trade and regional covenants, not by waging war and annexing territory. Brazil helps meet its energy needs at Itaipú; Venezuela sells oil and iron ore to the United States. Rivers provide unobstructed passage to the oceans for interior regions; the exchange of goods annually increases because of better transportation and a desire to expand trade.

- Heightened anticipation of economic rewards from regional integration seems evident. Brazil and Argentina appear bent on increasing binational cooperation in trade and other areas that could erect a stable framework for peace.

- Civilian and democratic governments may see more advantages in regional harmony than in checkerboard tensions. In addition, concentration on national development, which seems more the domain of politicians than of generals, could expand regionalism faster than militarism.

- The United States exerts only minimal impact on conflicts in South America, in contrast with its involvement in Middle America. Usually, the United States' lack of interest in South America encourages more tranquillity than dissension in the region because the void has encouraged accommodation between the South American nations.

- Finally, geopolitics seems useful as a method for studying and applying foreign policy derived from such geographic factors as position, space, topography, resources, and distance. In theory and practice, I fail to see a direct connection between geopolitics and conflict. Violence and aggression transpire when conflict cannot find a peaceful channel. Like other theories of international relations, geopolitics provides insight into both strife *and* harmony, an unbiased description and explanation rather than blame and proscription.

Discussions about nuclear weapons in South America rarely appear in the geopolitical literature of the United States, and the subject is almost never covered in depth by South American writers. Brazil and Argentina possess the technology for building nuclear bombs, although both republics have pledged in the Tlatelolco Pact never to develop such weapons. Nonetheless, one would think that under particularly unsettling regional and world conditions the two countries could easily gain a nuclear capability.

Child (1985: 101–103) maintains that Argentina probably has more incentive than Brazil for crossing the nuclear threshold because it may want something to "equalize" its neighbor's greater power resources. But Argentinean disincentives to nuclear arms include precipitating Brazilian retaliation and destroying the gains of integration and peace, inducing a costly and destabilizing Southern Cone arms race, and being censured by worldwide public opinion and the western alliance. Child believes Brazil would soon follow Argentina's construction and testing of a nuclear device, although it too could be driven to develop the bomb first to heighten its prestige as an emerging world power.

Another Argentinean inducement for developing nuclear weapons could stem from Buenos Aires' need to control the Plata basin. Steven Gorman (1979: 60 – 63) calculates that Brazil possesses a significant military advantage over its neighbor if such a struggle ensues. Brazil's economy is more stable and powerful, and its much greater population is not as concentrated as Argentina's and far enough from Argentina to be protected from exposure. In all of these cases, emergence of Southern Cone nuclear weapons would surely revive the South American checkerboard.

The Geopolitics of Smuggling, Illegal Immigration, and Pollution in South America

Smuggling, illegal immigration, and pollution become geopolitical activities when associated with frontiers, space, resources, and strategic locations.

Smuggling

Smuggling entails illicit transfer of goods and people across boundaries. It is common in South America because governments cannot effectively supervise distant and isolated hinterlands. Consequently, regional tensions sometimes arise, as in the Guajira Peninsula and on the Brazilian frontier with the buffer countries. But with the expansion of regional integration, the lowering of tariffs, and the growth of facilities that promote better exchange of goods and services, smuggling may wane. Nonetheless, it is important to a discussion of geopolitics in which resources are valued and frontier tensions could escalate.

Narcotics trafficking from South America to Europe and the United States has risen to major importance in foreign affairs. Coca leaves, grown in the poor, isolated, mountains of Peru and Bolivia and then transported to Colombia for refining, produce cocaine, which renders huge profits and, in some cases, political power. Drug dealers take advantage of both the poverty and the terrain in growing areas, and they dominate local governments and finance insurgent groups in Peru and Colombia. National unity and integration are weakened as a result. Colombian cartels have tied themselves to Middle American pariah states (for example, to Manuel Noriega's

Panama and Fidel Castro's Cuba), tempting the United States to act to stop the narcotics flow.

Illegal Immigration

Illegal migration in South America happens where populations cluster at frontiers and economic and political conditions on one side are better than on the other side. For instance, Colombians in recent decades have sought jobs in Venezuelan farm communities and oil fields, and Brazilians have illegally crossed into Uruguay, Bolivia, and Paraguay. Northern Uruguay, eastern Paraguay, and western Bolivia all contain large numbers of Brazilian squatters and business enterprises; in many cases, these dominate the frontier provinces. Unauthorized colonization could portend territorial expansion and encourage external intervention. Further, it might destabilize regional harmony and integration.

Pollution

Pollution represents a newly recognized element in the geopolitics of South America. Since many mining, industrial, and population centers are distant from international frontiers, this problem has not drawn widespread appreciation as a regional issue. But mercury from Brazilian gold mines contaminates fish and drinking water from the Paraguay River, and the slash-and-burn farming of illegal squatters depletes tropical soils. Worst of all, the Amazon *selva* faces rapid destruction by new developers, as the area along roads and rivers and on gigantic plantations is deforested. The ensuing global warming may cause a shortage of oxygen worldwide. Potential ecological collapse is clearly relevant to war and peace.

Democracy and Revolution in South American Geopolitics

Democracy seems to dwell more comfortably in South America than in Middle America, if we use the Fitzgibbon-Johnson-Kelly surveys of Latin America since 1945 as a basis for judgment (Kelly 1992d: 3). These surveys place more of the original ten South American countries in the top half of the democracy scales in eight of the eleven indices. Two of the surveys record even levels of democracy between the two regions, and only one, the 1980 survey, reveals a higher democracy quotient for the Middle American states. Greater size and

Table 3. South America's Democracy Rankings

No. of Countries Listed among 10 Most Democratic,
South America and Middle America, 1945–1995

Survey Year	South America	Middle America
1945	5	5
1950	5	5
1955	5	5
1960	5	3
1965	6	4
1970	6	4
1975	6	4
1980	4	6
1985	6	4
1991	7	3
1995	7	3

Cumulative Democracy Rankings for
South American Countries, 1945–1995

1. Uruguay	6. Brazil
2. Chile	7. Peru
3. Colombia	8. Ecuador
4. Venezuela	9. Bolivia
5. Argentina	10. Paraguay

power, more isolated frontiers, higher levels of wealth and development, and greater distance from the United States may offer some geopolitical explanations for the greater democracy in the South American countries.

If we use the rankings at the bottom of table 3, Uruguay shows the highest tendency for democracy, Paraguay, the least. The two landlocked republics, Bolivia and Paraguay, score lowest on democracy. These two plus eighth-ranked Ecuador also tally at the bottom of the ten in national wealth. In all, the buffer nations sans Uruguay have stronger authoritarian traditions.

Countries of predominantly European culture and those located at the continent's northern and southern extremes tend toward more constitutionalism. The two largest and most powerful countries, Brazil and Argentina, hold middle positions on the democracy continuum.

Revolution likewise seems conditioned in part by position, resources, and other geographic features. For example, uneven terrain, isolated and distant hinterlands, natural wealth located near frontiers, weak and repressive governments, smuggling and illegal colonization, foreign control over national resources, and distrust of the United States all make for potential rebellion in South America. Such strife is present in the backlands of Peru and Colombia now, and, during the late 1960s and early 1970s, in fairly mild levels in Bolivia, Brazil, Uruguay, and Argentina, the last three being urban examples. But revolutionary success during this century seems more characteristic of Middle America than of South America, for example, in Mexico (1910), Guatemala (1945), Cuba (1959), and Nicaragua (1979). Only Bolivia in South America had a successful revolution in this century (1952).

Regional Economic Cooperation and Integration

Not all of South American geopolitics consists of frontier controversy, checkerboard tensions, and warfare. A cooperative and unifying orientation in the form of integration also commonly appears in the literature and in the practice of foreign affairs. In fact, cooperation, more than conflict, seems prominent in contemporary South American geopolitics.

Integration clearly fits within our definition of geopolitics because it focuses on policies that deal with frontiers, resources, and communication over distance. Many of the Southern Cone writers, in particular, Bernardo Quagliotti de Bellis, Nicolás Boscovich, Luis Dallanegra Pedrazo, and Julia Velilla de Arréllaga, advocate coordination of regional economic policies dealing with trade, industry, pollution, water usage, transportation, hydroelectric power, and fiscal policy to bring about long-term peace, development, and even political confederation in the Southern Cone.

Integration occurs at several levels of complexity and advances in steps toward complete regional and political economic cooperation (Masi 1987: 3 – 6):

a. a system of preferential tariffs, under which customs are reduced according to bilateral or multilateral negotiations;

b. free-trade zones, in which tariffs on commerce disappear between participating states, but in which there is no common external tariff;

c. a customs union, that is, a free-trade zone combined with a common external tariff;

d. a common market, that is, a customs union that also guarantees free movement of the factors of production across the borders of member nations;

e. an economic union, in which monetary, fiscal, and similar policies are coordinated within a common market system; and

f. complete economic integration, in which all participants apply a single economic policy.

Attempts at Latin American integration during the 1950s and 1960s are still active, although many are languishing. The Central American Common Market, the Caribbean Free Trade Area, the Andean Pact, the Latin American Free Trade Association and its successor, the Latin American Integration Association, all began with aspirations of coordinating policies and resources in hopes of members gaining more in regional development than they could attain by their own efforts. But problems dampened aspirations. For instance, geographic obstacles prevented physical contact and heightened the costs of communication. Weaker states felt overwhelmed by the demands of larger countries; national autonomy became their protection. In some cases, free trade, which eliminated revenue-rendering tariffs, lessened fiscal balances, again mostly in the smaller republics. Leaders and governments lacked the skills and resources to administer joint projects. In addition, rewards from integration failed to materialize.

A second integrationist trend has emerged in the hemisphere since the middle 1980s. Pres. George Bush's Enterprise of the Americas and other factors initiated the North American Free Trade Agreement (NAFTA) in 1993 among Mexico, Canada, and the United States, which may produce long-term results in fostering North American trade. Chile may be the first South American nation to join NAFTA officially.

In South America the greatest evidence of momentum toward

integration now lies in MERCOSUR, or the Mercado Común del Sur (the Southern Cone Common Market), which originated in the 1991 Treaty of Asunción, signed by Brazil, Uruguay, Paraguay, and Argentina. Under the terms of the treaty interregional tariffs have largely disappeared since 1995. The interesting question is whether NAFTA and MERCOSUR will someday join?

With a record of failure at hemispheric integration, why has this surge of integrationism now risen in South America? First, without the current Brazil-Argentina rapprochement, Southern Cone integration simply could not have advanced. Both countries have shifted away from confrontational foreign policies toward a "common list" of cooperative undertakings (Bartolomé 1989). Argentina wanted Brazilian heavy machinery, processed food and beverages, and leather and footwear, whereas the Brazilians sought Argentinean beef and wheat. A clear strategy has gradually emerged of (1) multinational conventions that steadily increase the common list, (2) careful avoidance of pricing and trade-imbalance distortions, and (3) periodic presidential-level negotiations to stimulate further integration.

A wide spectrum of agreements in other areas (Baumann 1988; Welch 1988) accompanies the erection of trade incentives: binational commerce associations, cooperation in nuclear and hydroelectric energy policies and in transportation, plans to create a common currency (the gaucho) and a biotechnology center, and the creation of a Brazil-Argentina investment fund and other fiscal and monetary instruments to help stabilize binational commerce.

Second, the great expanse of South America continues to open up. Paved highways expand (although in many cases railroad construction has faltered because of higher maintenance expense), and eventually cross-continental auto, truck, and bus travel will facilitate more dependable and less costly commercial, tourist, and other contacts. The ambitious Brazilian road network, still under construction, will span the Amazonian basin and link the interior to the coastal cities. The Hidrovía of the Paraguay-Paraná River systems, completed in 1990, now allows barges to travel 3,442 kilometers from Porto Cáceres in southwestern Brazil through the waters of Bolivia, Paraguay, and Argentina to the Atlantic port of Nueva Palmira, Uruguay (Gauto and Casco Carrera 1989). The Carretera Marginal Bolivariana de la Selva (the Marginal) will extend from Venezuela to Bolivia along the eastern Andean foothills (Glassner 1988: 164).

Other new road systems could be described as well. This process of spatial opening clearly parallels and promotes successful integration.

Third, factors endemic to Southern Cone nations have increased the desirability of regional policy coordination. The compactness of the territory, centered on the Plata River watershed, and a common need for hydroelectric power have all encouraged unity. Committed leadership in Brazil and Argentina, by far the dominant economies, almost guarantee the continuation of integration. A sense of community, created by common racial and historical backgrounds, further enhances cooperation. National leaders also have come to recognize that free trade, not economic nationalism, spells success in development.

Fourth, major domestic groups have come to recognize that without South American integration, local economies could be exposed to a global "marginalization." Mariano Bartolomé has this to say on the subject (1989: 38): "The union of Brazil and Argentina is condemned to success lest we disappear commercially from the world." In other words, join integrationist blocs and reap the consequent benefits of trade, or suffer from marginality and economic stagnation.

Fifth, the ending of the cold war probably exposed South America to more, not less, economic vulnerability from the United States and elsewhere. Recent trends indicate higher Latin American dependency on the United States for exports, imports, and foreign investment (Hurrell 1992: 365–369), at the same time that the United States appears less interested in becoming involved in South America. Mexico's "defection" and free-trade merger with North America left its Latin siblings feeling isolated and fiscally endangered. Economic security, consequently, may lie in regional unity, which can be used as a bargaining chip for eventual access to the North American free-trade market.

Finally, how would integration affect South American geopolitics, assuming eventual achievement of some regional economic cooperation? Certainly, frontier tensions and checkerboard balances would diminish, and the buffer states could find independence by exposing themselves to transnational agreements. Territorial disputes might atrophy because national conflict over space loses vitality when nations cooperate. Ecuador and Bolivia, for example, could reach their Amazonian and Pacific goals and objectives through continental union, with Ecuador gaining the Marañón and Bolivia attaining an outlet to the sea.

There might be a spurt in development, and interiors might be brought closer to coasts with further integration. A unified South America might wield greater economic leverage in world affairs, although, to me, the continent would still lack sufficient resources to compete effectively with Japan, Europe, and North America or to attain autarky. Eventual confederation, a political collaboration arising from successes in economic undertakings, possibly lies in a distant geopolitical future; the continent could become unified, dynamic, and peaceful, and thus prepared for meeting the challenges of the twenty-first century.

T his chapter first looks at three distinct Americas: the northern, middle, and southern parts, and how each differs geopolitically. It then turns to a geopolitical comparison of U.S. and Latin American development and why the north, at least in part, experienced more rapid industrialization. A discussion of the continental magnitude of Brazilian expansion, the potential for South American confederation, and the 1492 discovery of America follow. For the most part, these themes are wrapped in a strategic format in which South American geopolitics project into the geopolitical systems of other global regions.

The Three Americas

America appears so fragmented geographically, culturally, and politically that the northern and southern extremes and a middle sector display geopolitical distinctiveness (Kelly 1986b). Two largely disconnected American continents, the northern and the southern, reach from the Arctic to the Antarctic and separate the Atlantic and the Pacific Oceans. Because of the lack of land corridors in the hemisphere's jumbled central portion, this north-south chasm is widened by great distances, sometimes harsh climates and topographies, contrasting development patterns, and the historical proclivity of both regions to look first toward Europe rather than to one another. The middle section, the Caribbean and Central America, exhibits qualities very different from either of the flanking continents, yet geopolitically it tends to align more closely to the north.

Different peoples inhabit this tripartite American landscape, and cultural and national traits have become more pronounced as the years have passed. Fully thirty-two sovereign countries arose in America, each unique, and these formed into dissimilar regions and subregions. A unique blending of human traits has also occurred, within contrasting geographic environments, historical migrations, traditions, and foreign policies.

The Northern Section

The United States, for example, is located in a hemisphere of largely weak states, distant from Eurasia, yet positioned in a prosperous northern temperate zone between Europe and Asia. The United States possesses great advantages in terms of climate, topography, river and lake systems, and natural resources. Consequently, the country's geopolitical situation elevated the territory to a world power, if a political authority administered these advantages properly. Militarily dominant in the New World, the United States sometimes finds it necessary to intervene in Latin America and on the fringes or the interior of Eurasia to maintain favorable balances of power that support U.S. security. Interestingly, much of the evolution of U.S. foreign policy rested in the country's relations with Middle and South America.

The Southern Section

South America separates into four or five fairly clear subregions: the countries of the Plata River valley, the Southern Cone, the Andean, the Amazonian, and the Caribbean sectors. Little connects these sections, with the Caribbean northern tier particularly isolated from states to the south. South America's terrain produces much less wealth and industry than North America's. The continent suffers from poorer soils, harsher climates and topography, ill-positioned lakes and rivers, and global marginality. These factors, as well as the need to protect national borders, has kept foreign and security policies largely focused on continental affairs.

The Middle Section

Middle America is a geographic quagmire, extremely fragmented racially, culturally, and politically; possessing a very weak resources infrastructure (except for petroleum in certain areas); chaotic and repressive governments; and countries divided by seas and mountains. Attempts at economic and political cooperation among the nations of Central America and the Caribbean have failed repeatedly, and probably will continue to do so unless they somehow succeed at union or join the United States in some sort of association. In location, on the southern flank of the United States, the region normally comes under the domination of the Yankees.

The South and the Middle Compared

In comparing South America with Middle America, the former holds fewer but larger and more politically stable countries and has less diverse racial and national characteristics. In terms of regional power as measured in resources, technology, and industry, the prize easily accrues to the southern sector. Regional integration appears a more likely outcome in the south; conversely, serious interstate strife for the present seems more probable in the Caribbean watershed. In sum, a clear geopolitical delineation exists between South and Middle America; below this line lies geopolitical transformation, above it, stagnation and U.S. interference.

The Geopolitical Status of Middle America

From a broader strategic perspective, Middle America since its discovery by Columbus has alternated in international geopolitical status between a shatterbelt configuration (table 4), a region of local turmoil and rivalry between outside great powers, and a great power's sphere of influence, where the area is enveloped within the regional and strategic interests of a powerful foreign state (Kelly 1986b: 69). The first of the two Caribbean shatterbelts included rivalries among Spain, England, and France. In the second, the Soviet Union faced the United States for dominion of the Caribbean and Central America.

Since the arrival of the Spaniards, Middle America has not experienced autonomy, and independence from foreign domination, particularly from the United States, likely will not occur in the foreseeable future. This history of persistent outside intervention stems from Middle America's central position between oceans and continents and its location on the United States' southern border. In this rugged, fragmented terrain with overlapping racial and cultural settlements, competition for the control of interoceanic transit, and recurring political and economic instability, the region is vulnerable to foreign intrusion. Hence, in a geopolitical sense, Middle America is much more strategically involved than South America.

Specifically, the geopolitical importance of Middle America lies in

Table 4. Caribbean Spheres of Influence and Shatterbelt Eras

1520s–1650s	Spanish sphere of influence
1620s–1820s	Shatterbelt
1820s–1890s	British sphere of influence
1890s–1960s	U.S. sphere of influence
1960s–1980s	Shatterbelt
1980s–	U.S. sphere of influence

the potential for local disputes or instabilities to escalate into strategic conflict between the United States and threaten Eurasian countries or coalitions; this U.S. concern is reflected in the Monroe Doctrine. The United States simply cannot tolerate any Eurasian rivals erecting a foothold in Middle America. Thus, the region oscillates between shatterbelt and sphere-of-influence status, with at present, the United States as primary intervenor. One sees these strategic connections in the 1945 CIA intervention in Guatemala, in the 1962 Cuban missile crisis, and in the alleged Grenadan and Nicaraguan Sandinista ties to the Soviet Union.

In global affairs Middle America will react and not act, will continue to be divided, depressed, and unstable, and will remain under the thumb of some outside great power or powers. With Russia no longer a strongly involved strategic force, the previous shatterbelt over the region has reverted to a U.S. sphere of influence that could persist well beyond this century.

The weak strategic association between South America, the Caribbean, and Central America has had a great impact on hemispheric geopolitics. One example is the inability of South America to counterbalance U.S. interventions in Middle America. This has forced the central republics either to align with the United States or to seek protection against the Yankees within a shatterbelt; the latter choice is a dangerous alternative if the Eurasian sponsor someday departs, as Cuba has learned during the 1990s. In either case, Middle America geopolitically is tied more firmly to the north than to the south. U.S. involvement in the Caribbean shelters South America, particularly the Southern Cone, from the need for an intercontinental security commitment, except for the limited possibility that a South Atlantic shatterbelt might arise.

The Geopolitical Status of South America

The wealthier, less-fragmented South America of today is independent in global geopolitics, isolated from northern great-power strategic rivalry and interference, largely at peace internally, beginning economic and political integration, and potentially able in the near future to exert a stronger international influence than previously (Bartolomé 1989). This autonomy will likely continue in light of the rapprochement developing between Brazil and Argentina (Selcher 1985) and the progress toward integrating the Plata River basin's security, energy, and trade policies.

The United States holds a significant power advantage over both areas of Latin America. The United States settled a potentially extremely wealthy territory, destined for eventual great-power status if its resources were developed, its domain extended from the Atlantic to the Pacific, and its political system remained united, stable, and progressive. By the turn of this century, that combination was realized, allowing the United States to begin its rise to global leadership. The United States' supremacy represents the dominant strategic factor within the geopolitics of the Western Hemisphere.

With the recent exception of Brazil, and previously of Argentina, no such claims of world status have ever risen from the larger countries of Latin America, for their wealth, size, and geographic features do not compare to the strength that emerged in the United States. In their traditional competition for South American leadership, Brazil and Argentina tended to checkmate each other's rise to a greater role in world affairs, thus maintaining South America's position on the global-power periphery. For similar reasons of geography, Central America and the Caribbean are divided today into odd patchworks of small and middle-sized powers, with Mexico in the twentieth century less conspicuous in international relations because of its envelopment within the mighty shadow of its northern neighbor.

South America, however, may have greater world impact under joint Brazilian-Argentinean leadership (Kelly 1990a). Brazil, for example, in 1990 ranked ninth in the world in gross national product. Argentina and Brazil together rank close to eighth. Ray Cline rated Brazil as the sixth-greatest global state in 1975. Again, Brazil and Argentina combined would have ranked fifth. Although Southern Cone integration remains at present more promise than fact, progress toward Brazilian-Argentinean rapprochement during the 1980s and 1990s built a momentum that does not appear to be faltering. At the least, the ideal of both countries integrating their developmental and foreign policies offers food for interesting geopolitical thought, a topic that will be discussed at more length in a later section. Nevertheless, the United States seems content to ignore this South American potential for greater world impact and how this impact might work to the advantage or the disadvantage of the United States' strategic position.

A Geopolitical Comparison of
North and South American Development

The United States enjoys higher levels of industrial development than do most areas of Latin America. In geopolitical terms, five explanations may account in part for this contrast.

The Northern Advantage in Resources

For most minerals utilized in industry, Latin America ranks rather low among world regions. In this regard, one commentator (Atkins 1977: 33) notes "a continuing myth, dating from the discovery of the New World, [that] pictures the Latin American region as possessing immense mineral resources, which need only capital and skills to be developed. [But] The region is not generally rich in minerals, although a minority of states are especially well endowed in certain resources." Specifically, comparisons (table 5) of South American and U.S. mineral production help illustrate the wide differences in natural wealth (Espenshade and Morrison 1986: 41–47).

In all of the cases except iron ore, the United States holds a clear advantage, and for iron ore as well as for cobalt, copper, lead, nickel, and zinc, it can import additional supplies from immediate neighbors Canada and Mexico. South America outstrips the north only in bauxite, chromite, manganese, tin, and tungsten, primarily from Brazil and Bolivia, and the United States easily obtains these from Australia, southern Africa, and Middle America.

Not only do more resources abound in the north, but their locations facilitate industrial utilization. Location made a crucial difference particularly during the initial years of U.S. industrialization. Centrally placed lakes, rivers, and canals provided cheap access from oil, coal, and iron ore fields to the early industrial centers on the East Coast and in the Ohio Valley. Transport by water also facilitated

Table 5. Mineral Wealth Production as % of World Production

Mineral	North America	United States	South America
Coal	20.0	18.0	—
Uranium	46.6	27.5	—
Aluminum	32.1	24.2	—
Vanadium	—	9.7	—
Iron ore	12.8	5.8	16.8
Petroleum	24.2	16.4	5.1
Natural gas	36.1	29.5	2.5

internal and international export capacity; the Ohio, Missouri, and Mississippi Rivers and the Great Lakes connected the Erie Canal, the Saint Lawrence River system, and a series of barge networks.

Most of these advantages are normally not evident when we examine the different and difficult terrain of South and Middle America. With limited exceptions in the Southern Cone, the regions south of the United States lack abundant industrial materials, and in all situations where oil, coal, iron ore, and other manufacturing necessities exist, they are located distant from the others and are not linked by natural or inexpensive transit. Rivers normally connect coasts with uninhabited interiors, efficient lake cartage and coastal barge traffic simply do not materialize, and canal and superhighway systems have yet to be built in great numbers.

In the United States, fertile soils and a temperate climate in the middle regions, supplemented by available river and lake transport, allowed for surplus food output, which boosted industrialization and the national economy. There were no impassable mountains, jungles, and deserts in North America to prevent or fragment strongly grounded social and economic ecumenes on the East Coast and the eventual spread of settlers to the rich Midwest and beyond. The Appalachian range barred westward expansion only until the seaboard colonies were firmly established. Not only did interior rivers provide the westward-moving pioneers a relatively simple mode of travel, but they likewise offered a facility for cheaply carrying midwestern goods to domestic and international markets through the port of New Orleans and onto seagoing barges and ships beyond.

Nor did the western and southwestern plains and the Rocky Mountains prevent U.S. settlement of the continent's Pacific rim. North American Indian tribes proved militarily ineffective against eastern immigrants, and free land and gold offered strong incentives for reaching California. Maritime trade routes on both sides of the continent were also more direct from the United States to prosperous Eurasian markets. Excellent deepwater ports along all coasts further helped the United States fulfill its maritime and global destinies.

The abundant agricultural output of the Atlantic watershed of the Southern Cone equals that of the U.S. breadbasket. But total South American food production falls well below U.S. levels. Nor do fluvial transit systems connect harvest zones to industrial centers, except for Buenos Aires and the fertile pampas connected by the Plata River. The steep Andean mountains, the vast Amazonian *selva*, isolated hinterlands, and great distances between industrial centers have helped restrict the development of a coordinated regional and continental system for economic growth, development of transportation and communications, and substantial industrialization. Only recently have these begun to appear, again mainly on the Atlantic side of South America.

While South America languished during the last century, development and industrialization spurted in North America. The north not only became industrialized a century earlier than did the south, but the United States also extended itself from ocean to ocean, developed a more democratic and a more stable political system, established a mighty technological infrastructure, and exhibited interventionist-strategic international relationships. All of these events and many others related directly to geographic position and resources; U.S. industry benefited from these geopolitical factors; the southern republics normally did not.

The United States did not have the great topographical and climatic obstacles that worked so mightily against the national and regional unity of Latin America. Brazil and Argentina failed to reach the Pacific coast, a profound conditioning factor in South American geopolitics in general, because mountains and deserts limited their movement westward and eastward. Unlike in the United States, where the west coast was for the most part sparsely colonized, European settlement in Peru and Chile would have made further Portuguese expansion more difficult.

Doubtless, circumstances beyond favorable terrain assisted U.S. expansion, for instance, the crumbling Spanish Empire, the small numbers and inferior weaponry of the northern Plains Indians, Napoleon's sale of Louisiana and Seward's purchase of Alaska, an unstable balance of power in Europe, and successful territorial wars with Mexico and Spain. These advantages seemed exclusively North American; South America was isolated, divided, impoverished, and controlled by outsiders in comparison. But had the Portuguese gained Pacific and Caribbean footholds, or had the Spanish left a united Spanish America, how differently might local and strategic geopolitics have evolved. The geographic landscape of both continents, again measured in terms of position and resources, proved a major factor in the success or failure of continental projection.

Western territorial expansion assisted the United States in generating political stability as well as economic growth. Pressures and problems that might have emerged on the east coast were relieved by access to opportunities in the hinterland. Fertile but cheap land attracted skilled and hardworking settlers, and the resulting labor shortages increased wages throughout the country. Products from the farm belts and mines fed industry in the East, and prosperity built substantial domestic markets for industrial products during most decades. These advantages did not accrue as readily to South America, again, in part because of resource availability.

Colonial-Period Geopolitics

Early explorers in North America found no gold, silver, or advanced indigenous empires. As a result, English policymakers considered the region of little economic or strategic importance and neglected North America for that reason. Had these types of resources existed, probably a more restrictive mercantilist rule might have been imposed, similar to Spain's rigid management of the abundant resources in Latin America. When England attempted to restrict its administrative system in the 1770s, the North Americans, preferring the freedom and flexibility of neglect and peripheral status, rebelled.

By 1776 British uninterest had allowed North Americans the chance to develop indigenous industries, export primary goods, develop shipbuilding capacity for international trade, create a system for internal communications, exploit a resources-rich interior, and cultivate a nationalist spirit of autonomy and self-sufficiency. In most ways, the colonies resembled a free nation well before it gained statehood through military rebellion. Economic expansion immediately followed independence. Distance from England and a European perception that North America lacked resources and strategic position—all components of geopolitics—engendered opportunities for the United States that Latin Americans would never have.

From the perspective of European leaders during the discovery and exploration, the southern regions, from Peru to Mexico, proved enormously rich in gold and silver, the form of wealth then sought most vigorously. Advanced and tightly administered indigenous empires provided the Spanish an available labor supply for mines, for food production, and for transporting goods, and a hierarchical structure for governing. Even the English considered the Spanish colonies a better investment, and they encouraged smuggling, convoy raiding, and seizure of strategic enclaves where possible.

The Spanish took their American colonies very seriously and established in their sectors of the New World the most advanced bureaucratic structures of the time. A tight and stifling administration gave the Spanish colonists little freedom on which to base later development. Consequently, after independence, the Latin Americans did not possess the North Americans' self-confidence or infrastructure for local development.

The Hispanic territories emerged as regions intended only for advancing the metropolitan center in Spain. Impressed indigenous labor mined for gold and silver; agriculture and transportation systems serviced this exporting requirement. Tying primary goods to overseas trade and importing products manufactured in Europe became the prime economic incentive, a linkage that Latin Americans are still trying to break. Spanish leaders forbade industry in the colonies and discouraged self-government. Internal trade, travel, and development did not arise during the period, reflecting an intentional policy of isolation, mercantilism, fragmentation, subservience, and bureaucratization. Only in certain peripheral areas, such as in Chile, Venezuela, and Argentina, did some flexibility and innovativeness appear that would later spark a progressive and industrial consciousness. The Spanish discounted these areas because gold, silver, or advanced indigenous peoples were absent, so the population engaged in illegal smuggling with the Dutch, French, English, and North Americans, which sparked some motivation for indigenous industry.

The mercantilist trade sentiment ultimately served Spain and its

American colonies ill, according to Stanley Stein and Barbara Stein (1970), for American gold and silver instead helped finance English industrialization. They describe the inability or unwillingness of the Spanish to erect protective tariffs. The resulting exposure to cheaper and better English manufactures minimized Spain's capacity to provide such goods for its own market and for its American dependencies. This helps explain why the Spanish sphere of influence over Latin America so quickly reverted to British hegemony after independence in the early nineteenth century.

A variety of geopolitical factors contributed to Latin American independence:

- the isolation of Latin America, a peripheral location at great distance from Spain, gave rise to local autonomy and to illegal contacts with other nations;

- the costs of administering so vast a territory impoverished the Spanish crown and reduced its staying power;

- the rugged topography facilitated the guerrilla tactics of revolutionary forces and exposed the peninsular armies;

- Napoleon's invasion of Spain and Portugal created a power vacuum that encouraged American rebellion; and

- Britain's naval strength helped prevent Spain and its South American continental allies from reestablishing control over America. Once the center weakened, the periphery folded inward to force a fragmenting of the whole.

Following independence, most of Latin America suffered fifty years of political chaos, disunity, and social and economic collapse. This was the legacy of the long colonial period, which exploited natural wealth at whatever cost and left voids that would take years of national introspection and sacrifice to fill.

But despite the dissolution of the Spanish Empire in America, the international relations of the region stayed largely the same: manipulation of Middle America by outside forces and peripheral status for South America. For the remainder of the century, Britain made Middle America its sphere of influence, despite U.S. attempts to inhibit such European interference. Had the United States challenged British hegemony, the Caribbean might have reverted to a shatterbelt. But whatever its configuration, Middle America remained tied to the strategic objectives of the northern powers, in either sphere of influence or shatterbelt, because of its location and its volatile politics.

For South America, however, the British, and later the United States, never filled the position left by Spain and Portugal. For the past one hundred years, neither a shatterbelt nor a sphere of influence has emerged in South America, although foreign economic and at times political manipulation continue. The region, protected strategically by the United States, and without sufficient power to have an impact very far beyond its immediate bounds, continues to be an independent force in global politics, although on the international margin.

One further geopolitical feature from the colonial period needs brief mention: the ill-drawn frontier boundaries separating the Spanish and Portuguese administrative jurisdictions. Borders were seldom clearly delineated, a problem in large part stemming from the vast empty spaces between the early population ecumenes. Clear lines of separation simply lacked importance. But as territories became more populated and integrated, and national characteristics diversified, disputes and occasional warfare erupted over resources and passages claimed by competing republics. This evolution has yet to conclude, for most contemporary conflict still revolves around disputed boundary markings.

America and the European Balance of Power

The power configurations of one region affect other world areas as well; these strategic linkages were particularly important to an America on the verge of independence from Europe. This connection is still vital to the geopolitics of the Western Hemisphere, for European struggles normally have accrued to the advantage or disadvantage of the Americas. For reasons inherent in European rivalries, the Americans of both continents were assisted in their rebellions, the British colonists by the French and Spanish, the Spanish and Portuguese colonists by the English.

Napoleon sparked Latin American independence when his forces occupied Spain and Portugal. He prevented England's reconquest of North America in the War of 1812 and significantly boosted the United States by selling Louisiana. The United States' possession of the port of New Orleans as a sea outlet for the Mississippi watershed gave it important access to international markets for industrial and agricultural goods. Additionally, the Napoleonic wars provided infant U.S. industries and midwestern and southern farmers access to a lucrative trade with all contenders in the European struggle, which the United States would take advantage of in subsequent balance-of-power disruptions in Eurasia.

English warships later blocked Bourbon ambitions for the lost Spanish colonies, and England likewise helped terminate the African slave trade to America, both factors again associated with America and the European balance of power. Wars in Europe and poor harvests stimulated substantial immigration to the New World, advanced industry and technology, and brought new peoples to the cities and interior. Russian distrust of the British delivered strategically important Alaska to the United States. And German unification and military power caused France to withdraw its military forces from Mexico and England to leave the Caribbean under North American control. Where European monies had contributed heavily to U.S. industrialization, the borrowing needs of the Europeans during World War I quickly shifted the United States from debtor to creditor. Many other examples of benefits to America from European difficulties could be cited. Needless to say, such geopolitical repercussions significantly elevated the security, prosperity, and independence of the New World.

The United States' share of the benefits was disproportionate for reasons of its more advanced industry and shipbuilding, its more stable government and greater food production, and its resource wealth and abundant skilled labor. Most of the new Latin republics, still plagued by political chaos, isolation and disunity, and economic and social underdevelopment, languished for decades while the United States exploded industrially. Finally, political rivalries and weaknesses in Europe enabled the United States to spread its authority to the Caribbean, Arctic, and Pacific Oceans and beyond and to become in less than a century after independence the only American continental power and great-power aspirant. In contrast, Brazil and Argentina were unprepared for such expansion until much later, after many of the advantages of nineteenth-century industrialization had passed.

Immigration Patterns to the New World

Immigration to America also falls within geopolitical analysis. Wars, floods, and drought prompted migrations. Overpopulation, promises of wealth and of vacant lands, new modes of transport, all caused humans to move as well. Impressed African slaves added substantially to this drama. The new settlers filled unoccupied spaces, they congested cities and spurred industrialization, they developed and utilized natural resources, and they created pressures for territorial expansion and boundary conflict.

Immigrants impeded national unity when they could not, or refused to, assimilate, as happened in Argentina and elsewhere, although South America, for the most part, has not faced major problems of irredentism, or efforts to change state boundaries to conform to ethnic lines. But Brazilian fear of displaced Asians in the Amazon territory, the Mennonite "states within a state" of the Paraguayan Chaco, and calls for restoration of the former Inca Empire are examples of this geopolitical topic.

Immigration left a hodgepodge of nationalities and races in America. Indeed, one has difficulty labeling most American countries as unified "nations," since cultural and national identities have often not melded well. Indigenous peoples were decimated, exploited, isolated, and resentful. Mestizos, or mixed races, fared somewhat better, and in Latin America often acted as intermediaries between European bosses and village Amerinds. They also worked in factories and consumed processed goods. Most Europeans, the recent arrivals particularly, kept to the cities and engineered advancements in industry. Asians came as farmers or small merchants. In many parts of Latin America, rugged topography and lack of resources prevented closer integration of races and nationalities, but where large cities and extensive farmlands predominated, as in the United States and the Southern Cone, diversity tended more strongly to help advance modernization.

Immigrants, particularly to the United States and the Southern Cone, created a dual system of labor, important for stimulating industry. Recent arrivals worked for lower wages, enabling the middle classes to afford manufactured goods. In both areas, this process stimulated profits in and expanded commerce and agriculture. Labor duality was less common in Middle and Andean America because the abundant supply of Amerinds and mestizos dampened wages and discouraged formation of capital and technology.

Investment and Head Start

These comparisons help explain the more substantial industrialization of the United States. North America clearly provided a better place for local and European capital investment, possessing as it did greater natural resources and better transport systems, higher agricultural productivity, a strong dual-labor facility with an abundance of skilled workers, a more stable and efficient government, and a larger middle-class market of consumers. Except for the War of 1812 and the Civil War, the United States remained peaceful and largely immune to foreign invasion, thanks to the European balance of power and to weak neighboring states. Peace and prosperity came because the continent was united and integrated under one political system. South America could not match these benefits. The ability of the United States to take advantage of the European collapse in World War I erased the industrial debts accumulated in previous decades, releasing the north from the repayments Latin Americans later had to make. And once ahead of the southern republics in terms of development, the United States could impose liberal trade, cheaper products, and military abuse on its neighbors, thereby extending the industrial gap between the two continents.

The Territorial Expansion of Brazil

We turn in this section to a closer view of Brazilian territorial expansion because this topic is at the core of South American geopolitics. Brazil's central position and great expanse, its industry, resources and population, control of the Amazon, and geopolitical instincts, have made the country dominant in regional foreign affairs. Indeed, in matters of war and peace, political stability and economic prosperity, boundary tensions and regional integration, global marginality and status, Brazil counts as the primary determiner of the continent's destiny.

But this geopolitical uniqueness also contributes to suspicion and fear of encirclement (Kelly 1988b: 192): "As colony, empire, and republic, Brazil traditionally has been viewed by Spanish neighbors with envy, dislike, and suspicion. To many of them, Brazil possessed an alien European heritage [in being Portuguese], she was envied for her potential power and wealth, and above all, she was seen to be a threat to continental stability and even as aggrandizer of certain bordering territories."

Brazil has responded in various ways to its position as "Portuguese American island in a Spanish American archipelago . . . surrounded by latently hostile . . . neighbors" (Hilton 1975: 14). Sometimes, it has separated itself from Latin America and sought close linkages with the United States or aspired to major power status. Toward Spanish America, Brazil has usually played a disinterested or low-key role. If it perceived activism in South America as desirable, Brazil instituted policies that ranged from vigorous territorial expansion to hegemonic leadership and balance-of-power manipulator to stimulator of interior economic development with its Spanish neighbors.

Brazil could adjust its ambitions according to perceived opportunities: its central location in South America; its ability to project sufficient power beyond its frontiers; the frequent disunity, weakness, or turmoil of its Latin American neighbors; its frontiers isolated from external threat; and diplomats who understood geopolitical relationships and usually exploited them to great advantage. By the 1970s, these factors had become particularly clear, and Brazil found itself poised and willing to assert its leadership among the nations of the Southern Cone.

Variations of six foreign policies—(1) imperialist, (2) South American balance-of-power participant, (3) U.S. surrogate, (4) major power aspirant, (5) South American hegemon, and (6) regional integrator—have assisted South American stability and peace. Brazil could affect regional conflict in the role of imperialist or balance-of-power participant, or reduce tensions as South American hegemon or integrator. All geopolitical, these policies impinge on the theme of territorial expansion.

Brazil as Imperialist

Territorial conquest distinguishes the imperialist state, which forcefully seizes lands owned by other countries. Lewis Tambs dramatically forecasted this role as Brazil's (1965: 179):

> March to the West; inspired by the spirit of the *bandeirantes* [early Portuguese slave raiders] and guided by the wiles of Portuguese statecraft, Brazil stands poised on the far-flung parapets of its colonial redoubts, tempted by a vision of grandeur. The question is: "Will Brazil take the plunge toward the Pacific and transcontinental empire?" Only time will tell. But, if the past serves as a model for the future, the history of Brazil's expanding frontiers assures that the attempt will be made.

Four expansionist doctrines—the doctrine of organic frontiers, the South American heartland, Brazilian manifest destiny, and the law of valuable areas—appear prominently in the writings of Brazilian geopoliticians who closely follow imperialist theses.

The organic theory of the state, which imagines nations as living entities, justifies territorial aggrandizement as a necessary requisite of "young," and thus "growing," countries. This doctrine draws the particular interest of the major Brazilian theorists (Meira Mattos 1989, 1975; Golbery 1981; Backheuser 1952) because it legitimizes the country's historical expansion and classifies its present far-flung boundaries as either "living" or "dead." But this doctrine increases Spanish suspicion and heightens hemispheric tension. The encircling countries, for example, see Brazil's interest in occupying the Bolivian heartland as a device it will use to control the entire continent as well as gain a land corridor to the Pacific (Bond 1981; Ferris 1981; Moneta and Wichmann 1981). Travassos' "symbolic" or "magic" triangle, Tambs' Charcas triangle, both formed by the Bolivian towns of Sucre, Cochabamba, and Santa Cruz de la Sierra (map 14), and Golbery's "continental welding zone" (map 3), which encompasses large portions of Bolivia and Paraguay, attest to this alleged conspiracy.

Child (1985: 98) heard this reflection of Spanish fear of Brazil's destined "westward march" from a Peruvian official: "Brazil, which is like the United States a hundred years ago, believes she has a manifest destiny to occupy the continent and reach the Pacific, and Peru is California." Tambs (1965: 42) argues that Brazil moved its capital inland to Brasilia as part of a carefully designed strategy to secure passage to the Pacific through the Charcas triangle. Expansion likewise threatens by means of illegal colonization of isolated and uninhabited lands across frontiers, followed by eventual arbitration and annexation (Child 1985; Pittman 1981a; Tambs 1965). Contemporary examples of this potential exist in the northern provinces of Uruguay, eastern Paraguay, and the Santa Cruz region of Bolivia (Nickson 1981).

Brazil as South American Balance-of-Power-Participant

Traditionally, Brazil has aligned itself with Chile against Peru and Argentina (Burr 1955) as a way of preventing Spanish encirclement and of preserving the Southern Cone buffer states. Such an equilibrium, nevertheless, has probably obstructed expansion to the Pacific for both Brazil and Argentina, threatened a continentwide escalation of conflict and a South American shatterbelt, and stymied a greater international role for Brazil.

Brazil as U.S. Surrogate

South Americans commonly allege that Brazil seeks a *"barganha leal,"* or deal, with the United States (Child 1985: 35 – 36; Perry 1976: 39 – 43) that is beneficial to both countries in terms of status, economics, and security. The "key nation" concept, a variant of this claim (Child 1985; Myers 1984; Mutto 1971), charges that Brazil chooses to act in league with the United States as enforcer of regional peace and controller of economic and military resources.

Brazil as Major-Power Aspirant

Although great-power status for Brazil represents a traditional aspiration, fervor for such prestige rose to a higher pitch in the 1970s, during the country's spurt in national development. Contemporary financial and political difficulties have muted these declarations. Yet the potential exists for Brazil's eventual rise to the status of a world power.

Brazil as South American Hegemon

Unlike an imperialist state, a regional hegemon (Modelski 1982; Gilpin 1975) possesses the greatest military and economic power among the countries of a region; designs and enforces the primary political and economic "rules of the game" as recognized by the region's other members; and guarantees peace and independence among neighbors. Brazil seems bent on playing this role in contemporary South American foreign affairs. Compared military capabilities (table 6) reveal Brazil's strength in South America (Manwaring 1981: 71 – 72, 95 – 96; for similar comparisons concerning the country's economic supremacy, see Selcher 1985: 27).

One sees evidence of Brazil's interest in asserting a hegemonic role in the way it tries to reduce South American conflict and increase cooperation in regional development (Kelly 1988b; Selcher 1985; Bond 1981). Gorman offers a good example of the rising authority of Brazil in the area (1979: 53): "Not U.S. intercession but Brazilian power diplomacy seems more responsible to date for preventing the outbreak of violence in the region. If this is true, there may exist some basis for beginning to think of South American relations in terms of a regional balance of power (in which Brazil plays the role of balancer), rather than the more conventional framework

Table 6. Relative Military Capacity Scores

1. Brazil	13,406
2. Argentina	2,021
3. Cuba	1,039
4. Mexico	918
5. Peru	185
6. Venezuela	140

Note: Scores taken from population, military strength, industrial productivity, and gross national product variables.

of North American hegemony." Consequently, this hegemonic role makes regional turmoil less probable, encourages interstate integration, and replaces U.S. influence with Brazilian.

Brazil as Leader of Integration

Integration, unlike territorial expansion, best describes contemporary Brazilian foreign policy. This transition emerged during the 1970s, after decades of associating with the United States, ignoring regional development, and intimidating neighbors. Wayne Selcher (1985) claims that domestic economic difficulties, a vision of development opportunities in South America, and disillusionment with U.S. sponsorship prompted this change. As shown in table 7, I estimate that current Brazilian foreign policy has moved to the non-expansionist side of a stability-conflict spectrum. Chances remain high that, for the immediate future, the republic will assume an integrationist stance in its international relations with neighbors, with minimal threat of frontier instability.

Brazil, in its role as regional peace and integration advocate, and not as expansionist threat, appears to me to be a geopolitically satisfied state, with secure frontiers and no serious territorial disputes with neighbors. It seems to have more to gain from continental stability and prosperity than from conflict. Likewise, its power, prestige, and position look sufficiently strong to assert leadership and bring results.

A continuation of Brazil's historical growth, either as a piecemeal extension of its frontiers by diplomatic means, or by a more forceful enlargement by means of military intimidation, could ensue if Peruvian or Argentinean intrigue were active along its frontiers, or if the

Table 7. Brazilian Foreign Policy Spectrum

South American Stability ◄────────► South American Conflict

(6)	(5)	(4)	(3)	(2)	(1)
Regional integra- tionist	South American hegemony	Great Power aspirant	U.S. surrogate	Balance-of- power participant	South American imperialist

Importance in Brazil's Current Foreign Policy

70%	30%	0%	0%	0%	0%

region destabilized, particularly in Bolivia, Uruguay, Suriname, and Paraguay.

The cutting off of hydroelectric power from Itaipú or of some other vital resource would also invite Brazilian intervention, as might a hostile Spanish encirclement. The United States could encourage expansion by resurrecting its key-nation policy or by encouraging alliance or higher status, which would detach Brazil from its Latin associates. Serious domestic instability or a coming to power of imperialist or revolutionary leaders likewise might spur aggressiveness.

If perchance Brazil succeeded in expanding its territory for a significant distance westward and northward and became a continental power with its authority consolidated over the Pacific and Caribbean coasts, certain geopolitical outcomes might arise. Serious rebellion could occur in the newly acquired territories, as the imperial thesis predicts. An attempt at Spanish encirclement most likely would again emerge, under Argentinean leadership. The traditional checkerboard could perform prominently in this drama, with the United States either endorsing Brazilian dominance or attempting to counter it by assisting the bloc of Spanish rivals. A Brazil with territory on both coasts would certainly achieve its goal of great-power status. And through Brazilian leadership, one could also foresee a consolidation of South American integration, if Brazil's Spanish neighbors acquiesced, and from here, some type of continental confederation.

South American Confederation

Economic integration was discussed in chapter 4 because it seemed to belong more to the regional dimension than to the global. But the effects of a political collaboration among neighboring states could extend beyond regional bounds into the strategic arena. Successful economic integration brings expanded power and prestige, which becomes more political than economic in nature, as, for example, when common policies toward other economic and political blocs are established, or confederation members are protected from outside discriminatory practices. Increased unity on the political dimension simply elevates bargaining to a higher, international, level of involvement, which is, in part, an intention of integration. Hence, the political factor in integration more closely fits this chapter's emphasis on larger-scope strategic questions.

As the present century closes, economic integration continues to receive strong support in South America. Momentum toward expanding Southern Cone integration into noneconomic realms, based on successes already achieved, also has begun. It seems appropriate, therefore, to carry this analysis further by touching on the possible political and strategic ramifications of integration in South America. Could economic collaboration someday grow into a more structured political collaboration or confederation, and, if so, how might South American geopolitics change?

First, does South America offer fertile ground for greater political cooperation? Points raised earlier speak to the appropriateness of predicting greater South American unity, among these, for example, the Brazil-Argentina rapprochement, river basin communications plus increasing access to the hinterland, the region's autonomy and common heritage, a unifying focus on hydroelectric power, the fear of marginality, and a desire to enter the North American free-trade market. By effectively utilizing local resources and technology, the Plata and other nations could duplicate, on a much smaller scale, the industrial successes of North America.

With regional economic structures in place and successful, normally transnational political institutions arise, a "spillover" from economic rewards to political collaboration. South America surely would correspond to this model as well. The private sector, in fact, probably could pilot the process more assertively than could bureaucrats because it reaps the major rewards and seems better organized for pushing ahead.

It is obviously an advantage that decision making appears largely confined to Brazil and Argentina, since together they dominate the system. The buffer states would be seriously isolated if they opposed the leader states, and their defections, as well as those of the other states, could not seriously hamper progress.

Guarantees do not exist that the United States would favor closer economic association with South America. The Asian and European blocs might decide similarly because their commercial interests seem to lie elsewhere, even though Chile probably will be invited to join NAFTA. Hence, the atmosphere seems appropriate for indigenous cooperative ventures. On the other hand, if all the South American states ever entered the North American market, again as Chile apparently will, this process would more easily derive from continental unity, not segmentation, which provides yet another stimulant for tighter regional focus.

On the whole, South American political collaboration, or confederation over the long run, might alter the continent's geopolitics in several ways. Without a doubt, fewer frontier tensions and disputes among member countries would transpire, possibly coupled with more regional prosperity and additional political and economic clout in global bargaining. But the most interesting speculation may center on U.S. relations with its southern neighbors. Would the United States continue to ignore Latin America in preference to Eurasia? Would rivalry materialize over Middle America? Would the United States and South America compete in world organizations and trading blocs? Or would South American unity and enhanced power bring eventual association with North America? These queries at the moment appear unanswerable, because the hemispheric relationship since colonial times has remained distant, weak, and unequal. An interesting future awaits if southern economic and political consolidation emerges.

South American Ties beyond the Hemisphere

South American isolation runs thematically throughout our discussion of geopolitics. The continent's detachment derives from its distance from northern core areas, its marginal position, and its limited resources, markets, and industry. But benefits also accrue to peripheral location. Whereas isolation might breed stagnation and limited access to technology and trade opportunities, marginality could safeguard the area from conflict originating elsewhere and help the republics focus on developing their own niche and opportunities.

The United States is South America's closest ally, *and* its greatest

threat. The southern republics fear northern indifference and interference. This tradition has swung from dependency to enmity to in-
souciance. The relationship must continue to be dynamic, complex,
and difficult, for each hemisphere's geopolitics points in different directions, that of the United States to the strategic, that of South
America to the regional and the subregional. South American unity,
when and if it arises, not only may stabilize the north-south linkage,
but also may shift South American geopolitics to a blending of the
regional and the strategic. Again, the future South America – United
States relationship bears watching in this regard. My hunch turns
more to a harmonic transition than discordant.

Geopolitically similar to the United States in their relations with
South America, the countries of Europe normally show much more
interest in North America, the Middle East, and even Africa, Middle
America, and South Asia, than in South America. At times, Europe
has played a balancer role between the Americas and within South
America, but this is infrequent recently. Likewise, the European balance of power has much less impact on South American affairs than
it does in North America, a reflection again of the regional nature of
South American geopolitics.

Africa, spatially close to South America, lacks economic attractiveness in comparison to Europe, the United States, and the Pacific
Rim. Only Brazil has taken an interest in the continent—in trade,
resources, and security matters—but this connection has atrophied
since the end of the cold war and the transition to economic bloc rivalries. Antarctica is also a potential resource but much too costly
to exploit at present. Andean geopolitical writers predict the future value of South America in Pacific Rim development, although
whether the republics would profit from this connection remains to
be seen. The Middle East and South and Southeast Asia are little no-
ticed in South America's foreign affairs.

Geopolitics and the Discovery of America

One of the epic events of history occurred with Christopher Columbus' journey in 1492 across the Atlantic to America. Subsequent
global affairs, including strategic geopolitical structures, were dramatically changed after that voyage. Several major transformations
can be traced to Columbus' vision and courage.

The discovery of America greatly increased the strategic or intercontinental dimension of geopolitics by showing spatial relationships that operated for the first time within a world system. Eurasia

and America became linked, events in one area affected happenings in the other. Soon, as Halford Mackinder proclaimed in a 1904 paper, this Earth system became closed and thus more interrelated, such that geopolitical theories (such as the heartland thesis and Modelski's one hundred-year cycles) could be proposed that covered all foreign affairs involvement.

America buffered maritime contact between western Europe and eastern Asia, which helped keep Eurasia separated. The United States eventually was strong enough to balance the political forces on the larger continent and insert itself as a counterweight to prevent imperial domination of Eurasia, and thus Earth. Diverse migrant peoples have created in America a great racial and cultural experiment (albeit with millions killed in the process of conquest and settlement) of living together in a "melting pot" unique in human history and perhaps vital to future global peace. Furthermore, the wealth of the New World allegedly caused western Europe to leap ahead of Eurasia in commerce, industry, and technology (Blaut 1992; Frank 1992) and establish European colonization and political domination that only in this century is being challenged and overcome.

The main thrust of this chapter is images and perceptions of hemispheric geopolitics rather than actual diplomacy and inter-American events. I have sought to register the viewpoints of leading theorists and policy practitioners with, when useful, my own descriptions added. Since in orientation U.S. geopolitics is more strategic and South American geopolitics more regional, U.S. views of South America take up two thirds of this chapter. Occasionally, the strategic opinions of my sources may seem biased and antiquated, as well they may be. Yet, they are part of my geopolitical explanation and, as such, deserve a place in this account.

North and South American geopolitics diverge markedly, in fact, so markedly that the two continents seem worlds apart. But this divergence provides good comparative insights into both systems. Where a strategic and British emphasis appears in the north, a regional and Germanic accent characterizes the south. Halford Mackinder inspires the Yankee; Friedrich Ratzel models for the Latin. Sea power and Eurasia predominate in the United States; organic frontiers and development prevail in South America. The United States, unchallenged in North and Middle America, has taken on an assortment of challenges in Asia and Europe, whereas the South Americans appear mired in a fragmented, multipolar, checkerboard configuration.

The United States projects its substantial power to Asia and Europe and attempts to maintain American security through Eurasian division. South America counts on the U.S. military shield because the republics are unable to extend their authority to the strategic level. Yankee geopolitical axes today pass westward and eastward, whereas the Latin axis stays internal to the hemisphere. Consequently, the two routes seldom cross, and a strategic or regional coordination of security policies between north and south based on a common geopolitics seems irrelevant at the present time.

Albeit difficult to locate, certain geopolitical similarities do occur. Although boundaries and territorial expansion (two prime qualities of South American geopolitics) now hold little importance in the north, the changing frontiers of Florida, Louisiana, Texas, and Oregon once were immensely relevant to U.S. security, and the potential for shatterbelts in all three American sectors helped formulate the Monroe Doctrine, a cornerstone of U.S. strategic calculations. Might South America's frontiers someday become as stable and development as successful as in these North American areas and the republics' foreign affairs hence turn more to the strategic?

In addition, both continents value American free-trade associations and fear economic exclusion from the Asian and European blocs. Above all, both north and south find themselves within Mackinder's peripheral "outer crescent," which binds the two Americas in a common position of continental defense, although the United States is much more dominant in this theater than its southern neighbors.

Will the global post–cold war transitions alter hemispheric geopolitics? In my opinion, probably not substantially for either South America or for the South America–United States relationship, because the cold war rivalry in large part only indirectly entered the Southern Hemisphere. In contrast, in Middle America, where the Monroe Doctrine is more relevant, more cold war reverberations were felt. Now, with less Yankee fear of Eurasia, the region may face uncharacteristic northern neglect, uninterest, and isolation in strategic matters. The United States could disregard all of its southern neighbors, both Middle and South American, as it faces internal problems in addition to meeting the new challenges of the emerging multipolar world.

Perhaps future economic prosperity in South America, successful industrialization, regional integration led by Brazil and Argentina, political stability, and democracy may come to exert a greater impact on hemispheric geopolitics than did the cold war's end. Such changes in the south could propel South America to a larger strategic role, in sync with a gradual strategic withdrawal by the United States. Ultimately, some new pattern of cooperation could emerge, with both continents adjusting to dawning regional and strategic realms that might encourage a more productive association among the northern, middle, and southern portions of America.

North American Geopolitical Views of South America

South America Is Seen as Peripheral

Eurasia, its immediate rimlands, and North America hold the world's most "nodal," or pivotal, locations, according to a majority of northern geopolitical observers. "What counts" in international affairs occurs in these areas. In contrast, South America, according to the Yankee, occupies a peripheral location, unimportant when compared to other territories. George Kennan reflects this northern ethnocentrism (Luers 1984: 6): "It seems unlikely that there could be any other region on the earth in which nature and human behavior could have combined to produce a more unhappy and hopeless background for the conduct of human life than in Latin America." Henry Kissinger's debate with the Chilean foreign minister supports this perspective (Hersh 1983: 263):

> "Mr. Minister, you make a strange speech. You come here talking of Latin America, but this is not important. Nothing has ever come from the South. The axis of history begins in Moscow, goes to Bonn, crosses over to Washington, and then goes on to Tokyo. What occurs in the southern world is not important. It is not worth the time."
>
> "I said," remembers Valdés, "Mr. Kissinger, you know nothing of Latin America." "No," Kissinger replied, "and I don't care."

Other commentators recognize an epicenter of civilization, originally in the Mediterranean, now shifted northwestward to the North Atlantic and Western Europe, the present cultural and political "centers" of the world. Again, Latin America is excluded (Spykman 1942; Semple 1903).

Lucile Carlson (Carlson and Philbrick 1958: 286) attributes Latin America's negligible importance to lack of land and natural resources and contends that "most of the southern hemisphere is only a desolation of water, and hence, cannot act as the home of man. Where [a majority of] men live, things become important." The isolation of South America has caused history, prosperity, and international politics to pass by the southern lands, leaving subservience, stagnation, and depression as a residue of the northern advantage.

A Conventional Defense Cannot Achieve American Safety

Hemispheric security rests on the ability of the United States to project its power onto Eurasian territory and to maintain in Asia and Europe a stable and favorable balance of power.

Because Washington saw Soviet expansion as its most dangerous postwar threat, strategists naturally stressed Eurasia, and not Latin America, in their immediate military calculations. Defense policy since 1947 has essentially aimed to project military force effectively onto Eurasia to prevent its absorption into the Soviet empire (Gray 1981; Atkeson 1976; Spykman 1942). Three particular regions hold contemporary American interest—Western Europe, the Persian Gulf, and East Asia—although additional Eurasian zones have emerged from time to time. Consequently, the security perimeter of the United States extends to Asia, Europe, and the Middle East, not to America, and a "fortress America" conception, a "quarter-sector sphere" enveloping the hemisphere, and other configurations in which Latin America becomes a military partner to the United States have never received support from Pentagon analysts (Child 1976).

George Kennan illustrates the strategic guidelines envisioned by North American planners (1951: 10):

> It [becomes] essential to us, as it was to Britain, that no single Continental land power should come to dominate the entire Eurasian landmass. Our interest has lain rather in the maintenance of some sort of stable balance among the powers of the interior, in order that none of them should effect the subjugation of the others, conquer the seafaring fringes of the landmass, become a great sea power as well as land power, shatter the position of England, and enter—as in these circumstances it certainly would—on an overseas expansion hostile to ourselves and supported by the immense resources of the interior of Europe and Asia.

Within this Eurasia nucleus, Latin America's contribution to North American defense, from the U.S. geopolitical perspective, rests only in these areas: (a) keeping Eurasian military footholds out of the hemisphere; (b) providing volunteer bases, matériel, and troops when necessary; and (c) assisting in protecting maritime routes that bring resources to America and that project North American power overseas (Ronfeldt 1983). But these roles receive scant notice from northern strategists, who instead watch over the core strategic regions beyond the New World.

Focusing on Latin America's peripheral status, and the southern liability to North America, Spykman provides this insight (1942: 457):

> There is no possibility of achieving an adequate integration of the states of the new World in the face of German opposition, and even if there were, the balance potential of the Americas would still be inadequate to balance the Old World. Because of the distribution of land masses and military potentials, a balance of power in the transatlantic and transpacific zones is an absolute prerequisite for the independence of the New World and the preservation of the power position on this side of the oceans. Hemisphere defense is no defense at all. The Second World War will be lost or won in Europe and Asia. The strategic picture demands that we conduct our military operations in the form of a great offensive across the oceans. If our allies in the Old World are defeated, we cannot hold South America; if we defeat the German-Japanese Alliance abroad, our good neighbors will need no protection.

Spykman predicted encirclement and eventual defeat of the United States if "the three land masses of the Old World can be brought under the control of a few states and so organized that large unbalanced forces are available for pressure across the ocean fronts" (1942: 448). In such an attack on the New World, Latin America would provide minimal assistance, and the United States could suffer eventual defeat by virtue of the vast resources of the encircling nations.

This geopolitical scenario significantly influenced the containment policies devised by Kennan and others, who proposed blocking such expansion by erecting "rimland dikes" around the Russian heartland. Distant South America is very peripheral to this design.

Latin America Does Not Threaten the United States

Writers describing U.S. geopolitics acknowledge the advantages of America's "splendid isolation" from Eurasian power struggles and of the absence of military threat from a weak and divided south. This isolation and safety from neighbors' attacks bring unique benefits to security, as Frederick Hartmann and Robert Wendzel note (1985: 22–23):

> The fact of *where* the American nation is physically located has had a profound and continuing effect, for the United States is the sole great power in the world without great power neighbors nearby. . . . This freedom from close neighbors possessing sufficiently significant military power to challenge the United States was not true in America's initial decades . . . , but it was an accomplished fact before the time of the Civil War. . . . For the rest of its history until recent times the American people gave little thought to dangers arising close to home. . . . But this kind of freedom, geopolitically induced by the absence of large military forces directly across American frontiers, is a very unusual experience. What other great powers could say the same (or think in the same fashion about its vulnerability)?

With its southern perimeter not in immediate danger, the United States can focus beyond America to Eurasia. This enables it to concentrate on maritime projection, on bolstering rimland allies and balancing distant enemies, on emphasizing trade and industry, and, in general, on picking the most effective interest to fulfill.

Political Vacuums in Latin America
Pose Potential Threats to the United States

Not unusual among nations, the United States has sought stability on its frontiers. This desire grew in reaction to a weakened Spanish Florida and French Louisiana, in which the English could have encircled the defenseless North Americans. Shatterbelt possibilities around the Great Lakes, in Texas, on the Pacific coast (Bemis 1943), and, more recently, within the entire Caribbean basin as well as in Korea, Vietnam, and the Persian Gulf have created greater alarm. Either absorb these lands oneself or align them against the Eurasian opponent seem to be the best solutions to the problem of frontier shatterbelts.

As described earlier, shatterbelts link local dissension to international rivalry and create the necessary conditions for conflict escalation and, possibly, warfare. Within this perspective, security threats arise not immediately from frontier power vacuums themselves but from possible military alliances that might cause Eurasian bases to form in these vacuums (Cohen 1973; Spykman 1942). Hence, contemporary revolution and depression in Middle and South America do not endanger U.S. security directly, but they could invite serious challenge if they attracted enemy involvement in the turmoil in these states.

Saul Cohen saw the possibility of a "counter encirclement" against the United States from a political and military Soviet presence in the Caribbean (1973: 139–140): "The actual military threat posed by a hostile country like Cuba is negligible, but the success of its revolutionary policies could tap widespread anti–United States sentiment." And this political opposition, "coupled with Russian bases in Middle America, is not entirely inconceivable." Advising against U.S. military intervention against these bases, Cohen instead recommended diplomatic strategies for strengthening a U.S. sphere of influence and for preventing Soviet participation in the region.

Although shatterbelts have not appeared in South America since those at the Amazon and Plata estuaries in the eighteenth and nineteenth centuries, leaders of the southern republics fear the escalation possibilities of a Caribbean shatterbelt, as occurred during the 1960s and 1980s, when it seemed the United States had become ensnared in a series of Middle American quagmires. Nonetheless, in its geopolitical isolation, South America remains peripheral to great-power conflict beyond its borders, and shatterbelts, even those close by, have exerted less impact on the continent's immediate foreign affairs.

Attempts to prevent or to fill these frontier vacuums and to exclude hostile foreign penetration reflect an important expression of U.S. policy toward Latin America. Examples of such geopolitical impact abound: the application of the geopolitical principles that led to the Louisiana purchase and subsequent territorial expansion; the no-transfer resolution of 1811; the Monroe Doctrine; the Rio Pact and the charter of the Organization of American States; the CIA's campaign against Salvador Allende in Chile; President Carter's blocking of uranium fuel sales to Brazil; the Cuban missile crisis of 1962; military assistance to the Nicaraguan Contras. Literally, all U.S. security actions toward its neighbors derive from this northern dread of frontier vulnerability.

Latin America Embodies a Natural U.S. Sphere of Influence

Since independence, the United States has claimed leadership over the Western Hemisphere. In this respect, Richard Walton (1972: 27) found "a widespread belief that the American flag should fly over most of the continent, including Canada to the north and large parts of Latin America to the south. Even that was not enough for the most romantic of American boosters. They believed that it was God's will that the Stars and Stripes flutter over the two continents from the Arctic to the Antarctic." Similarly, a *Chicago Tribune* editorial in 1922 (Aguilar 1968: 43) asserted: "We do not wish to anticipate the future, but everything leads us to surmise that sooner or later Mexico will bow to our sovereignty. If we cared to be prophetic, we would say that all nations to the south will feel our attraction by virtue of the law of political gravity. Penetration and absorption could be gradual or union might be borne out of a crisis. A country like Mexico cannot remain in a state of economic stagnation and political chaos." Samuel Flagg Bemis (1943) felt such U.S. confidence in the inevitable annexation of Cuba, Canada, and other adjacent territories probably stalled such aggrandizement and preserved their independence.

The Monroe Doctrine and its corollaries likewise assert this ideal of U.S. paramountcy, a good example being Secretary of State Richard Olney's 1895 declaration (Mecham 1965: 64): "Today the United States is practically sovereign on this continent, and its fiat is law upon the subjects to which it confines its interposition. . . . The safety and welfare of the United States are so concerned with the maintenance of the independence of every American state as against any European power as to justify and require the interposition of the United States whenever that independence is endangered."

So strong has been this U.S. feeling of leadership and superiority that Yankee leaders have at times exaggerated the Eurasian threat in America to institute escalatory and inconsistent policies that themselves have helped create more problems than solutions in hemispheric relations (Luers 1984).

The United States Sees Naval Power as Crucial to Protecting Vital South American Territories and Resources

Commentators find the Panama Canal still the most vital South American strategic location, although in recent decades, this prominence has waned in light of the canal's increasing obsolescence (Child 1980) and its control by the Republic of Panama. The several Caribbean maritime straits—Mona, Yucatán, Florida, Windward, and Abnegada—have been sources of concern over the years, particularly when Caribbean shatterbelts figured in hemispheric geopolitics. Likewise, the Galápagos Islands, the passages at the southern tip of South America, the Atlantic Narrows, the bulge of Brazil, the lesser Antilles, Jamaica, Guantánamo Bay, Key West, the Virgin Islands, Nicaragua, and Mexico have been of particular concern for their pivotal importance (Komorowski 1973; Eliot 1938; Dupuy and Eliot 1937; Lea 1909; Mahan 1897).

Latin America as a resources and labor reserve for U.S. defense purposes draws additional attention. For instance, Raymond Komorowski (1973) lists various critical minerals, military labor and facilities, and emerging industrial systems, all of which could broaden the defense of the United States in time of war. From an air power perspective, Alexander de Seversky (1942) posits the growth of U.S. influence through dominance of global air space, with Latin America becoming integrated within this framework as a supply source for strategic materials.

For protecting important straits and maritime lines of communication, assuring imports of strategic minerals and energy products, controlling hemispheric political stability, and defending against possible Eurasian challenge, naval power is important in the North American geopolitical literature relative to Latin America. The *U.S. Naval Institute Proceedings*, one of the best sources for analysis of U.S. strategic interests in the region, has published a variety of insightful articles on this geopolitical topic (Valenta 1982; Scheena 1978; Komorowski 1973).

Latin America Is a Primary Market and Source of Primary Materials for U.S. Industry

U.S. leaders have traditionally resisted intrusions of Asian and European businesses into Latin America for reasons of security and commerce. Congress endorsed the "Lodge corollary" to the Monroe Doctrine, for example, in reaction to a Japanese firm's attempt to lease property near Mexico's Magdalena Bay. "Dollar diplomacy" and "gunboat diplomacy" further illustrate this demand for market exclusiveness. During the oil scarcity crises of the 1980s, Mexican and Venezuelan oil reserves assumed special value as available replacements for Middle Eastern sources.

Common assertions of northern economic hegemony over the southern republics carry the message that Latin America should consider itself a restricted business and trade zone for the United States. The Alliance for Progress, the Caribbean Basin Initiative, and the North American Free Trade Agreement give this objective an official structure.

Brooks Adams, in a turn-of-the-century article (1903), predicted serious rivalry among European nations and the United States for leadership of a globally integrated, self-supporting economic empire, one containing a "base," or raw materials source, a "central market," or industrial center, and a "terminus" market of consumers. Whichever industrial power center dominated this system would control global political affairs as well, he, like Mackinder, maintained. To Adams, abundant and cheap minerals and labor in China offered the most promising base for the system, Latin America, the best market. Both of these tied to U.S. industrial might would balance America against Europe and eventually bring the former world hegemony.

This particular scheme appears in much of the traditional U.S. thinking about Latin America. The southern continent is viewed as serving this country as a reliable pan-regional source of natural resources, a market and investment outlet, and a provider of labor to the exclusion of Eurasia and to the benefit of U.S. prosperity and power.

Latin America Offers a Primary Area for U.S. Expansion

Homer Lea (1909: 30) enlisted the Monroe Doctrine to explain a desirable organic thrust of U.S. frontiers: "It was recognition of U.S. national spirit and vigor that led Monroe to enunciate his doctrine providing for the inviolability of the Western Continents. By removing them from the sphere of European expansion, he hoped to prevent the widening boundaries of these militant powers from coming into contact with the natural growth of the Republic. No doctrine proclaimed by a statesman of this nation or of the Old World ever portrayed truer insight into the nature of national life." Elsewhere (p. 103) he asserted United States hegemony over Hispanic America as a right of a "virile" nation in need of "virgin and unexploited territories": "The territorial dominions of the United States are not only those possessions governed by its laws, but that vast region of Mexico, the West Indies, Central and South America, which as far as being causative of war, are as much under the political sovereignty of the United States as are the states of the Union."

Admiral Alfred Thayer Mahan argued in favor of expansion in a similar vein. He compared the United States of 1900 as being like the ancient Roman Empire in terms of historical growth, bent as it was on aggrandizement and greatness: "If we do not advance we recede." The United States, he pleaded, could not gain world eminence without first dominating the Caribbean basin and adjoining strategic positions in Middle America and beyond (1897: 33–36, 102–104). Such perspectives seem to have remained in the geopolitical vocabulary of North Americans.

Geography and Race Have "Conspired against Latin America"

Tropical environments create human weakness and corruption, according to many early twentieth-century U.S. perceptions of the south (Eliot 1938; Lea 1909; Mahan 1897). I remember a panel discussion with the Brazilianist Jordan Young, who recalled the seventeenth-century case of two ships carrying Puritan settlers to America. Driven off course from their Massachusetts destination by Atlantic storms, one ship eventually landed in temperate southern Brazil, the other on a small tropical island in the Caribbean. The Brazilian Puritans developed into prosperous farmers and industrialists, whereas the Caribbean Puritans eventually became vicious pirates, later destroyed by Spanish authorities for menacing life and property in the region. Whether truth or fiction, to me his account underlines a North American stereotype of the ill-effects of the tropics on human behavior and performance.

The rugged terrain of Latin America, allege several geopolitical writers from the United States, hampers transportation, retards a coordinated industrial infrastructure, and restricts commercial agriculture and minerals exploitation. It scatters and isolates natural resources vital to modernization and prevents integration of the hinterland. Difficult terrain, in the political view, allegedly assists the staying power of feudalism, prevents democracy, gives sanctuary to revolutionaries, and hinders national and regional unity (Carlson and Philbrick 1958: 285; Walton 1972: 7–11).

A majority of the earlier geopolitical writings on Latin America clearly do not set Latin races and civilizations on an equal par with those in the United States. Bemis (1943: 9) exemplifies a common theme of this perspective when he writes: "Racial mixture has been . . . a volatile element in the amalgam of inter-American solidarity." He implies that miscegenation among Indian, African, and Hispanic peoples is responsible in part for the region's lack of unity. He argued that "favorable climate is a necessary basis of modern civilization," and that tropical lowlands "present a barrier to white civilization" and help explain the instability and backwardness of the Ibero-American republics (Bemis 1943: 7).

Mahan and Spykman offer two other examples of this racial aspect. Mahan (1897: 33–38), describing in Manifest Destiny terms "our natural, necessary, irrepressible expansion" in territory to the Pacific, saw U.S. growth "arrested on the south by the rights of a race wholly alien to us." Apparently, they viewed the presence of such races as restricting the advancement of Anglo-Saxon penetration into lands already inhabited by lesser peoples.

Spykman (1942: 46, 218–230, 253–256) could not entrust hemispheric defense to the Latin Americans. In the following passage he notes the prominent differences between the two spheres:

> It is perhaps unfortunate that the English and Latin speaking parts of the continent should both be called America, thereby unconsciously evoking an expectation of similarity which does not exist. Only if it is realized that the countries to the south are different from the United States in essential geographic features, in racial and ethnic compositions, in economic life, and in social customs, ideology, and cultural traditions can we evaluate the significance of this area for our national life and estimate correctly the likelihood of an effective cooperation in a common policy of hemisphere defense.

Because of such variance, Spykman doubted that cooperative ties could stand on just "sentiment" and "friendly feelings." Instead, he believed hemispheric alliances must conform to power politics, "in terms of geography and balance of power." He even advocated North American occupation of parts of Latin America during security crises when mutual assistance compacts would not be in force.

Latin American Residents of the United States Represent a Valuable Asset in the Inter-American Relationship

At present, sixteen million Hispanic Americans live in the mainland United States, more than 6 percent of the population. Their numbers have nearly doubled since 1970. Although Chicanos, or Mexican Americans, constitute 60 percent of this figure, residing chiefly in the border states of Aztlán, or the Aztec homeland, most South

American states have contributed to this total. This demographic reality, neglected by policymakers until recently (Villarreal and Kelly 1982; García and de la Garza 1976), identifies these peoples as distinctive to North America and marks them as cultural and diplomatic bridges for creating hemispheric ties to the southern republics.

The United States and Latin America Share a Heritage, Interest, and Destiny

Visualizing an American system in which unifying factors dominate cleavages in the United States–Latin America relationship, Russell Fitzgibbon recommended a "Union of the Americas," a potential "de facto confederation," somewhat on the British Commonwealth design (1942: 60, 65–67, 73). He reasoned that all American states suffered "external political pressure" from Europe, all shared "a relatively self-sufficient economic area," all felt "a sometimes cynical and usually sophisticated European Weltpolitik" or foreign interference, and all possessed "a sense of youth and vigor (some might call it naïveté and brashness), a feeling that the hemisphere's destiny is yet to be unfolded, the American spirit is formed in part of an attachment to idealism—social, political, even spiritual." Fitzgibbon's emphasis clearly focused on a positive, beneficial North and South American relationship, devoid of hegemony, exclusion, and superiority.

Another rendition of American unity, drawn by Arthur Whittaker (1954: 1–21, 30, 22), traced a "Western Hemisphere idea" to Enlightenment origins, to an "anti-American" bias that alleged Europe's superiority over America, and to later commercial and political revolutions. From these an "American system" had emerged, based on the assumption that, "because of certain definable geographical, political, and other factors, Europe and America constituted separate, distinct, and mutually antagonistic spheres, and each of these spheres possessed an inner unity denoted by the word 'system.' Hence, the peoples of this Hemisphere stand in a special relationship to one another which sets them apart from the rest of the world."

Despite gradual acceptance of the Western Hemisphere idea by the U.S. foreign affairs establishment during the interwar period, Whittaker claimed northern neglect of the inter-American relationship during the cold war and its subsequent overt and covert interventions destroyed what potentially could have become a hemispheric confederation. Instead, the larger sphere fragmented and new antagonisms within the relationship arose.

Still contained in this area of geopolitical literature is a unifying objective, from the standpoints of geographic isolation from Eurasia, resistance to unwanted European intrusions, sharing a common environment and New World destiny, and a potential for integration and economic cooperation, all references to a persistent dream for hemispheric friendship and accommodation.

South American Geopolitical Views of the United States

South America Cannot Challenge the Power, Position, and Status of Its Northern Neighbor

One does not see in the South American geopolitical literature any southern wish to challenge North America for hemispheric political and economic leadership. Rather, South American geopoliticians seem to acknowledge the greater power of the north, derived from its superior resources and from its more pivotal world location. Gen. Julio Londoño of Colombia, for instance, claimed that geography has caused this divergence (1977: 12–14; 195?: 57–73; 1948: 6–45). The United States, he declared, possesses a more strategic location and higher energy, minerals, and agricultural productivity, its river and lake systems link population centers, and its seacoasts make it a more likely sea power, the latter quality a prime requisite for world power. Lamenting South America's isolation, poor harbors, paucity of fertile farmlands, and lack of internal river systems, he asserted: "We are a distant continent . . . [we have] no history." Brazilian authors, often bent on conferring great-power status on Brazil, have also never declared a rivalry or superiority to the Yankee in geopolitical terms.

Most of the South Americans seem satisfied to reside distant from northern contentions and strategic responsibilities. They find security in distance and isolation, although they admire the resources and developmental successes of Europe and the United States. Nuclear weapons, for example, so much a part of U.S. foreign affairs, receive very little mention in the southern literature. The United States appears less threatening to the republics than immediate South American neighbors (Brazil the usual antagonist), and the strategic doctrines of Mahan, Spykman, and Cohen are positively received, notwithstanding the fact that they do not calibrate well with the national geopolitical arguments of South America.

South American Geopolitics Usually Favored the United States in the Cold War

As with other strategic geopolitical areas, the Soviet Union – United States rivalry largely bypassed South America. Southern geopolitics looked inward to local sources and issues, primarily frontier disputes, checkerboard rivalries, and regional integration. Not surprisingly, Brazilian, Argentinean, and Chilean geopolitics receive most strategic interest, largely because of their locations near strategic waterways, the Atlantic Narrows and the southern passages, their foreign policy traditions of Southern Cone leadership, and the antisocialist orientations of their armed services. In this last regard, South America's armed forces, so prominent in the continent's geopolitics, normally exhibit conservative, anti-Communist, and pro-U.S. values, since they have been closely tied to their U.S. counterparts and have been socialized into the traditional ethos of the military corporation.

General Carlos de Meira Mattos of Brazil, for instance, commanded the Latin American contingent of the U.S.-led inter-American peace forces sent to Santo Domingo in 1964, allegedly to quell pro-Castro radicalism, and he served as vice-director of the Inter-American Defense College in Washington, D.C. (Kelly 1984: 444 – 445). Meira Mattos, Therezinha de Castro, and Golbery do Couto e Silva all link Brazil to the United States, contending that only Brazil among the South American republics possesses the power and the position to assist the United States in setting up containment policies, especially in securing the South Atlantic sea lanes and in stabilizing Southern Cone politics. Norberto Ceresole declares that (1988: 56) "Argentine geopolitical thinking has traditionally . . . viewed the South Atlantic as a maritime containment barrier against Soviet 'expansionism' coming out of the Indian Ocean basin, West Africa, and the Southern Pacific Ocean (Indochina Peninsula). All that Argentine civilian and military 'strategists' asked for (and continue to ask for) was a political arrangement with Great Britain for the recovery of formal sovereignty of the Malvinas Islands."

Several authors saw advantages to South America in the United States – Soviet Union competition. Londoño suggested that the continent's distance from northern power rivalries allowed for a better chance of South American unification and development as well as greater security from nuclear war (1977: 22–28, 169–171; 195?-: 10–27, 123–131).

Likewise, the continent's peripheral position seemed better situated than most northern areas for involvement in a future prosperity of the "Pacific Era." Southern Cone authors in particular visualized wealth for continental development coming from the adjacent southern oceans and from the Antarctic, areas very peripheral to northern great-power interests.

Within the perspective of forcing the return of the Malvinas Islands to Argentina, Ceresole (1988: 57–59) urges a national policy of nonalignment in the East-West conflict:

> Under present conditions, given the military hegemony which Western powers exercise over the [South Atlantic] region, any fracture which is introduced and which would be a discontinuity in the exercise of power by the capitalist maritime world, is not only beneficial for our national interests, but is also a basic condition for our own power that can mean, at some point, the sovereign use of that strategic space . . . the elements of fracture and discontinuity the Soviet naval presence in the region might introduce, will be, in all cases, objectively favorable to Argentine national interests, regardless of the ideological perception one might hold of them.

Examples abound of this desire to take advantage of distance and peripheral position and to balance the Soviet Union against the United States for South America's gain, a theme the Monroe Doctrine purported to avoid but which recent geographic realities have made available to the South Americans.

On the other side of the geopolitical coin came fear of a great-power condominium, with a Soviet and U.S. spheres of influence or pan-regional conspiracy that could "freeze" the global economic and political power structure to the impairment of the southern states. João Augusto de Arujo Castro (1971) and Gen. Juan Domingo Perón (1971: 11) claimed that such a contract in fact had taken place. To counter this possibility, Latin American states worked to avoid northern exclusiveness at the San Francisco United Nations conference in 1945 by insisting on the establishment of the Economic and Social Council. Later, in the various "Group of 77" conferences, they continued to suspect this condominium.

South American Geopolitical Writers Fear U.S. Political Interference and Possible Armed Intervention

Many examples exist of northern interference in South America. Since 1945, closely contested elections in which "leftist" parties compete attract U.S. money and intrigue. A good case in point is the one billion dollars allegedly paid to various Chilean groups by the Central Intelligence Agency for taking votes from the socialist candidate, Salvador Allende. The United States has encouraged the rise of military regimes in places with unstable constitutional governments, as, for instance Chile, Brazil, Bolivia, and Argentina. Throughout South America, the United States now presses for democracy, development, and integration, and against arms races, nuclear weapons, narcotics trafficking, and excessive debt accumulation.

The number of such northern interferences in South America does not appear aberrant, for the larger imperial and strategic nations such as the United States seem naturally bent on intercession as an important part of their foreign policy. Indeed, even if we possessed a complete inventory of U.S. military and covert activity, we would probably discover that the southern countries may seem much less pertinent to United States concerns than those in Europe, the Middle East, and the Asian rimland. Except for limited detachments of troops in Panama and in Cuba's Guantánamo Bay, and small intelligence-gathering facilities on certain Caribbean islands, the United States expends a minimal military effort in Latin America as a whole, and almost none in South America.

Never has the United States forcibly inserted combat troops into the local affairs of any of the southern continent's republics. Obviously, South America differs from the Caribbean basin in this respect, for U.S. armed intervention in Middle America has persisted throughout much of the twentieth century. Why this propensity for northern intercession in the Caribbean and not in South America?

Seven Middle American countries have suffered U.S. armed intrusions: Cuba (1898, 1904–1925, 1962); Haiti (1904–1934, 1994–); Mexico (1846–1848, 1915–1917); Panama (1904, 1990); Grenada (1983); Nicaragua (1904–1933, 1980s); and the Dominican Republic (1910–1928). All of these interventions seem associated with political instability that the United States considered insupportable so near its southern frontier. With the exception of Mexico, all to some degree touched on trans-Isthmian routes through the Caribbean, particularly the Panama Canal. Here, the strategic rationale for intervention—the "soft underbelly" vulnerability of the United States, which conceivably lies exposed to interference from Eurasian opponents—invited northern concern. Accordingly, for the Caribbean basin South American states, including Guyana, Suriname, and Venezuela, but not for the Southern Cone, U.S. intrusion seems plausible, but in a very removed sense. When we distance from Middle America, these strategic rationales for intervention disappear. U.S. military intercession far from Middle America appears very unlikely, for strategic value in South America simply does not exist at present.

South America remains largely detached from U.S. frontiers and from Caribbean passages, and normally its republics possess more power, territory, and stability than do most of the countries of Middle America. No transit areas vital to U.S. strategic interests pass through the middle or southern portions of the continent. Furthermore, Brazil has taken a leadership role among the South American nations, strengthening the autonomy of the South American states. Mounting diplomatic unity, which may lead to greater integration, further diminishes U.S. influence in South America. Hence, unwanted outside intervention has largely bypassed the southern continent.

In resisting the potential for U.S. interference, South Americans have enlisted a variety of tactics. A common front against the Yankee is a favorite response to alleged "divide and rule" and "Balkanization" maneuvering, which, at times opens the way to intervention (Ferrer 1967). Recent momentum toward regional cooperation, in addition to the Brazil-Argentina rapprochement and Brazil's withdrawal from U.S. sponsorship, has increased enfranchisement. Another tactic, gaining trade and investment access to the North American Free Trade area, may reduce South America's isolation, improve its bargaining position with the United States (as well as with Japan and the European Community), and heighten its prosperity and development. All these factors should expand the continent's independence.

Finally, Latin America has sought protection from international law and international organizations. These sources favor nonintervention and peaceful settlement of disputes and oppose unilateral intercession (Bailey 1965). One would expect that tack to continue. However, the greatest security seems to rest in South America's peripheral location and paucity of resources coveted by North America, plus the continent's growing potential for unity, prosperity, and stability.

The United States Is Perceived as Purposefully Fomenting Division in South America

An environment for fragmentation certainly characterizes the region, whether or not encouraged by outside forces. Four or five dissimilar regions, each with contrasting terrains and climates, diverse cultures and local political structures, and different national identities and regional demeanor, clearly define the continent's landscape. Vast distances, jungles, and uplands maintain sectional distinctiveness and impose great barriers to continental unity. A general commitment to confederation lingers, seen in repeated calls for this objective and evidence that continental cooperation could bring reward. Perhaps the republics of South America never will tightly merge policies and resources, for the obstacles in the south appear to be extreme when compared with those faced by the United States.

Proof exists of occasional U.S. "divide and conquer" strategies toward South America, similar to those formerly perpetrated on the republics by imperial Spain and England. South America's multipolar foreign affairs structure facilitates this strategy. The "special relationship," or *"barganha leal,"* between Brazil and the United States offers a good example of this strategy, as the United States raised Brazil to a higher diplomatic status and drew it away from Spanish America until recently. In addition, the Nixon administration's key-nation strategy sought to make Brazil a regional enforcer of cold war stability (Mutto 1971: 21–22). Maintaining equal arms levels in the Southern Cone states and protecting the buffers of Uruguay and Ecuador are additional examples of this strategy.

Nevertheless, there is also evidence of U.S. endorsement of South American harmony. U.S. sponsorship of the Pan American movement, of inter-American highway systems, and of regional economic cooperation attest to this strategy. Although perhaps not attuned to all of the consequences of its ambitions, the United States may be more comfortable dealing with one stable, coherent, and friendly South America than with twelve diverse states with varying levels of prosperity and steadiness and inhabiting a very fragmented and shatterbelt-prone continent. Of course, a united but hostile South America could be dangerous to U.S. interests, but advantages also certainly accrue in unity.

Both U.S. policy directions—the divide and conquer and the unifying—seem plausible and potentially fruitful, for both, under differing circumstances, could achieve northern security and trade goals. The fragmenting environment, although probably the more dangerous for the United States, does allow a higher degree of manipulation, although it also introduces a shatterbelt possibility. The harmonious milieu impedes Eurasian alliance but lessens northern control. In either case, the outcome seems of minimal risk to the United States. Again, in a strategic sense, South America matters very little. The most important local security concern emerges in Middle America, and not farther to the south, where the expending of U.S. resources on the world periphery would not render large profits.

Finally, the South American checkerboard structure expedites, if not guarantees, a potential for outside intervention. As long as twelve separate nations inhabit the continent in opposition and without regional coordination, a shatterbelt or sphere-of-influence configuration could dominate South American foreign affairs. At present, independence arises from isolation and minimal strategic resources, but this could change. Long-term security, instead, seems tied to continental solidarity, which the republics appear bent on maintaining.

South America Depends on the United States Economically

The traditional path to development for most South American nations followed one of two approaches. The first, mercantilism, bound the republics to producing unprocessed goods and purchasing manufactured items from outside capitalists. The second, economic nationalism, sought to exclude the disadvantages of trade and instead to protect and promote certain indigenous industries. Although both are still present in Latin America, a third technique, regional trade and development cooperation, possibly tied to access to the North American market, appears to be most favored at present.

Balance and strength seem good ways of avoiding economic vulnerability to outsiders and the waste and distortions of protectionism. Accessing northern markets, with potential rewards lying in greater South American prosperity and independence, has gained support in the major republics. But serious obstacles lie in the path of increased market access.

1. Latin America does not offer the United States a good consumer market, nor do the two economic systems seem compatible in terms of trade and level of development. Significant profits from hemispheric commerce seem distant and unlikely.

2. Perhaps with North American free trade now officially structured, the United States may align its economic priorities only with Mexico. Going farther south with free trade could jeopardize contact with Japan and the European Community, two vastly more important markets than Latin America.

3. With the exception of oil, Latin America lacks the strategic materials desired by the United States. Australia and southern Africa, as well as North America itself, satisfy most of the United States' minerals requisites.

4. With neither a strategic position nor ample power, South America cannot assist the United States in stabilizing the balance of power in Eurasia. Hence, trading cooperation in security matters for economic concessions from the United States becomes difficult because the United States can ignore its southern neighbors without jeopardizing its security and prosperity.

Yet, South America appears at present ready to avoid economic isolation and stagnation. Most governments now endorse free-market capitalism as a strategy for national and regional development and security. Fear of continued attachment to peripheral status leads them to look for ways to avoid separation from northern financial sources. The republics now favor regional integration and a cooperative continental approach to development. In sum, they seem prepared for trade association with the United States, but whether it will reciprocate this interest remains uncertain.

Accordingly, several strategies seem available to South Americans. Autarky or near self-sufficiency, even if attainable, probably would plummet the region into economic depression and solitude, although, of course, it would make the continent independent, albeit at high cost. This does not appear to be a popular choice at the present moment. Diversification, or South America's search for economic sources beyond North America, has not yielded significant dividends because Asians and Europeans, like people in the United States, have found greater profits elsewhere. Regional confederation merits attention because it unifies markets and communications within policy coordination. Yet, there have been few successes here either, for economic coordination requires a higher level of industrial and technological sophistication than South America now has. Recent suggestions for direct admittance into the North American economy could prove a promising alternative, considering the protectionism and competition of the European and Japanese economies and the interest in hemispheric free trade, although, once again, U.S. interests may lie elsewhere.

The perception of development as tied to national security traditionally has represented a cornerstone of South American geopolitics. Without development, defense falters. Generals Pinochet, Londoño, Guglialmelli, Meira Mattos, Golbery do Couto e Silva, and others have linked national security issues (internal as well as external) to development and national cohesion and demanded for the armed services a prominent role in these endeavors. Development means power, they argue, and power resolves rebellion, internal disunity, access to energy resources, occupation of virgin territories, subservience to outside investors, and frontier defense. But with momentum toward regional integration, amidst the Brazil-Argentina rapprochement and the declining influence of the armed forces in foreign affairs, this thesis is no longer as prominent as it once was.

New Regional and International Opportunities Await South America in the Evolving Postwar Multipolar World

The security preoccupations of the cold war period appear less relevant now, particularly in the case of the American states. For possibly the first time, the United States may find itself designing a completely new political and economic relationship with its southern neighbors, as the nonmilitary questions no longer pertain as directly to hemispheric defense.

A multipolar world, with the poles in Japan, China, Russia, Germany/Europe, and the United States, likely will not turn on exclusive regionalism (for instance, northern-dominated pan-regions or spheres-of-influence condominiums). Flexible and friendly, but rather stiff, competition may well exist, with South America an "open market" for leading countries' trade and investment. Consequently, the southern continent could expect fairly strict noninterference from North America in its domestic affairs and, a "new era of good feelings" (Hakim 1992: 49) that will not only strengthen South American independence but will also advance its bargaining position with the north.

South America may take on equal importance in the Caribbean in U.S. eyes. A prominent North American writer about interhemispheric relations (Smith 1991: 88) shows the possibility of this dynamic: "Thus the geopolitical concerns that once riveted United States attention to the Caribbean basin have largely disappeared. While the area will remain important to the United States because of its proximity, the focus of American attention [in Latin America] is likely to shift to South America and to new problems." Drugs, debt, and environmental concerns, Wayne Smith maintains, have moved the southern continent higher on the North American priority list.

A majority of new inter-American issues will turn on economic and social matters now that the importance of security has diminished. This direction, particularly if bolstered by open international competition, can improve the bargaining advantage of the South Americans, who possess a strong potential for growth and development.

Global multilateralism could work to the advantage of Brazil because it is the best positioned among the South American states to compete internationally and within the continent, and its development rate seems the most substantial. Brazil could represent the regional future, a conduit of trade, technology, and investment. Furthermore, with its central location and control of the Amazonian transport core, it serves as integrationist leader for the continent, as the other republics apparently accept its role.

The U.S.–South American Geopolitical Connection: A Final Comment

The United States and South America share a hemisphere distant from the power struggles of Eurasia. Their cultural and political traditions parallel in many ways, as settlers of both continents arrived in a new world as immigrants who created civilizations that rejected those of their ancestors, erected new systems of government and foreign affairs, and feared European invasion and discrimination. In such a climate, the two continents have evolved, not as antagonists but as distant partners.

But their contrasting geopolitical bases have prevented substantial security cooperation and economic union. The wealth, more central position, and strategic orientation of the United States point it to Eurasia, not to South America, as its foreign policy priority. The inward-directed geopolitical orientations of the South American republics reflect their peripheral position and absence of great unity and wealth.

In large measure, these inter-American geopolitical linkages continue, but with a steady trend toward a more stable and cordial association under new circumstances. For instance, if the South Americans could prosper economically, govern themselves more democratically, and build a successful structure for integration and confederation, the United States might look south more often in its global designs. If Eurasia became peaceful and, as a result, the United States' focus on that area became less intense, Latin America could deepen its economic and political connection with North America. But to my mind, South America never will be of great interest to the northerners, and the relationship will largely continue its present course.

I n this last chapter, I first briefly summarize geopolitics in South America, and then forecast the
direction of South American geopolitical thinking from the national, continental, and international perspectives.

Summary

Checkerboards and shatterbelts have formed the basic structure of
South American geopolitics since colonial times, the former internally in the continent's multipolar balance-of-power configuration,
the latter externally in its original separating of the Spanish and Portuguese empires in America and its later isolating of South America
from the Middle American shatterbelt and beyond. The predominant checkerboard kept the continent's geopolitics largely focused
inwardly on frontiers, resources and development, and the prevention of two-front wars and an escalation of conflict. There are no
longer any shatterbelts in South America, but they have left South
America divided, isolated, and dependent on foreign resources and
technology.

Fortunately, South American diplomacy may be moving away
from checkerboards and toward accommodation more than mandala rivalry. Brazil's recent shift toward rapprochement with Argentina and its promotion of an Amazonian consensus may bring a
better chance of continental integration and eventual confederation
of some type. The end of the cold war and the successful passage of
the North American Free Trade Agreement might also stimulate the
growth of a new American regionalism.

But South America, traditionally isolated in southern oceans, not
well connected to the northern and middle sectors of America, and
distant from major northern trade routes and great-power interests,
still inhabits the periphery. The continent is not particularly unified

politically or economically, nor does it contain especially sought-after strategic positions or resources. Accordingly, South America lacks a single cohesive geopolitics, and its subregional and national geopolitics, which are internally consistent and may be studied and applied, are much more local than global in thrust. Its world impact is further restricted by the tremendous authority of the United States, its northern neighbor, benefactor, rival, and threat. Hence, the placement of the continent encourages the foreign policies of South American nations to focus on border issues, national resources and development, checkerboard or positional balancing, and sometimes even survival as a country.

Forecast of National Geopolitics

Most trends in national geopolitics will persist into the coming century. I believe the near future portends evolutionary change in public policy that will gradually move it from border security to cross-border integration.

Growing emphasis on internal development and integration, with more civilians than military in the process of planning and implementation, will reflect gradual expansion in communications and transportation and in industry and technology.

Yet, neglect of isolated hinterlands and the continental core will continue, for the most part because of the expense of accessing such lands and popular preference for coastal and currently productive regions. Development in the Andean republics likewise will normally lag behind that of the Southern Cone nations.

There will be less focus on frontier protection. Border tensions should ease. Communications and industrial growth likely will enhance regional peace and integration more than they will encourage cross-national friction, since economic cooperation will become more vital to national interests than borders will be.

Most boundary disputes will be settled by negotiation, although rivalries over national ownership of marginal seas could persist. Nuclear weapons and conventional arms races should not become major issues in domestic politics, since the cold war has ended and the South Americans seem strongly supportive of the antiproliferation regimes.

Greater governmental response to the marginal seas will reflect new fishing and mining technologies as well as pooled resources resulting from regional integration.

Particularly in the Andean hinterlands and in the larger cities, terrorism, rebellion, and irredentism may linger, although better national integration and successful economies and democratic governments may partly stem this social disintegration. With less isolation and heightened trade interchange, the buffer states of Bolivia, Ecuador, Guyana, and Paraguay should gain stronger democratic systems as a result.

Barring domestic turmoil, a factor not easily predicted, I do not foresee Brazil's territory expanding, its overt interference in the affairs of smaller neighbors, or renewed antagonism toward Argentina. This transition began two decades ago and translates into eased border tensions, greater success in continental integration, diminished chances for checkerboard and shatterbelt conflict, and moving South America from the world periphery.

Despite growing international demands for protection, the neglect of ecological matters, including destruction of Amazon rain forests and pollution of air and waters near mining, transport, and industrial areas, will continue.

The respect for geopolitics as an important facet of national policy making will persist, and civilians will become more involved in the expansion of geopolitical theory and application. I doubt that the new geopolitical theories described in the British journal *Political Geography* and like sources will receive much acceptance among South American academicians, who will likely continue to follow traditional geopolitical thinking.

Continental Geopolitics

The present checkerboard structure of multipolar regional diplomacy will shift to a more integrated structure. Regional cooperative aspirations and diminished competitiveness between the checkerboard alignments should grow, which represents a substantially different picture of South American geopolitics from that of thirty years ago.

There should be a shift from the prior emphasis on borderlands security toward national integration connected to regional integration. I do not envision major escalation of South American tensions or frontier warfare; the possibility of shatterbelts and of outside military intervention is minimal.

The enlargement of continental economic integration and increased interaction with the North American market may occur along two dimensions: the gradual strengthening of MERCOSUR in the Southern Cone, and the connecting of North and South American trade and investment, with perhaps Chile leading the way in cementing ties between the two blocs. Both of these developments could prompt an emergence of some type of loose South American confederation.

The conflicts over the Malvinas / Falklands and Bolivia's quest for an ocean outlet will likely be resolved; resolution is far from likely for disputes over Antarctica, the Marañón, and the Essequibo. However, the latter disputes will not lead to lengthy armed strife or regional-international conflict escalation because the regions remain relatively isolated and the technology and capital for developing them is not available in South America.

International air, road, and canal linkages will gradually expand, particularly in the Southern Cone and adjacent to the coasts. For instance, superhighways could connect the capital cities of Peru, Chile, Brazil, Argentina, and Venezuela, and paved roads will soon allow access to the continental core. Improved transportation will enhance integration, improve access to markets and resources, and bolster harmonious regional relations, although the environment will suffer.

Isolation among South American subregions will lessen, with Brazil acting as primary bloc connector. Improved transport networks, common access to North American free trade, regional peace and integration, and growing political and economic maturity also should lessen isolation.

As a theoretical paradigm of continental geopolitics, a spectrum of checkerboard-regionalism outcomes can be drawn (table 8) that portrays a linkage between national and regional alignments or structures and the type of environment or pattern one might expect from certain of these structures, for example between regional strife and interstate harmony. If checkerboard configurations emerge to the exclusion of regionalism, tension and even warfare might follow, with unstable frontiers, the possibility of shatterbelts, and the absence of substantial integration. Were regionalism to dominate, confederation could become a distinct prospect, with calmer boundaries, less subservience to extracontinental pressures, and heightened economic collaboration among nations and regional blocs.

Between the two extremes of war and confederation, the current South American geopolitical position shows a transition from checkerboard tension to regional accommodation, originating in

Table 8. Checkerboard-Regionalism Outcomes Spectrum

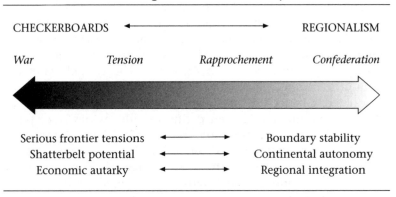

CHECKERBOARDS			REGIONALISM
War	*Tension*	*Rapprochement*	*Confederation*

Serious frontier tensions	⟷	Boundary stability
Shatterbelt potential	⟷	Continental autonomy
Economic autarky	⟷	Regional integration

part from the Brazil-Argentina decision in the 1970s to drop their earlier antagonism in favor of cooperative development of their respective resources. The present direction indeed appears to be toward increasing continental rapport, a good chance for peace and further regional integration.

International Geopolitics

For the next several decades, South America will remain peripheral to the global power centers and marginal to Japanese, European, and U.S. interests. Its relationship to the United States will continue as its most important contact with other continents and great-power matters.

Nonetheless, a unified voice is emerging in continental affairs and confidence in its political and economic destiny is growing. This, of course, will have the greatest impact on ties with the United States, and the least on communications with nations of the former Soviet bloc. This new unity could someday congeal into a loose confederal union.

The current global balance-of-power structure moving from cold war bipolar or "bipolycentric" to immediate post–cold war unipolar, with the United States as sole superpower, could easily shift in several decades to a multipolar structure wherein the United States is joined by Japan and Germany as primary great powers (Layne 1993). This transformation could increase the political and economic bargaining power of the South Americans by giving them more sources to balance or to align with and by giving them an opportunity to loosen ties to North America.

Ambivalence toward the Yankee will continue. Entry into the North American common market may diminish distrust, but suspicion and resentment will persist because of differing economic, cultural, political, and strategic perspectives. The United States will continue to be uncertain about which blend of strategic axes should be adopted. Greater Pan American compatibility will probably appear in economic, rather than political, undertakings since post–cold war competition seems more technological than military.

South American impact on global affairs will increase if the following circumstances continue or emerge: (1) Brazil's assumption of a greater international status; (2) continuation of Brazilian-Argentine cooperation; (3) widespread national political maturity, particularly in the larger states; (4) economic expansion, especially within an integrative plan; (5) some type of continental confederation established and in operation; (6) U.S. sponsorship of a greater South American role in world affairs; and (7) world peace and prosperity wherein, within the United Nations, the South Americans may come to hold a greater sway in international matters.

South America's global involvement will decrease for these reasons: (1) a return to checkerboard diplomacy and the failure of continental and hemispheric integration; (2) North American focus on Eurasia; and (3) resumption of bipolar or multipolar structures at the strategic level of geopolitics.

The Contribution of Geopolitics to the Study of South American International Relations

The South American environment, since colonial times and very probably before the Columbian epoch as well, has proved to be fertile ground for the study and practice of geopolitics. The continent's resources and topography, the spatial placement of its republics and regions, its isolation and peripheral location, its reactive position adjacent to the great powers, and its blending of continental and maritime and European and British/North American geopolitical traditions have spawned a distinctive geopolitics, one lending itself to checkerboards and shatterbelts, buffer states and spheres of influence, frontier conflict and regional economic integration. Can other regions equal South America's unique and rich geopolitical heritage?

The South American landscape provides a fertile field for describing geopolitical concepts and theories. New writers will expand on the works of past decades, and a Pan American exchange of geopolitical ideas beyond my initial efforts and those of Jack Child, Howard Pittman, Carlos de Meira Mattos, Bernardo Quagliotti de Bellis, and many others will increase the cross-fertilization. European authors, for example, Klaus Dodds, will further this dialogue. In fact, one of my hopes has been not only to describe South American geopolitics, but also to clarify the major concepts and theories so that the study and practice of hemispheric and global geopolitics can expand.

My evaluation of the contribution of geopolitics to South American diplomacy is a positive one, particularly since the 1970s. It appears that once the leading writers and practitioners recognized that a checkerboard structure had contributed to frontier conflict, spatial expansion and contraction, national autarky and economic stagnation, and international vulnerability, they envisioned a new direction. Having viewed the choices among geopolitical structures, South Americans at present seem bent on shifting from previous patterns of strife and rivalry to something perhaps more productive, an accommodative regionalism. If, indeed, greater harmony and progress is the legacy of geopolitics, what better way to end this discussion than to predict that geopolitics will continue to give insight and direction to the continent's foreign affairs.

Bibliography

Abente, D. (1987). The war of the triple alliance: three explanatory models. *Latin American Research Review* 22: 47–69.

Adams, B. (1903). War as the ultimate form of economic competition. *U.S. Naval Institute Proceedings* 29: 829–881.

Ael, R. (1988). Dr. Karl Haushofer—¿Atlántico o Pacífico? El Océano Pacífico como futuro mar mediterráneo del acontecer mundial. *Geopolítica* (Buenos Aires) 37: 84–89.

Aguilar, A. (1968). *Pan-Americanism from Monroe to the present: a view from the other side.* New York: Monthly Review Press.

Arujo Castro, J. de (1971). Congelamento de poder mundial. *Segurança e Desenvolvimento* 20 (Rio de Janeiro).

Atencio, J. (1986). *¿Qué es la geopolítica?* Buenos Aires: Editorial Pleamar.

Atkeson, E. (1976). Hemispheric denial: geopolitical imperatives and Soviet strategy. *Strategic Review* 4: 26–36.

Atkins, G. (1977). *Latin America in the international system.* New York: Free Press.

Backheuser, E. (1952). *A geopolítica geral do Brasil.* Rio de Janeiro: Biblioteca do Exército.

Badía Malagrida, C. (1919). *El factor geográfico en la política sudamericana.* Madrid: Establecimiento Tipográfico de Jaime Ratés.

Bailey, N. (1965). *Latin America: politics, economics, and hemispheric security.* New York: Praeger.

Baptista Gumucio, M. (1983). Geopolítica de Bolivia: mediterraneidad y destino. *Geopolítica* (Buenos Aires) 26: 5–18.

Bartolomé, M. (1989). Las relaciones Argentina-Brasil: del conflicto a la cooperación. *Geopolítica* (Buenos Aires) 39: 30–38.

Bemis, S. (1943). *The Latin-American policy of the United States.* New York: W. W. Norton.

Blaut, J. (1992). Fourteen ninety-two. *Political Geography* 11: 355–385.

Bond, R. (1981). Brazil's relations with the northern tier countries. In *Brazil in the international system: the rise of a middle power* (Wayne Selcher, ed.), pp. 123–141. Boulder: Westview.

Boscovich, N. (1992). Las regiones en una estrategia para el desarrollo argentino. *Geopolítica* (Buenos Aires) 45: 21–29.

—— (1991a). El eje hidroeconómico del Alto Paraná: ¿integración o desintegración? *Geopolítica* (Buenos Aires) 44: 26–37.

—— (1991b). La alternativa integracionista en el Cono Sur. *Geopolítica* (Buenos Aires) 43: 18–28.

—— (1990). El futuro argentino en la Cuenca del Plata: la hidrovía Paraguay–Paraná–Rio de la Plata. *Geopolítica* (Buenos Aires) 40: 38–51.

—— (1986). Pensamiento geopolítico brasileño: Travassos, Golbery, Meira Mattos. *Geopolítica* (Buenos Aires) 34: 37–44.

—— (1984). Río Bermejo: su aprovechamiento múltiple, racional y amplio. *Geopolítica* (Buenos Aires) 29: 35–49.

—— (1983a). La Argentina en la Cuenca del Plata. In *Los países del Atlántico Sur: geopolítica de la Cuenca del Plata* (Luis Dallanegra Pedraza, ed.), pp. 57–122. Buenos Aires: Editorial Pleamar.

—— (1983b). Geopolítica y geoestrategia en la Cuenca del Plata. *Geopolítica* (Buenos Aires) 27: 18–24.

—— (1979). *Geoestrategia de la Cuenca del Plata—para la creación del gran litoral argentino*. Buenos Aires: El Cid Editor.

—— (1974). Un proyecto regional argentino y la salida natural de Bolivia al mar. *Estrategia* 30: 28–43.

—— (1973). *Un proyecto regional argentino—canalización del Bermejo para una geopolítica argentino del Cono Sur*. Buenos Aires: Editorial Ciencia Nueva.

—— (1960). *Soluciones argentinas: análisis de la realidad política económica nacional*. Buenos Aires: Prólogo.

Briano, J. (1977). *Geopolítica y geoestrategia americana*. Buenos Aires: Editorial Pleamar.

Burr, R. (1955). The balance of power in nineteenth-century South America: an explanatory essay. *Hispanic American Historical Review* 35: 37–60.

Bushnell, D. (1975). Colombia. In *Latin American foreign policies: an analysis* (H. Davis and L. Wilson, eds.), pp. 401–418. Baltimore: Johns Hopkins University Press.

Butland, G. (1960). *Latin America: a regional geography*. New York: John Wiley and Sons.

Cañas Montalva, R. (1981). Chile: el país más austral en la tierra. *Geosur* 23: 22–35.

—— (1979). Chile, el más antártico de los países del orbe y su responsabilidad continental en el Sur-Pacífico. *Seguridad Nacional* 14: 89–118.

—— (1972/1973). Los hombres y el territorio en el trascendente devenir geopolítico de Chile. *Revista Geográfica de Chile "Terra Australis"* 23/24: 52–71.

—— (1970–1971). Los hombres y el territorio en el trascendente devenir geopolítico de Chile. *Revista Geográfica de Chile "Terra Australis"* 21: 51–77.

—— (1960). Trascendencia geopolítica de Canal Beagle. *Revista Geográfica de Chile "Terra Australis"* 18: 6–20.

—— (1959a). Los mapas y la visión geopolítica del Pacífico. *Revista Geográfica de Chile "Terra Australis"* 17: 3 – 4.

—— (1959b). Fronteras: la política internacional de Chile frente a los imperativos geopolíticos desprendidos de su trascendente posición en el Pacífico Sur antártico. *Revista Geográfica de Chile "Terra Australis"* 17: 15 – 36.

—— (1956 – 1957a). La Antártica: visionaria apreciación del General O'Higgins. *Revista Geográfica de Chile "Terra Australis"* 14: 5 – 21.

—— (1956 – 1957b). Chile en el Pacífico—Argentina en el Atlántico, factores de estabilidad continental. *Revista Geográfica de Chile "Terra Australis"* 14: 65 – 94.

—— (1955). El Pacífico, epicentro geopolítico de un nuevo mundo en estructuración. *Revista Geográfica de Chile "Terra Australis"* 12: 11 – 17.

—— (1953a). Misión o dimisión de Chile en el Pacífico sur-antártico. *Revista Geográfica de Chile "Terra Australis"* 10: 9 – 12.

—— (1953b). El valor geopolítico de la posición antártica de Chile. *Revista Geográfica de Chile "Terra Australis"* 6: 11 – 16.

—— (1949). Agrupación o confederación del Pacífico. *Revista Geográfica de Chile "Terra Australis"* 2: 15 – 20.

—— (1948). Reflexiones geopolíticas sobre el presente y el futuro de América y de Chile. *Revista Geográfica de Chile "Terra Australis"* 1: 27 – 40.

Carlson, L., and A. Philbrick (1958). *Geography and world history.* Englewood Cliffs, N.J.: Prentice-Hall.

Carpio Castillo, R. (1981). *Geopolítica de Venezuela.* Caracas: Editorial Ariel-Seiz Barral Venezolana.

—— (1980). *El Golfo de Venezuela y el Tratatado [sic] Herrera Campins-Turbay.* Caracas: Venediciones.

—— (1974). *Fronteras marítimas de Venezuela.* Caracas: Comisión Organizadora de la III Conferencia de las Naciones Unidas sobre Derecho del Mar.

—— (1961). *México, Cuba y Venezuela: triángulo geopolítico del Caribe.* Caracas: Imprenta Nacional.

Castro, T. de (1992). *Nossa América: geopolítica comparada.* Rio de Janeiro: Colégio Pedro II, Instituto Brasileiro de Geopolítica e Estadística.

—— (1988). The Southern Cone and the international situation. In *Geopolitics of the Southern Cone and Antarctica* (Philip Kelly and Jack Child, eds.), pp. 85 – 99. Boulder: Lynne Rienner Publishers.

—— (1986a). *Geopolítica: principios, meios e fins.* Rio de Janeiro: Colégio Pedro II, Secretaria de Ensino.

—— (1986b). *Retrato do Brasil: atlas-texto de geopolítica.* Rio de Janeiro: Bibliex.

—— (1986c). A dinâmica geopolítica do monroísmo. *A Defesa Nacional* 724: 10 – 20.

—— (1985a). Dinâmica territorial brasileira. *A Defesa Nacional* 718: 97 – 112.

—— (1985b) Bacia do Prata: polo geopolítico do Atlântico Sul. *A Defesa Nacional* 721: 42–53.

—— (1985c). O Brasil e a bacia do Prata. *A Defesa Nacional* 704: 73–91.

—— (1984a). O Atlântico Sul: contexto regional. *A Defesa Nacional* 714: 91–108.

—— (1984b). O Cone Sul e a conjuntura internacional. *A Defesa Nacional* 712: 17–34.

—— (1983a). *Brasil da Amazônia ao Prata*. Rio de Janeiro: Colégio Pedro II, Secretaria de Ensino.

—— (1983b). Directrices geopolíticas de Brasil. *Geosur* 47: 32–42.

—— (1983c). La crisis de las Malvinas y sus reflejos. *Geopolítica* 26: 29–34.

—— (1983d). Relações Brasil–Estados Unidos em face das dicotomias nortesul e lesteoeste. *A Defesa Nacional* 706: 15–29.

—— (1983e). O mar; enfoque geopolítico. *A Defesa Nacional* 708: 31–46.

—— (1982a). *O Brasil no mundo atual*. Rio de Janeiro: Colégio Pedro II, Secretaria de Ensino.

—— (1982b). Antártica: suas implicações. *A Defesa Nacional* 702: 77–89.

—— (1981a). Directrices geopolíticas de Brasil. *Geosur* 26: 28–41.

—— (1981b). Directrices geopolíticas do Brasil. *A Defesa Nacional* 693: pp. 33–47.

—— (1979). Vocação Atlântica da América do Sul. *A Defesa Nacional* 681: 53–74.

—— (1977). Antártica: carta-aberta a Carlos Mastrorilli. *A Defesa Nacional* 672: 15–19.

—— (1976). *Rumo a Antártica*. Rio de Janeiro: Livraria Freitas Bastos.

—— (1972a). Considerações gerais sobre a Antártica. *A Defesa Nacional* 641: 113–116.

—— (1972b). A Antártica e os desafios do espaço. *A Defesa Nacional* 645: 133–140.

—— (1969). O mundo atlântico e seus imperativos estratégicos. *A Defesa Nacional* 622: 61–65.

—— (1968). Comunidade luso-brasileira: aspecto geopolítico. *A Defesa Nacional* 619: 129–134.

Caviedes, C. (1988). The emergence and development of geopolitical doctrines in the Southern Cone countries. In *Geopolitics of the Southern Cone and Antarctica* (Philip Kelly and Jack Child, eds.), pp. 13–29. Boulder: Lynne Rienner Publishers.

Ceresole, N. (1988). The South Atlantic: war hypothesis. In *Geopolitics of the Southern Cone and Antarctica* (Philip Kelly and Jack Child, eds.), pp. 55–66. Boulder: Lynne Rienner Publishers.

Child, J. (1988a). *Antarctica and South American geopolitics: frozen lebensraum*. New York: Praeger.

—— (1988b). South American geopolitics and Antarctica: confrontation or cooperation? In *Geopolitics of the Southern Cone and Antarctica* (Philip Kelly and Jack Child, eds.), pp. 187–202. Boulder: Lynne Rienner Publishers.

────── (1986). Geopolitical conflicts in the Southern Cone. Paper presented for the National Defense University Symposium on Inter-American Security Policy, Washington, D.C.

────── (1985). *Geopolitics and conflict in South America: quarrels among neighbors*. New York: Praeger.

────── (1980). Strategic concepts of Latin America: an update. *Inter-American Economic Affairs* 34: 61–82.

────── (1979). Geopolitical thinking in Latin America. *Latin American Research Review* 14: 89–111.

────── (1976). Latin America: military-strategic concepts. *Air University Review* 27: 27–42.

Clark, M. (1988). Cooperation on ice: the potential of collaboration in the Southern Cone. In *Geopolitics of the Southern Cone and Antarctica* (Philip Kelly and Jack Child, eds.), pp. 203–213. Boulder: Lynne Rienner Publishers.

Cline, R. (1975). *World power assessment: a calculus of strategic drift*. Washington, D.C.: Georgetown University Press.

Cohen, S. (1994). Geopolitics in the new world era: a new perspective on an old discipline. In *Reordering the world: geopolitical perspectives on the 21st century* (G. Demko and W. Wood, eds.), pp. 15–48. Boulder: Westview Press.

────── (1973). *Geography and politics in a world divided*. 2nd edition. New York: Oxford University Press.

Conde, C. (1983). Brazil in Suriname: see how a regional power acts. *World Paper* 10: 14.

Connell-Smith, G. (1984). Latin America and the Falklands conflict. *Yearbook of World Affairs* 38: 73–88.

Corbett, C. (1975). Toward a US defense policy: Latin America. *Military Review* 55: 11–19.

D'Adesky, S. (1979). Brazil's rise to dominance in Latin America. *Fletcher Forum* 3: 46–65.

Dalby, S. (1990). American security discourse: the persistence of geopolitics. *Political Geography Quarterly* 9: 171–188.

Dallanegra Pedraza, L. (1983). Situación energética Argentina y la Cuenca del Plata. In *Los paises del Atlántico Sur: geopolítica de la Cuenca del Plata* (L. Dallanegra Pedraza et al., eds.), pp. 11–56. Buenos Aires: Editorial Pleamar.

Da Rosa, J. (1983). Economics, politics, and hydroelectric power: the Paraná River basin. *Latin American Research Review* 18: 77–107.

de Hoyos, R. (1988). Malvinas/Falklands, 1982–1988: the new Gibraltar in the South Atlantic? In *Geopolitics of the Southern Cone and Antarctica* (Philip Kelly and Jack Child, eds.), pp. 237–249. Boulder: Lynne Rienner Publishers.

de Seversky, A. (1942). *Victory through air power*. New York: Simon and Schuster.

Dodds, K. (1994). Geopolitics and foreign policy: recent developments in Anglo-American political geography and international relations. *Progress in Human Geography* 18: 186–208.

Dodds, K., and J. Sidaway (1994). Locating critical geopolitics. *Environment and Planning D: Society and Space* 12: 515–524.

Dupuy, R., and G. Eliot. (1937). *If war comes*. New York: Macmillan.

Eliot, G. (1938). *The ramparts we watch: a study of the problems of American defense*. New York: Reynal and Hitchcock.

English, A. (1981). Latin American power balances and potential flash points. *International Defense Review* 14: 1273–1281.

Espenshade Jr., E., and J. Morrison (1986). *Goodes world atlas*. Chicago: Rand McNally.

Ewell, J. (1982). The development of Venezuelan geopolitical analysis since World War II. *Journal of Inter-American Studies* 24: 295–320.

Ferris, E. (1981). The Andean Pact and the Amazon treaty: reflections of changing Latin American relations. *Journal of Inter-American Studies and World Affairs* 23: 147–175.

Fitzgibbon, R. (1942). Union in the Americas. In *Global Politics* (R. Fitzgibbon, ed.), pp. 57–75. Berkeley and Los Angeles: University of California Press.

Frank, A. (1992). Fourteen ninety-two once again. *Political Geography* 11: 386–393.

García, F., and R. de la Garza. (1976). *The Chicano political experience: three perspectives*. North Scituate, Mass.: Duxbury Press.

Gauto, J., and R. Casco Carrera (1989). El costo de la mediterraneidad. *ABC Color* (Asunción), 29 August, p. 9.

Gilpin, R. (1975). *U.S. power and the multinational corporation*. New York: Basic Books.

Glassner, M. (1988). Bolivia's orientation: toward the Atlantic or the Pacific? In *Geopolitics of the Southern Cone and Antarctica* (Philip Kelly and Jack Child, eds.), pp. 154–169. Boulder: Lynne Rienner Publishers.

——— (1985). The view from the near north—South Americans view Antarctica and the southern ocean geopolitically. *Political Geography Quarterly* 4: 329–342.

Golbery do Couto e Silva (1981). *Geopolítica do Brasil*, 2nd ed. Rio de Janeiro: Livraria José Olympio Editora.

Gorman, S. (1982). Geopolitics and Peruvian foreign policy. *Inter-American Economic Affairs* 36: 65–88.

——— (1979). Present threats to peace in South America: the territorial dimensions of conflict. *Inter-American Economic Affairs* 33: 51–71.

Govea, R., and G. West. (1981). Riot contagion in Latin America, 1949–1963. *Journal of Conflict Resolution* 25: 349–368.

Grabendorff, W. (1982). Interstate conflict behavior and regional potential for conflict in Latin America. *Journal of Interamerican Studies and World Affairs* 24: 267–294.

Gray, C. (1981). The most dangerous decade: historic mission, legitimacy, and dynamics of the Soviet empire in the 1980s. *Orbis* 25: 13–28.

———— (1977). *The geopolitics of the nuclear era: heartlands, rimlands, and the technological revolution.* New York: Crane, Russak.

Guglialmelli, J. (1986). Geopolítica en la Argentina. *Geopolítica* (Buenos Aires) 34: 22–28.

———— (1982). ¿Fabrica el Brasil una bomba atómica? *Estrategia* 70: 5–12.

———— (1980–1981). Islas Malvinas. Exigir definiciones a Gran Bretaña en las negociaciones sobre soberanía. *Estrategia* 67/68: 5–17.

———— (1980a). Energía y geopolítica. *Estrategia* 66: 5–25.

———— (1980b). Argentina-Brasil y resto de los países del Cono Sur. Intercambio comercial. *Estrategia* 63: 5–26.

———— (1979–1980). Corpus-Itaipú. Tres batallas perdidas por la Argentina y, ahora peligrosas perspectivas: el papel de socio menor del Brasil. *Estrategia* 61/62: 7–29.

———— (1979a). *Geopolítica del Cono Sur.* Buenos Aires: El Cid Editor.

———— (1979b). El General Savio. Industrias básicas, poder militar y poder nacional. *Estrategia* 60: 5–36.

———— (1979c). Patagonia. A cien años de su ocupación no podemos conmemorar su vertebración a la nación. *Estrategia* 59: 5–36.

———— (1979d). Argentina. Geopolítica y fronteras. *Estrategia* 57: 5–15.

———— (1978a). Argentina ratifica el tratado de Tlatelolco, mientras las superpotencias condicionan su adhesión al segundo protocolo adicional. *Estrategia* 52/53: 5–30.

———— (1978b). Economía, poder militar y seguridad nacional. *Estrategia* 51: 7–29.

———— (1977a). El área meridional del Atlántico suroccidental, la geopolítica del Chile y el laudo del Beagle. *Estrategia* 48: 5–18.

———— (1977b). Geopolítica en la Argentina. *Estrategia* 46/47: 5–14.

———— (1977c). Carlos Pellegrini: protección para la industria nacional. *Estrategia* 45: 5–32.

———— (1976a). Argentina: plan nuclear y presiones externas. *Estrategia* 42: 5–19.

———— (1976b). ¿Argentina insular o peninsular? *Estrategia* 41/42: 5–25.

———— (1976c). Golbery do Couto e Silva, el "destino manifiesto" brasileño y el Atlántico Sur. *Estrategia* 39: 5–24.

———— (1975–1976). Argentina, política nacional y política de fronteras. Crisis nacional y problemas fronterizos. *Estrategia* 37/38: 5–21.

———— (1975a). Argentina-Brasil, enfrentamiento o alianza para la liberación. *Estrategia* 36: 1–29.

———— (1975b). ¿Y si Brasil fabrica la bomba atómica? *Estrategia* 34/35: 5–21.

———— (1975c). Itaipú-Corpus. Operar en el frente principal y no confundirse con los frentes secundarios. *Estrategia* 33: 5–16.

———— (1974). Argentina, Brasil y la bomba atómica. *Estrategia* 30: 1–15.

—— (1973–1974). Banzer–Buenos Aires–Brasilia. *Estrategia* 25/26: 5–10.

—— (1973a). Chile. Los sucesos del 11 de setiembre. *Estrategia* 24: 49–52.

—— (1973b). Fuerzas armadas para la liberación nacional. *Estrategia* 23: 7–30.

—— (1972–1973). Argentina frente al "operativo misiones" del Brasil. *Estrategia* 19/20: 7–16.

—— (1972). Las FF. AA. en América Latina (FF. AA. y revolución nacional). *Estrategia* 17: 9–19.

—— (1970–1971). Nuestro tema central. *Estrategia* 9: 56–57.

—— (1970). Relaciones argentino-brasileñas. *Estrategia* 5: 48–57.

—— (1969a). Responsibilidad de las fuerzas armadas en la revolución nacional. *Estrategia* 4: 7–17.

—— (1969b). Fuerzas armadas y subversión interior. *Estrategia* 2: 7–14.

—— (1969c). Función de las fuerzas armadas en la actual etapa del proceso histórico argentino. *Estrategia* 1: 8–19.

Guillén, A. (1967). *Dialéctica de la política.* Montevideo: Editora Cooperativa Obrera Gráfica.

Hakim, P. (1992). The United States and Latin America: good neighbors again? *Current History* 91: 49–53.

Hartmann, F., and Wendzel, R. (1985). *To preserve the republic: United States foreign policy.* New York: Macmillan.

Hennig, R., and Körholz, L. (1977). *Introducción a la geopolítica.* Buenos Aires: Editorial Pleamar.

Hensel, P., and Diehl, P. (1994). Testing empirical propositions about shatterbelts, 1945–76. *Political Geography* 13: 33–51.

Hepple, L. (1990). Metaphor, geopolitical discourse, and the military in South America. Unpublished manuscript, 1–26.

—— (1988). The geopolitics of the Falklands/Malvinas and the South Atlantic: British and Argentine perception, misperception, and rivalries. In *Geopolitics of the Southern Cone and Antarctica* (Philip Kelly and Jack Child, eds.), pp. 223–236. Boulder: Lynne Rienner Publishers.

—— (1986). The revival of geopolitics. *Political Geography Quarterly* 5: S21–S36.

Hersh, S. (1983). *The price of power: Kissinger in the Nixon White House.* New York: Summit Books.

Hilton, S. (1975). *Brazil and the great powers, 1930–1939: the politics of trade rivalry.* Austin: University of Texas Press.

Hoge, W. (1981). Brazil's busy factories forge a labor firebrand. *New York Times* (April 3), A2.

Hurrell, A. (1992). Latin America in the new world order: a regional bloc of the Americas? *International Affairs* 68: 363–380.

Hurtado, S. (1993). *Ecuador y Peru: vecinos distantes.* Quito: Corporación de Estudios para el Desarrollo.

Kantor, H. (1969). *Patterns of politics and political systems of Latin America.* Chicago: Rand McNally.

Keen, B., and Wasserman, M. (1984). *A short history of Latin America.* Boston: Houghton Mifflin.

Kelly, P. (1992a). Fronteiras e geopolítica: uma discussão das teorias do Gen. Meira Mattos. *A Defesa Nacional* 757: 41–49.

——— (1992b). La geopolítica de la confederación: los escritos del Gral. colombiano Julio Londoño. *Geopolítica* (Buenos Aires) 46: 40–50.

——— (1992c). Los ciclos mundiales de Modelski y el futuro de Sudamérica. *Geosur* 143/144: 3–13.

——— (1992d). Measuring democracy in Latin America: the Fitzgibbon-Johnson index. Paper presented before the Midwestern Association for Latin American Studies, Edwardsville, Ill.

——— (1991). La tierra de corazón de Mackinder: el concepto aplicado a Sudamérica. *Geosur* (Montevideo) 135/136: 33–47.

——— (1990a). La geopolítica de América Latina: eslabones regionales y estratégicos. *Geopolítica* (Buenos Aires) 40: 16–28.

——— (1990b). Los patrones ciclos internacionales y la geopolítica sudamericana. *Estudios Paraguayos* (Asunción), accepted for publication.

——— (1989). A "idade de ouro" do Brasil. O modelo de ciclos prolongados de Modelski e a América do Sul. *Política e Estratégia* 7: 15–24.

——— (1988a). Traditional themes of Brazilian geopolitics and the future of geopolitics in the Southern Cone. In *Geopolitics of the Southern Cone and Antarctica* (Philip Kelly and Jack Child, eds.), pp. 111–122. Boulder: Lynne Rienner Publishers.

——— (1988b). Geopolitical tension areas in South America: the question of Brazilian territorial expansion. In *Inter-American relations: the Latin American perspective* (Robert Biles, ed.), pp. 190–209. Boulder: Lynne Rienner.

——— (1986a). Escalation of regional conflict: testing the shatterbelt concept. *Political Geography Quarterly* 5: 161–180.

——— (1986b). Buffer systems of Middle America. In *Buffer Systems in World Politics* (J. Chay and T. Ross, eds.), pp. 67–84. Boulder: Westview.

——— (1984). Geopolitical themes in the writings of General Carlos de Meira Mattos of Brazil. *Journal of Latin American Studies* 16: 439–461.

Kelly, P., and Boardman, T. (1977). Intervention in the Caribbean: Latin American responses to United Nations peacekeeping. *Revista/Review Inter-Americana* 6: 403–411.

Kelly, P., and Child, J. (1988). An overview: geopolitics, integration, and conflict in the Southern Cone and Antarctica. In *Geopolitics of the Southern Cone and Antarctica* (Philip Kelly and Jack Child, eds.), pp. 1–10. Boulder: Lynne Rienner Publishers.

Kelly, P., and T. Whigham (1990). La geopolítica del Paraguay: vulnerabilidades regionales y respuestes nacionales. *Perspectivas Internacionales Paraguayas* (Asunción) 3: 41–78.

Kennan, G. (1951). *American diplomacy 1900–1950*. New York: New American Library.

Komorowski, R. (1973). Latin America—an assessment of U.S. strategic interests. *U.S. Naval Institute Proceedings* 843: 150–171.

Kurian, G. (1990). *The new book of world rankings*, 3rd ed. New York: Facts on File.

Layne, C. (1993). The unipolar illusion: why new great powers will rise. *International Security* 17: 5–51.

Lea, H. (1909). *The valor of ignorance*. New York: Harper Brothers.

Levine, R. (1982). Brazil: the dimensions of democratization. *Current History* 81: 60–63, 86–87.

Liss, S. (1975). Venezuela. In *Latin American foreign policies: an analysis* (H. Davis and L. Wilson, eds.), pp. 419–437. Baltimore: Johns Hopkins University Press.

Londoño, J. (1981). Nueva geopolítica de Colombia: sus fronteras. *Geosur* 28: 5–13.

——— (1979). Geopolítica de Colombia. *Geopolítica* (Buenos Aires) 13–14: 18–28.

——— (1978). *Los fundamentos de la geopolítica*. Bogotá: Talleres de la Imp. y Publicaciones de las Fuerzas Armadas.

——— (1977). *Geopolítica de Sudamérica*. Bogotá: Impr. y Publicaciones de las Fuerzas Militares.

——— (1973). *Geopolítica del Caribe*. Bogotá: Impr. y Litografía de las Fuerzas Militares.

——— (1969). *Geografía política de América*. Bogotá: Universidad Nacional, Dirección de Divulgación Cultural, Colección Textos, no. 5.

——— (1967). *Integración del territorio colombiano*. Bogotá: Lerner.

——— (1965). *Nueva geopolítica de Colombia*. Bogotá: Sección Impr. y Publicaciones de las Fuerzas Militares.

——— (195?). *Fundamentos de la geografía política*. Bogotá: Servicio de Imprenta y Publicaciones de las Fuerzas Armadas.

——— (1950). *La visión geopolítica de Bolívar*. Bogotá: Impr. del Estado Mayor General.

——— (1949). *Geopolítica de Colombia*. Bogotá: Impr. del Ministerio de Guerra.

——— (1948). *Suramérica; o, la geografía como destino*. Bogotá: Impr. del Ministerio de Guerra.

Luers, W. (1984). The Soviets and Latin America—thirty years. *Washington Quarterly* 7: 3–32.

Mackinder, H. (1919). *Democratic ideals and reality: a study in the politics of reconstruction*. New York: Henry Holt.

——— (1904). The geographic pivot of history. *Geographical Journal* 23: 421–444.

Mahan, A. (1897). *The interest of America in sea power past and present*. Boston: Little, Brown.

Manwaring, M. (1981). Brazilian military power: a capability analysis. In *Brazil in the international system: the rise of a middle power* (W. Selcher, ed.), pp. 65–98. Boulder: Westview Press.

Marini, J. (1990). *Estrategia nacional*. Buenos Aires: Editorial Pleamar.

——— (1988). Cuenca del Plata. *Geosur* 101–102: 3–10.

——— (1987). *Geopolítica latinoamericana de integración*. Buenos Aires: Editorial Humanitas.

——— (1982). *El conocimiento geopolítico*. 2nd. ed. San Miguel de Tucumán: Universidad de Tucumán.

——— (1980a). *Temas geopolíticos contemporáneos*. Río Cuatro: Departamento Imprenta, Universidad Nacional de Río Cuatro.

——— (1980b). *Desarrollo y seguridad de la Argentina en el marco geopolítico internacional*. Buenos Aires: Librería Hachette.

Masi, F. (1987). Lo político en la integración. *Primer seminario interno sobre naturaleza y alcances de la integración*. Asunción, pp. 3–6.

Mecham, J. (1965). *A survey of United States–Latin American relations*. Boston: Houghton Mifflin.

Meira Mattos, C. de (1990a). *Geopolítica e teoria de fronteiras: fronteiras do Brasil*. Rio de Janeiro: Biblioteca do Exército Editora.

——— (1990b). Geopolítica do Paraguai—um estúdio dos professores Philip Kelly e Thomas Whigham. *A Defesa Nacional* 748: 29–36.

——— (1989). Geopolítica de fronteiras—tipos de fronteiras. *A Defesa Nacional* 745: 35–46.

——— (1988). The strategic importance of the South Atlantic. In *Geopolitics of the Southern Cone and Antarctica* (Philip Kelly and Jack Child, eds.), pp. 214–222. Boulder: Lynne Rienner Publishers.

——— (1984a). *Geopolítica e trópicos*. Rio de Janeiro: Biblioteca de Exército Editora.

——— (1984b). O hemisfério sul e o equilíbrio do poder. *Política e Estrategia* 2: 115–120.

——— (1983). *O Marechal Mascarenhas de Moraes e sua época*. Rio de Janeiro: Biblioteca do Exército Editora, 2 vols.

——— (1982). Bacia do Prata ou Cone Sul? *A Defesa Nacional* 699: 37–43.

——— (1980a). *Uma geopolítica pan-amazônica*. Rio de Janeiro: José Olympio.

——— (1980b). La articulación de los pactos andino y amazónico. *Geosur* 15: 30–33.

——— (1979). A continentalidade do Brasil. *A Defesa Nacional* 682: 15–20.

——— (1977a). *A geopolítica e as projeções do poder*. Rio de Janeiro: José Olympio.

——— (1977b). Estratégia militar brasileira. *A Defesa Nacional* 673: 5–10.

——— (1975). *Brasil: geopolítica e destino*. Rio de Janeiro: José Olympio.

——— (1973). O poder militar e a política internacional. *Revista Brasileira de Política Internacional* 63/64: 63–80.

——— (1962). Portugal na África. *A Defesa Nacional* 581: 63–65.

———— (1960). O Brasil e o despertar afro-asiático. *A Defesa Nacional* 572: 114–118.

———— (1952). Aspectos geopolíticos de nosso territorio. *Boletim Geográfico* 4: 48–49.

Meira Mattos, C. de, and T. de Castro (1987). A problemática do Cone Sul. *A Defesa Nacional* 734: 63–88.

Meislin, R. (1982). Guyana outback a lure to miners and Venezuela. *New York Times* (September 28), p. 2.

Meneses Ciuffardi, E. (1991). Maintaining a regional navy with very limited resources: the Chilean case, 1900–1990. *Defense Analysis* (United Kingdom) 7: 345–362.

———— (1989a). As políticas externas e a defesa do Chile e seus efeitos sobre a segurança nacional. *Política e Estratégia* 7: 61–82.

———— (1989b). *Ayuda económica, política exterior y política de defensa en Chile, 1943–1983.* Santiago: Centro de Estudios Públicos.

———— (1989c). *El factor naval en las relaciones entre Chile y los Estados Unidos, 1881–1951.* Santiago: Ediciones Pedagógicas Chilenas, Librería Francesa.

———— (1989d). *Política de defensa: el caso de la adquisición de sistemas de arma.* Santiago: Centro de Estudios Públicos.

———— (1989e). América Latina: cooperación o conflicto. *Geopolítica* (Buenos Aires) 38: 24–36.

———— (1984). *América Latina, ¿cooperación o conflicto?* Santiago: Centro de Estudios Públicos.

———— (1983). Política exterior chilena: una modernización postergada. *Revista del Centro de Estudios Públicos* 2: 123–144.

———— (1982). Competenica armamentista en América del Sur, 1970–1980. *Estudios Públicos* 7: 5–41.

———— (1981a). Estructura geopolítica de Chile. *Revista de Ciencia Política* 1/2: 105–161.

———— (1981b). Política exterior, los fondos marinos y diversos intereses. *Revista de Ciencia Política* 1/2: 7–16.

———— (1977). *La Organización del Tratado del Atlántico Sur: una visión crítica.* Santiago: Instituto de Ciencia Política, Universidad Católica de Chile.

Mercado Jarrín, E. (1991). *Las nuevas relaciones internacionales y las fuerzas armadas sudamericanas.* Lima: Fundación Friedrich Ebert.

———— (1989). *Un sistema de seguridad y defensa sudamericano.* Lima: Centro Peruano de Estudios Internacionales.

———— (1985). *Hacia un proyecto nacional.* Lima: Instituto Peruano de Estudios Geopolíticos.

———— (1983). Cambios geopolíticos en el Cono Sur y nuestra seguridad nacional. *Estudios Geopolíticos y Estratégicos* 9: 27–29.

———— (1981a). Bases para una geopolítica peruana. *Geosur* 19: 3–35.

———— (1981b). El conflicto con Ecuador: problema definitivamente resuelta hace 39 años; (no obstante). *Estudios Geopolíticos y Estratégicos* 6: 9–31.

―――― (1980a). Comportamiento de los núcleos geohistóricos. *Estudios Geopolíticos y Estratégicos* 5: 84–103.

―――― (1980b). El desarrollo del "hinterland"—la selva central: dilatado vacio espacial. *Estudios Geopolíticos y Estratégicos* 4: 18–25.

―――― (1979). Proyecciones del Brasil. *Estudios Geopolíticos y Estratégicos* 3: 7.

―――― (1974). La política nacional y la estrategia militar en el Perú. *Estrategia* 27: 16–29.

―――― (1972). El tercer mundo. *Estrategia* 18: 46–51.

Modelski, G. (1982). Long cycles and the strategy of U.S. international economic policy. In *America in a changing world political economy* (W. Avery and D. Rapkin, eds.), pp. 97–116. New York: Longman.

―――― (1978). The long cycle of global politics and the nation-state. *Comparative Studies in Society and History* 20: 214–235.

Moneta, C., and R. Wichmann. (1981). Brazil and the Southern Cone. In *Brazil in the international system: the rise of a middle power* (W. Selcher, ed.), pp. 143–180. Boulder: Westview.

Morris, M. (1990). Great power military relations. In *Great power relations and Argentina, Chile and Antarctica* (M. Morris, ed.), pp. 144–160. New York: St. Martin's Press.

Mutto, C. (1971). Brazil's manifest destiny. *Atlas* 20: 21–24.

Myers, D. (1984). Brazil: reluctant pursuit of the nuclear option. *Orbis* 27: 881–911.

Nickson, R. (1981). Brazilian colonization at the eastern border region of Paraguay. *Journal of Latin American Studies* 13: 111–131.

Nunn, F. (1992). *The time of the generals: Latin American professional militarism in world perspective.* Lincoln: University of Nebraska Press.

Ó Tuathail, G. (1986). The language and nature of the "new geopolitics"— the case of U.S.–El Salvador relations. *Political Geography Quarterly* 5: 73–85.

Ó Tuathail, G., and J. Agnew (1992). Geopolitics and discourse: practical geopolitical reasoning in American foreign policy. *Political Geography* 11: 190–204.

Parker, G. (1985). *Western geopolitical thought in the twentieth century.* London: Groom Helm.

Pecci, A. (1990). Julio Chiavenato: Itaipú no pertenece al Paraguay. *Última Hora* (Asunción) 27 (January): 4–5.

Perón, J. (1971). El problema de la liberación. *Revista Latinoamericana de Geopolítica* (September) (Buenos Aires).

Perry, W. (1976). *Contemporary Brazilian Foreign Policy: The International Strategy Of An Emerging Power.* Beverly Hills: Sage Publications.

Pinochet Ugarte, A. (1984). *Geopolítica.* 4th ed. Santiago de Chile: Editorial Andrés Bello.

Pittman, H. (1988a). From O'Higgins to Pinochet: applied geopolitics in Chile. In *Geopolitics of the Southern Cone and Antarctica* (Phillip Kelly and Jack Child, eds.), pp. 173–180. Boulder: Lynne Rienner Publishers.

—— (1988b). Southern Cone Antarctic claims, territories, and the Ibero-American club vs. the common heritage of mankind theory. Paper presented to the Latin American Studies Association meeting, New Orleans.

—— (1986). The impact of democratization on geopolitics and conflict in the Southern Cone. Paper presented to the Latin American Studies Association meeting, Boston.

—— (1983). Geopolitics in the ABC countries: a comparison. Paper presented to the Western Political Science Association meeting, Seattle.

—— (1981a). Geopolitics in the ABC countries: a comparison. Ph.D. dissertation, The American University, Washington, D.C.

—— (1981b). Geopolitics and foreign policy in Argentina, Brazil, and Chile. In *Latin American foreign policies: global and regional dimensions* (E. Ferris and J. Lincoln, eds.), pp. 165–178. Boulder: Westview.

Quagliotti de Bellis, B. (1990a). El acondicionamiento territorial para la integración regional. *Geosur* 117/118: 2–47.

—— (1990b). Las hidrovías de la Cuenca del Plata. *Geosur* 121/122: 1–56.

—— (1990c). América Latina y los nuevos esquemas internacionales. *Geosur* 123/124: 3–10.

—— (1989). Uruguay en la geografía de la circulación en el Cono Sur. *Geosur* 113/114: 3–18.

—— (1988). The La Plata Basin in the geopolitics of the Southern Cone. In *geopolitics of the Southern Cone and Antarctica* (Philip Kelly and Jack Child, eds.), pp. 125–143. Boulder: Lynn Rienner Publishers.

—— (1986a). Dinámicas en el Cono Sur. *Geosur* 63/64: 3–22.

—— (1986b). El Atlántico Sur en la historia. *Geosur* 63/64: 23–44.

—— (1983). Uruguay en la Cuenca del Plata. In *Los países del Atlántico Sur: geopolítica en la Cuenca del Plata* (L. Dallanegra Pedraza, ed.), pp. 161–196. Buenos Aires: Editorial Pleamar.

—— (1982a). Inglaterra–Estados Unidos y las Malvinas: ¿un nuevo estado tapón? *Geosur* 34: 3–23.

—— (1982b). Bases para geopolítica del Uruguay. *Geosur* 36: 3–64.

—— (1981). Uruguay: puerta atlántica del Cono Sur. *Geosur* 17: 7–25.

—— (1980). Evaluación del poder mundial. *Geosur* 13: 5–19.

—— (1979a). *Constantes geopolíticas en Iberoamérica.* Montevideo: Geosur.

—— (1979b). *Nacionalismo e integración.* Montevideo: Asociación Sudamérica de Estudios Geopolíticos e Internacionales.

—— (1978). Estrategia y geopolítica en el Atlántico Sur: poder naval y poder económico. *Geopolítica* (Uruguay) 5: 5–14.

—— (1977). Actualidad geopolítica del Canal Beagle: Argentina y Chile estudian soberanía marítima no fijado por el arbitraje. *Geopolítica* (Buenos Aires) 9/10: 36–39.

—— (1976a). *Uruguay en el Cono Sur: destino geopolítico.* Buenos Aires: Tierra Nueva—Colección Proceso.

—— (1976b). *Geopolítica del Atlántico Sur.* Montevideo: Fundación de Cultura Universitaria.

———— (1976c). *Cuenca del Tacuarembó: plan de desarrollo, informe preliminar.* Montevideo: Instituto Uruguayo de Estudios Geopolíticos.

———— (1976d). Actualidad geopolítica en América Latina. *Geopolítica* (Montevideo) 1: 29.

———— (1975). URUPABOL y el corredor del Paraná. *Geopolítica* (Buenos Aires) 2: 10 – 18.

Randall, S. (1992). *Colombia and the United States: hegemony and interdependence.* Athens: University of Georgia Press.

Richardson, L. (1960). *Statistics of deadly quarrels.* Pittsburgh: Boxwood Press.

Ronfeldt, D. (1983). *United States security policy in the Caribbean.* Santa Monica, Calif.: Rand Corporation.

Scheena, R. (1978). South American navies: who needs them? *U.S. Naval Institute Proceedings* 104: 61 – 66.

Schoultz, L. (1987). *National security and United States policy toward Latin America.* Princeton, N.J.: Princeton University Press.

Seckinger, R. (1976). South American power realities during the 1820s. *Hispanic American Historical Review* 56: 241 – 267.

Selcher, W. (1985). Brazilian-Argentine relations in the 1980s: from wary rivalry to friendly competition. *Journal of Inter-American Studies and World Affairs* 27: 25 – 53.

Semple, E. (1903). *American history and its geographic condition.* New York: Houghton Mifflin.

Slater, J. (1987). Dominoes in Central America: will they fall? does it matter? *International Security* 12: 105 – 134.

Smith, W. (1991). The United States and South America: beyond the Monroe Doctrine. *Current History* 90: 49 – 52, 88 – 90.

Spykman, N. (1942). *America's strategy in world politics: the United States and the balance of power.* New York: Harcourt Brace.

Stein, S., and B. Stein (1970). *The colonial heritage of Latin America: essay on economic dependence in perspective.* New York: Oxford University Press.

Stepan, A. (1989). *Democratizing Brazil: problems of transition and consolidation.* New York: Oxford University Press.

Sternberg, H. (1987). "Manifest destiny" and the Brazilian Amazon: a backdrop to contemporary security and development issues. *CLAG Yearbook* 13: 25 – 35.

Tambs, L. (1965). Geopolitical factors in Latin America. In *Latin America: politics, economics and hemispheric security* (Norman A. Bailey, ed.), pp. 31 – 49. New York: Praeger.

Travassos, M. (1947). *Projeção continental do Brasil.* São Paulo: Companhia Nacional.

Tulchin, J. (1986). Uruguay: the quintessential buffer state. In *Buffer states in world politics.* (J. Chay and T. Ross, eds.), pp. 213 – 230. Boulder: Westview.

Valencia Vega, A. (1976). Geopolítica en Bolivia. *Geopolítica* (Uruguay) 1: 44 – 54.

———— (1975). *Integración nacional y Latinoamérica*. La Paz: Librería Editorial Juventud.

———— (1974a). *Geopolítica en Bolivia*. 2nd. ed. La Paz: Empresa Editora "Urquizo Ltda."

———— (1974b). *Geopolítica del litoral boliviano*. La Paz: Editorial "Juventud."

Valenta, J. (1982). Soviet strategy in the Caribbean basin. *U.S. Naval Institute Proceedings* 108: 169–181.

Velilla de Arréllaga, J. (1988). An energy and iron community in the La Plata Basin. In *Geopolitics of the Southern Cone and Antarctica* (Philip Kelly and Jack Child, eds.), pp. 144–153. Boulder: Lynne Rienner Publishers.

———— (1982). *Paraguay: un destino geopolítica*. Asunción: Instituto Paraguayo de Estudios Geopolíticos y Relaciones Internacionales.

———— (1981). El Paraguay y la integración americana. *Geosur* 24: 22–27.

———— (1977). Paraguay y su destino internacional: URUPABOL es clave geopolítica de integración. *Geopolítica* (Uruguay) 4: 16–25.

Villacrés Moscoso, J. (1990a). *Las pretensiones peruanas en la Cordillera del Condor hasta los ríos ecuatorianos Puyango y Calamayo*. Guayaquil: Editorial de la Universidad de Guayaquil.

———— (1990b). *Invasiones y desmembraciones efectuadas por los estados limítrofes vecinos al territorio ecuatoriano*. Guayaquil: Editorial Justicia y Paz.

———— (1985). *Las ambiciones por las Islas Galápagos*. Guayaquil: Casa de la Cultura Ecuatoriana.

———— (1982). *Peligros para el Ecuador de la integración económica con los estados limítrofes*. Guayaquil: Escuela Superior Politécnica de Litoral.

———— (1979). *Problemas económicos y políticos internacionales del Ecuador*. Guayaquil: Escuela Superior Politécnica del Litoral.

———— (1975). *Geopolítica del estado ecuatoriano*. Guayaquil: Departamento de Publicaciones de la Universidad de Guayaquil.

———— (1963). *Geopolítica del mundo tropical sudamericano*. Guayaquil: Departamento de Publicaciones de la Universidad de Guayaquil.

———— (1962). *The Interocean routes through the Amazonian region*. Guayaquil: Tropical Geography Center of the University of Guayaquil.

Villarreal, R., and P. Kelly. (1982). Mexican Americans as participants in United States–Mexico Relations. *International Studies Notes* 9: 1–6.

Von Chrismar Escuti, J. (1988). Semblanza del General Ramón Cañas Montalva y síntesis de su pensamiento geopolítico. *Revista Chilena de Geopolítico* 4: 9–12.

Walton, R. (1972). *The United States and Latin America*. New York: Seabury Press.

Wesley, J. (1962). Frequency of wars and geographical opportunity. *Journal of Conflict Resolution* 6: 387–389.

Whittaker, A. (1954) *The Western Hemisphere idea: its rise and decline*. Ithaca, N.Y.: Cornell University Press.

Wood, B. (1966). *The United States and Latin American wars, 1932–1942*. New York: Columbia University Press.

Index